THE NEW GUITARSCAPE IN
CRITICAL THEORY, CULTURAL PRACTICE
AND MUSICAL PERFORMANCE

The New Guitarscape in Critical Theory, Cultural Practice and Musical Performance

KEVIN DAWE
University of Leeds, UK

ASHGATE

Published by
Ashgate Publishing Limited
Wey Court East
Union Road
Farnham
Surrey, GU9 7PT
England

Ashgate Publishing Company
Suite 420
101 Cherry Street
Burlington
VT 05401-4405
USA

www.ashgate.com

British Library Cataloguing in Publication Data
Dawe, Kevin.
  The new guitarscape in critical theory, cultural practice
  and musical performance. – (Ashgate popular and folk music series)
  1. Guitar. 2. Guitar–Social aspects.
  I. Title II. Series
  787.8'7–dc22

Library of Congress Cataloging-in-Publication Data
Dawe, Kevin.
  The new guitarscape in critical theory, cultural practice and musical performance
  / Kevin Dawe.
    p. cm. — (Ashgate popular and folk music series)
  Includes bibliographical references and index.
  ISBN 978-0-7546-6775-9 (hardcover : alk. paper) 1. Guitar. 2. Guitar—
  Social aspects. I. Title.
  ML1015.G9D43 2009
  787.87—dc22

                                                                    2009046526

ISBN 9780754667759 (hbk)

Mixed Sources
Product group from well-managed
forests and other controlled sources
www.fsc.org Cert no. SA-COC-1565
© 1996 Forest Stewardship Council

Printed and bound in Great Britain by
MPG Books Group, UK

Contents

List of Figures

List of Tables

General Editor's Preface

The upheaval that occurred in musicology during the last two decades of the twentieth century has created a new urgency for the study of popular music alongside the development of new critical and theoretical models. A relativistic outlook has replaced the universal perspective of modernism (the international ambitions of the 12-note style); the grand narrative of the evolution and dissolution of tonality has been challenged, and emphasis has shifted to cultural context, reception and subject position. Together, these have conspired to eat away at the status of canonical composers and categories of high and low in music. A need has arisen, also, to recognize and address the emergence of crossovers, mixed and new genres, to engage in debates concerning the vexed problem of what constitutes authenticity in music and to offer a critique of musical practice as the product of free, individual expression.

Popular musicology is now a vital and exciting area of scholarship, and the *Ashgate Popular and Folk Music Series* presents some of the best research in the field. Authors are concerned with locating musical practices, values and meanings in cultural context, and may draw upon methodologies and theories developed in cultural studies, semiotics, poststructuralism, psychology and sociology. The series focuses on popular musics of the twentieth and twenty-first centuries. It is designed to embrace the world's popular musics from Acid Jazz to Zydeco, whether high tech or low tech, commercial or non-commercial, contemporary or traditional.

Derek B. Scott
Professor of Critical Musicology
University of Leeds, UK

Foreword

If only Dr. Dawe's book might have accompanied my first guitar, as a Christmas present, in 1957. But it could not have done, because the guitar was not then to be taken seriously; and, outside the classical world, neither were many guitarists. The acoustic instrument, where engaged in socially acceptable practices, was puny in the company of proper instruments. Electric forms held their own, but alongside loud and vulgar friends who looked as if they were having a good time and often engaged in commerce.

Two questions:

How did the instrument achieve global popularity?
Why is this now a subject worthy of academic interest?

In a rapidly proliferating field where a mass of material and commentary, players, musics, technology, interactions social and commercial and political, virtual and hands-dirtied, seek to escape a unifying grasp, Dr. Dawe has my respect in achieving this impressive and considered overview.

Robert Fripp
Friday September 25th 2009

Preface

Newton Faulkner's *Hand Built by Robots* (Sony BMG, 2007) was, according to *Observer Music Monthly* magazine, '2007's perfect soundtrack'.[1] Faulkner, according to David Smyth of *Q* magazine, was 'one of 2007's brightest new artists' (2008:136). Smyth writes also of Faulkner's 'extraordinary guitar technique … playing the melody on the frets with his left hand, doing the bass and simultaneously beating out the rhythm on the guitar's body with his right' (Smyth, 2008). The significance of Faulkner's success in terms of his guitar playing is picked up by Douglas Noble in *Guitar and Bass Magazine*, where he notes that: 'Newton Faulkner is not the first to make prominent use of the percussive possibilities of the acoustic guitar, but with high-profile festival appearances and a number one UK album he has brought them to a new audience' (Noble, 2008:136).

Newton Faulkner's guitar skills, including the techniques described above (which extend and supplement more conventional methods of playing the acoustic guitar), are but one aspect of his work as a live performer and recording artist which have not only gained the attention of the press, but may also have helped him to reach the top of the UK album charts (with a CD that acquired platinum status at the time of writing). Although he has a highly distinctive style of playing, Faulkner is by no means alone in his exploration of the 'possibilities' of the acoustic guitar. For instance, North American guitarist Vicki Genfan, who won *Guitar Player* magazine's Guitar Superstar contest in 2008, also uses a wide range of playing techniques on acoustic guitar. Genfan says of her winning piece, 'Atomic Reshuffle': 'The piece shows off a broad spectrum of the techniques I use – finger-picking, harmonic tapping, slide, and guitar percussion' (Molenda, 2008a:17). Genfan, like Faulkner, draws attention to the wider world of guitar playing that now exits, and it is a world that often challenges conventional models, including those which, one might claim, have a seemingly inbuilt gender bias. And there are now several ways in which this wider world of the guitar is being made ever more accessible to people outside of close-knit guitar fraternities, often without the help of large record companies, at least in the first instance. In this guitar-driven world, the use of extended playing techniques (including percussive acoustic guitar as described above) is not uncommon.

In fact, a wide range of playing techniques, musical innovations, guitar designs and uses of technology seem to demonstrate the fact that the world of the guitar

---

[1]   Comments taken from the cover of the *Hand Built* CD. See also Chris Power, 'Rising Star', *The Observer*, Comments and Features, Sunday 24 June 2007:10. Power notes that Faulkner's album was '2007's perfect *summer* soundtrack' (my italics): www.guardian.co.uk/theobserver/2007/jun/24features.magazine27.

– acoustic *and also* electric as I shall demonstrate later – is being re-assessed if not redefined in the hands of musicians like Newton Faulkner and Vicki Genfan. Moreover, one might also claim that although many different approaches to guitar performance have been around for some time, they are now being exposed as never before, and are even achieving or contributing to considerable commercial success (at least in Newton Faulkner's case). The techniques, technologies and approaches to guitar performance used by Faulkner and his peers do not represent a totally new phenomenon. But several recent musical, cultural and technological developments around the guitar most certainly do. Such phenomena are already affecting the guitar universe, including its constitution, growth, development, operation, definition, dissemination, reception in the wider world and scholarship.

When Newton Faulkner notes that flamenco guitarists also use percussive techniques, he also highlights the fact that the guitar exists as an instrument of global performance. For a moment a hole in the fabric of the conventional model of the guitar universe opens up and invites engagement with the myriad virtuosi based in music cultures that lie not only on the fringes of Europe and North America, but also well beyond them, for example, acoustic guitarist Debashish Bhattacharya from North India (his especially designed guitars with added strings are similar to a slide guitar and are played with the instrument laid flat upon the lap) and acoustic fingerstyle player D'Gary (Ernest Randrianasolo) from Madagascar. *Guitar Player* magazine's 2008 Guitar Superstar contest included Hawaiian guitarist Makana playing in what is often described as a 'slack key' style, as well as Daddo Oreskovich, of Bosnian origin, playing a 'fusion of metal and ethnic folk music' (although the exact form of 'metal' or 'ethnic' music played is not discussed) (Molenda, 2008a:18). But as noted in just a few books, guitarists have felt the pull and attraction of the widely based cultures of the guitar for some time.

A burgeoning collection of studio and field recordings (increasingly sold at concerts by musicians or their entourages), live performances, compositions copyrighted and performed by the composer-guitarists themselves (the performing right automatically goes to them live, and avoids copyright permissions and fees on record), television, radio and press coverage, as well as the Internet (which more than any other phenomenon exposes the world to guitars, and guitarists to the world of music as never before), extends and makes more secure the role and agency of the guitar in music, culture and society. Not only is the virtual world of the guitar providing an insight into the complexity of the world of the guitar that lies outside of cyberspace, but the Internet (YouTube, MySpace, etc.) is also helping to reconfigure our perception and vision of the world of the guitar as a vital component of it. Mention must also be made of the *Guitar Hero* series of computer video games, and the more recent 'pocket guitar' (iPhone and iPod software) and video guitars, three examples among a legion of recent developments that force one to re-examine the role, significance and wider presence of the guitar in popular culture and in the minds of non-specialist musicians. Such developments are, of course, not without their critics or detractors.

Comprehensive studies that attempt to reveal the ways in which the guitar is manifest, its concomitant factors and its wider significance – the 'state of the axe' (after photographer Ralph Gibson, 2008) – are only very slowly emerging. My core objectives in this book are not only to document aspects of the guitar phenomenon as it now stands by the collation and synthesis of a great deal of diverse information, but also to try and extend the academic terms of reference by which the guitar might be studied. I write comparatively about the guitar among the cultures and societies of the world, whilst drawing on studies of material culture, technology, new media, the body and senses, cognition, gender and sexuality and globalization. Given the sheer scale and complexity of the guitar phenomenon, as noted in Chapter 2, I have tried to limit this study to the provision of preliminary overviews, suggested research strategies and discussion around core themes, as noted in Chapter 3, where I present a working model of 'the new guitarscape'.

In Chapter 4 I refer to some of the musical techniques and technologies which distinguish the new guitarscape, from extended techniques to polyphonic, hexaphonic and augmented guitars, and from particular genre-based and genre-crossing sounds to a discussion of the politics and poetics of hybrid guitars. I introduce ideas about materiality and virtuality in Chapter 5, taking my lead from studies of material culture and the Internet. More recent work on the study of sensual culture is discussed in Chapter 6, which explores the experiential nature of what it is to 'play', 'touch' and feel' the guitar as an instrument of both the mind *and* body (this is particularly relevant at a time when extended techniques make further intellectual and physical demands upon performers and cyberspace takes the guitar away from the body). In Chapter 7 I discuss how aspects of gender and sexuality are expressed in the new guitarscape, including discussion of the work of men, women and lesbian, gay, bisexual, transgender and transsexual guitarists. Chapter 8 brings notions of the guitar's power and agency (influence, affecting presence, utility) as an object of culture and society to the fore. My claim is that the guitar's role in cultural politics and social action is not only multifaceted, but also underestimated. Chapter 9 throws into relief issues surrounding the guitar as an instrument of global performance, an instrument at home in a world of motion, yet still rooted in numerous cultural contexts and local scenes. I note some of the ways in which guitars and guitarists move across cultures, times and places, confronting issues of travel and translation, appropriation and representation.

The ten performances that follow in Chapter 1 are intended to throw the world of guitar playing into relief, featuring distinct approaches to performance, uses of technology and methods of playing. These ten very different means of creating not only music but also, potentially, meaning on the guitar are examples of the rich and diverse musical and cultural practices that now revolve around the instrument. They not only reflect the various ways in which the guitar is valued, but also represent the myriad individual-collective worlds of music in which the guitar plays a prominent role. In these performances and those described elsewhere in the book, I note some of the ways in which the guitar continues to yield to the demands of the musical instrument makers, composers, performers, technicians, promoters, journalists and audiences who continue to embrace it in the twenty-first century.

Acknowledgements

This book was written whilst I was on leave funded by the Arts and Humanities Research Council (Research Leave Award, AID 121038) and also the University of Leeds. I am extremely grateful to both the AHRC and the University of Leeds for their support during this time.

I have also been grateful for the help and support of the following musicians (despite their heavy work commitments): Bob Brozman, Sue Foley, Dominic Frasca, Fred Frith, Robin Hill, Sharon Isbin, Patty Larkin, Lionel Loueke, Muset Özgen, Kamala Shankar, Robert Urban and I Wayan Balawan. Many thanks go to Bette Warner, Jack Leitenberg and Josee Dufour (all in artist management).

Richard Corr, Fred Frith, Ray Hitchins, Ian Kelleher, David Mead, Suzanne Ryan and Steve Waksman read various chapters in draft form. I have benefited greatly from their generous and insightful comments. Two long interviews with Fred Frith during a very early stage of the project were particularly helpful. Many thanks go to Andrew Grey at Wikipedia, Matt Brown at Fender Custom Furniture and Patrick Keating at Play Away guitars. All personal communications noted in this book were made between July 2006 and July 2009.

Julian Rushton, John Baily and Lucy Green provided essential help and support early on. Lucy Durán, Allan Greenwood, Lizzie Lidster and Simon Warner helped in various ways, as did numerous discussions with several of my students at the University of Leeds. Two anonymous readers for a different press made helpful comments on a partial manuscript. One, in particular, provided penetrating comments. I remain indebted to that person. Lessons learnt with Frank Denyer, David Ward, John Blacking and Martin Stokes remain inspirational throughout.

Robert Fripp has been of great support all along, despite a hectic schedule involving concerts, recording, teaching and much else. His enthusiastic responses to my early drafts and encouragement ever since have been pivotal to the writing process as well as highly instructive. His e-mail correspondence whilst on tour provided me with an insight into the life of the professional touring and recording guitarist. I thank him wholeheartedly for taking on the task of writing the foreword to this book.

Derek Scott, editor of the Popular and Folk Music Series, has also been of great support. I thank him for his particularly insightful comments on a penultimate draft of this book and his interest in my work. I also wish to thank the whole team at Ashgate, especially Heidi Bishop.

My parents nurtured my early interest in the guitar. I cherish their love and support. I also thank my cousin Roger for letting me borrow his beloved twelve-string guitar forty years ago. He never did get it back but, with characteristic generosity, let the matter go. This book is partly down to him *and* his guitar.

Heartfelt thanks go to my wife, Moira, and son, Craig, for their love, support, patience and understanding throughout the writing process. Moira also proofread the chapters. This book is dedicated to my family.

Chapter 1

Ten Musical Lives of the Guitar

A feeling of great joy came over the musician. He had guessed what was to come: the guitar would produce offspring everywhere, a family infinitely diverse, of the strangest shapes and materials, a family that would soon cover the planet. No shame, no sorrow, no silence would be able to withstand all those guitars. Guitarists were the knights of the tempestuous alliance between Earth and humanity. (Orsenna, 1999:19)

Robert Fripp emerges unannounced upon a Tokyo stage that is dimly lit in various shades of blue. Immediately there is applause, from an audience sitting but also still arriving. He places the guitar that he carries on stage upon its stand and reaches for another already there. He kisses the guitar and puts its strap over his head. The setting of the guitar strap takes some time. We zoom back out to look down upon the auditorium and then switch back to the stage again to see Fripp sitting down, wearing headphones and adjusting the controls of his guitar and Lunar Module (a rack of sound processors). This takes some time. The camera shows his foot poised on the volume pedal (one of several pedals). By now the audience sounds like a hive of bees. Fripp's hands are also poised, for some time. The picking right hand is ready to play. The left hand is muting the strings and holding the guitar at the higher frets. The camera draws back to show a meditative figure holding a guitar. Suddenly he moves into action. Or rather, his left hand moves into playing position. A synthesized sound comes out of the speakers, a sustained note to which Fripp adds vibrato with his left hand. The audience begins to fall silent. Fripp starts to layer the soundscape (see Figure 1.1).

A whistle from the crowd leads to further applause. Green and red lights flicker on the Lunar Module. Fripp reaches across to the Module and turns one of its controls. The camera fades to a full view of the stage, then fades back in to a view of Fripp (still turning). There is then a view of the Lunar Module's harmonizers with their luminescent green read-outs of pitches and cents. The underlying layers of the soundscape are in place and the guitarist proceeds to add a melody line on top of repeating motifs. To my mind, the result is an exquisitely beautiful, slowly built-up improvisation: it is atmospheric, meditative, cathartic, moving. The bass notes swell as a finale. Our soul mate's music fades out as the rest of the extraordinary band of musicians comes on stage.[1]

---

[1]   Robert Fripp, 'Introductory Soundscape', on YouTube.com. See also King Crimson, *Eyes Wide Open: Live in Japan*, DVD (Tokyo, Kouseinenkin Kaikan, DVD1), Sanctuary/ DGM SVEM0248 (2003). All URLs cited are subject to the possibility of being updated

I am struck by the apparent lack of egotism in Robert Fripp's soundscapes performance, and remain fascinated by the vision of a quite still performer totally absorbed in his music. This is not the usual image one has of a guitar hero. In terms of the audience, soundscapes seem to be about listening, and not about watching a musician cavorting around the stage. The liner notes to Fripp's CD *Love cannot Bear* state: 'Soundscape performances, typically visit several moods, areas of reflection, consideration and personal interest, such as: queer space (ambiguous environments); threnody [wailing, song] and lamentation; paradise, paradise lost and paradise regained; foreboding; mourning; quietude; sonic pleroma; affirmation'.[2] Fripp's approach has rich philosophical and cultural dimensions which find practical expression, advancement and dissemination through his work as a guitarist and guitar teacher (with students around the world on the Guitar Craft courses which he founded).[3]

Robert Fripp is, of course, also founder member of the progressive and experimental rock group King Crimson, which he has led since the late 1960s. Evidence suggests that this guitar-based group (at least since the 1980s) have constantly tried to push at the boundaries of musical performance and musical experimentation on their chosen instrument(s). Past and present group members, including guitarists and bassists Robert Fripp, Adrian Belew, Trey Gunn, Tony Levin, John Wetton and Greg Lake, appear to hold on to a concept of the guitar which is not limited by convention but has been, until now, perhaps, in tension with inertia in the development of guitars and guitar technologies. I contend that these musicians keep pushing forward in such a way as to provide a window onto what can and might be created musically with a guitar.

Kamala Shankar, a professional performer of Hindustani classical music, sits on a low concert platform that is decked out in royal blue. Dr Shankar on guitar is accompanied by Shri Pundik Bhagavat on *tabla* (a pair of North Indian small drums). Normally a *gat* performance like this opens with a slow unaccompanied improvisation on an instrument or voice (the *alap*). Then comes the *gat* (or melody) proper, which forms the basis for improvisation within a rhythmic cycle. The rhythmic cycle is kept in place by the accompanying tabla (using variations on set patterns), and these drums may also take a solo (accompanied by a melody carried by the other instrument or instruments). The rhythmic cycle (*tala*) consists of sixteen beats in this case, four groups of four (*teental*). Over this rhythmic layer set pieces and improvisations are played out. In this performance, the improvisation

---

or removed. I cannot guarantee, of course, that each and every YouTube link given here will be available after this book goes to print. The reader may have to seek out and order the DVD and CD material referenced in this book or on artists' websites and other Internet video sites.

[2] Robert Fripp, *Love cannot Bear: Soundscapes – Live in the USA*, DGM 0552 (2005).

[3] See the book by Eric Tamm: *Robert Fripp: From King Crimson to Guitar Craft*, London: Faber (1990).

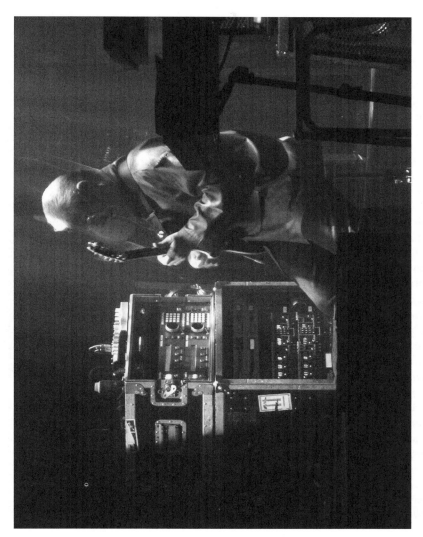

Figure 1.1   Robert Fripp, soundscape, Manchester 2004

and melody attend to pitch relations given by Rāg Yaman. Here Shankar's guitar not only functions as the main melodic instrument (I say 'main', because tabla drums are tuned percussion) but also adds rhythmic material. She says: 'I would call mine the Indian classical guitar. It has five strings, two chikari, and 12 sympathetic strings'.[4] *Chikari* strings provide a high-pitched drone and rhythmic punctuation. One or two strings of the guitar carry the melody, whilst other strings function as drones (also resonating in sympathy with the playing strings when not plucked). According to Shankar's web page, the 'Shankar-Guitar', as she also calls it – 'innovated by Dr. Kamala Shankar *and* designed by M.S. Rikhi Ram and Sons, New Delhi' – has a hollow body, with a thick soundboard, a new system of bracing and sound post, a flat back so it can be played on the lap, side walls of solid wood, and a 'one piece' structure, all of which appear to rule out the 'necessity of a hole on [the] sound board' (see Figure 1.2).[5]

The guitar sits across Shankar's lap. It appears as a red, thin-bodied guitar with an extra-thick neck. Its colouring is slightly darker than her sari. She moves a metal bar over the strings, which are positioned well above the frets – the guitar has a high action – to produce the melody notes. Her right hand plucks melody, drone and chikari strings. Her little finger rests on the soundboard of the instrument whilst she plucks the strings with the finger picks on her thumb and index finger. In this instance, a microphone on a stand is pointed at the instrument. She moves to and from the melodic material of the composition in her improvisation. She finishes with a flourish, the fast melodic improvisation and strummed accompaniment coming to a halt on the first beat of the rhythmic cycle, as is customary.[6]

Kamala Shankar, along with Brij Bhushan Kabra, Debashish Bhattacharya and Vishwa Mohan Bhatt, has been among the leading lights of Indian guitar players for some time. But until I discovered Kamala Shankar's video clip, I was unaware that female musicians played the guitar, let alone played with a slide in the North Indian classical music tradition. Shankar is the first woman to receive a doctorate in guitar from Banaras Hindu University. She might be called a 'classicist' or 'traditionalist', adhering to the principles of the Hindustani art music tradition. But that tradition has a history of innovation in instrumental performance, as well as in the design and development of musical instruments. She must also be seen as an innovator, developing her own approach to the guitar on an instrument of her own design, the 'Shankar guitar', in yet another male-dominated guitar world.

When asked: 'Does the guitar in any way help or hinder the playing of Hindustani music?' she replied: 'I don't think it hinders it in any way. In fact, the Hawaiian guitar is similar to the violin in that both are flexible and allow greater freedom than certain other string instruments. You can evoke up to five *swaras*

---

[4]   C.S. Sarvamangala, 'From Hawaii to Hindustan', the music magazine.com/kamala. html.

[5]   See www.kamalashankar-rajeevjanardan.com/.

[6]   Kamala Shankar, 'Dr Kamala Shankar (shankar-guitar): Raag Yaman', YouTube. com. See also www.kamalashankar-rajeevjanardan.com/.

Figure 1.2   Kamala Shankar

[pitches] with one stroke and there is immense potential to work on *gamak* and *meend* [ornaments]. I have developed my own way of blending the *gayaki ang* [vocal style] and *tantrakari ang* [instrumental style]. The guitar is also very close to the *veena*, which is a *dhrupad* instrument [instrument of song]. I want to now try out the *dhrupad* style [Indian classical singing style] and bring in the *nom-tom alap* [abstract syllables]'.[7]

Dominic Frasca's website intrigued me. I press 'play' on the still frame link to the video entitled 'Impossible Guitar'. By now I have surfed in and out of Frasca's website and back to YouTube, where 'Impossible Guitar' continues to feature (lifted from his website). In late May 2007, this same video in YouTube had received well over 3,000,000 hits and 5,684 comments, and had been saved to surfers' favourites 16,805 times. When accessed on 10 March 2009 it had been viewed over 20,000,000 times. By now, the video has loaded up and I hear the unmistakable sound of 'Dometude' coming out of the speakers. Just as strikingly different as the music which I am listening to are the images of Frasca playing his ten-string classical guitar. 'No loops. No overdubs. No other instruments. Just one person', is the message that fills the centre of the screen for a short while. 'Dometude' continues to play as footage of Frasca performing it returns. This is a minimalist piece, perhaps evoking the style of Philip Glass or Steve Reich. I recall that these composers were known for their ensemble writing, and Frasca's guitar sounds like an ensemble rather than one solo instrument.

Dominic Frasca's main guitar is a ten-string Thomas Humphrey-designed Martin Millennium acoustic classical guitar. The guitar features individual sensor saddles for each string which activate ten channels routed to a 1 GHz Apple Macintosh PowerBook running Logic Pro 6.4.3 with Waves and Blue Tube effects plug-ins. The ten strings can all be made to sound different through the great variety of sounds that can be patched into each one of the corresponding channels. This enables Frasca to set up the guitar like an ensemble. One hears multiple parts underlying his melodies. Notes are tapped on the fretboard using both hands – he is described as an 'Eddie Van Halen for Eggheads'– but both hands also stop notes and pluck strings in the conventional manner. 'Impossible Guitar' shows Frasca playing ten- and six-string guitars, both set up differently for each performance. Woodwork clamps and individual fretboard inserts act like mini-capos as they raise and set the pitch of the 'open' string. The positioning of these clamps is specific to each piece.

The music video finally enters its last phase as Frasca moves back to the ten-string guitar. He comments: 'My guitar technique is inspired by ensemble music, not by other guitarists.' He explains: 'For instance, the technique that allows me to play cross-string arpeggios with my fingers while at the same time playing percussion lines with my thumb came from listening to the music of Anthony Davis, with whom I studied composition at Yale' (Frasca, personal communication).

---

[7]   Sarvamangala, 'From Hawaii to Hindustan'.

Much of his music is based on instruments playing ostinati in different metres while a drummer lays down a groove to hold it all together.[8]

In a search for 'African guitarists' on the Internet, I came across the website of *Lionel Loueke*. I was immediately intrigued by his background and musical influences, for he was seemingly at home not just in his native Benin, but also in the world of the New York jazz scene. Of the videos of his work that I found on lionelloueke.com and YouTube, two performances, in particular, grabbed my attention.[9] The first shows Loueke performing in a 2006 concert as a member of the Herbie Hancock Quintet – this is his solo spot. Wearing what one takes to be a traditional African robe, he can be seen playing a sunburst Yamaha acoustic-electric arch-top guitar; he has a selection of pedals on the floor (including loop station, Digitech Whammy and Stereo Delay, facilitated also by the use of two Fender Twin Reverb amplifiers), and he makes use of a range of vocal articulations (including vocal clicks). Loueke's improvisation is rich and varied, utilizing both musical technologies and instrumental and vocal dexterity to achieve its goals. The improvisation appears structured but is 'completely improvised … of the moment … I think in colours … but I know how I am going to finish it' (Loueke, personal communication). The improvisation proceeds as follows: Loueke beats out rhythms on the strings and body of the guitar; atonal solo lead line section utilizing pitch bending and glissando; fast bebop-style guitar solo; tight vocal harmonies (utilizing vocal harmonizer on Loueke's voice); introduction to Loueke's composition 'Virgin Forest'; the band joins in (see Figure 1.3).

In the second video, Loueke can be seen explaining and demonstrating his guitar and vocal techniques in some detail. He is seen playing a Godin nylon-string acoustic-electric guitar in this clip. Of the many things to note about Loueke's guitar technique, the following facts intrigued me greatly. Loueke tunes his strings (highest to lowest) E, B, G, D, A (high A, a tuned G string), D. He usually plays with his right-hand fingers, exploring the chord voicings and arpeggiation possible with this tuning (imitating the West African harp-lute, the *kora*), whilst also inserting a piece of paper between the strings near the bridge to make them buzz, thus creating a sound reminiscent of the sound of the *kalimba* (hand or thumb piano) (Loueke, personal communication). Loueke played percussion for many years before taking up the guitar. He imitates the sounds of a wide range of percussion on the guitar, making use of the pitch bender, in particular, to recreate the sounds of the talking drum. 'The African element is who I am', he notes, and

---

[8]   www.dominicfrasca.com, 'Introducing Dominic Frasca'. See also 'Impossible Guitar' on YouTube.com. Dominic Frasca's quotes are taken from an interview with the title 'Guitar Hero 2005 Winner', in *Guitar Player* (November 2005), as featured on his website.

[9]   See the following YouTube videos: 'Lionel Loueke', 'Herbie Hancock Quintet – Virgin Forest' and 'Blue Note Act Lionel Loueke Part Two'. Lionel Loueke's CD output includes: Lionel Loueke, *Karibu*, The Blue Note Label Group/EMI 509950246526 (2008); Lionel Loueke, *Virgin Forest*, Obliq Sound OS104 (2006).

Figure 1.3   Lionel Loueke

he goes on to say: 'In the course of a concert I am both an African musician and a jazz musician' (Loueke, personal communication). Moreover, in my interview with Loueke, he notes that he has been inspired by African guitar players as much as by the jazz guitar masters, including among his influences Wes Montgomery and Franco. He is aware of what he calls the 'big sound' created by both these artists, particularly in Montgomery's chord voicings and Franco's arrangements for three or four guitars within a band context.

The spotlight shines centre-stage and encircles **Fred Frith**. The remainder of the Mexican stage is dark but for a row of soft blue lights back of stage. Frith has a semi-circle of effects pedals in front of him and a table full of pre-selected objects to his right. Behind him are two long Fender amplifiers/speaker cabinets with microphones hanging over them. Frith has his trusty sunburst '(1959) Gibson ES345' semi-acoustic guitar on his lap (Frith, personal communication). His right hand moves a violin bow across the strings of his guitar (above the pick-ups). He plays a series of high sustained notes. With his left hand he pulls at a 'thin piece of string threaded under one guitar string, which is somewhat detuned. The string simply pulls the [guitar] string upward to create precise pitches. The pulled string is bowed and the eerie sound of what you hear would not be possible without the pick-up mounted over the nut end of the guitar' (Frith, personal communication). My expectations are already transcended, and my preconceptions are in tatters. He combines and alternates bowing and pulling, bouncing the bow on the strings, playing with overtones and glissandi.

Frith then uses drum sticks on the guitar, which he plays on the strings just above the pick-ups (neck end). The rhythm and the distorted sound are constant. Like hail hitting a tin roof at 200 kph. Feedback comes and goes. He puts the guitar on its stand, and it continues sounding. He hunches forward and stares at his effects pedals. He is motionless for a short time. He then picks up the guitar and brings it to his body in standard playing position. Using a selection of objects he improvises over the loop. He suddenly shuts down the sound. The guitar is back on his lap. A soft buzzing sound can now be heard. This fades and closes the piece. The lights go up. Frith stands, bows, and leaves the stage to loud cheers and applause. I quickly rewind. Stop! Yes, that *was* 'the lid of a lozenge tin balanced on the strings with sound activated by an E-Bow' (Firth, personal communication).[10]

This concert was recorded by an audience member using mobile phone video capture. So the sections are artificial and fragment Frith's actual performance (which took place in Mexico City at the Teatro de la Cuidad de Mexico in March 2007). This particular example of Frith's work can only give an impression of the piece. But Frith caused a stir on the guitar scene as long ago as 1974 with the release of his *Guitar Solos* album (re-released on Fred Records, 2003). He was a founder member of the group Henry Cow (disbanded 1978), often described as an 'avant-garde' music ensemble. Frith, Professor of Composition at Mills College in

---

[10]   Fred Frith 'en el Teatro de la Cuidad de Mexico', March 2007, YouTube.com. See also www.fredfrith.com.

the USA, forces one to step back and re-assess the musical potential of the guitar and many of its technical conventions.

North American classical guitarist **Sharon Isbin** is no stranger to South America. She has travelled extensively throughout its lands, not only giving concerts but also exploring its interiors, including the rainforests. Her album *Journey to the Amazon* (Teldec, 1997) reflects her obvious and intense engagement with South American art music, involving collaboration between herself, Brazilian percussionist Gaudencio Thiago de Mello and saxophonist Paul Winter.[11] I am intrigued by the video of Isbin in concert with Thiago de Mello at the Ravenna Festival in Italy in 2007. Here they attempt to recreate some of the compositions featured on the album *Journey to the Amazon*, including pieces by Laurindo Almeida, Agustín Barrios Mangoré, Leo Brouwer and Antonio Lauro.[12]

I move to another YouTube video clip to see Isbin play the music of world-renowned Paraguayan composer-guitarist Agustín Barrios Mangoré (1885–1944).[13] This time, she plays the whole of his Vals Op.8 No.4. The camera fades in to show her hand placed over the soundhole of a six-string Spanish classical guitar (not that one can be certain that it was made in Spain). I look down at my score, which says: *tiempo de vals con brio*. I have a score; Isbin plays from memory. I look up just as she launches into the well-known melody that is the quaver passage. She sets the piece alight. Her technique is fluid, her phrasing seems utterly appropriate. Yet although she is clearly intent on what she is doing, she makes it look so easy. The Trio section calls for *muy expresivo*. Isbin delivers. The piece breathes in terms of its dynamic interpretation (loud/soft) but also in the way she speeds up and slows down in the 'Campanella' section. The coda leads to a *forte* finale on two strummed chords which are played with force and conviction.

Sharon Isbin is one of world's leading classical guitarists. In the past eight years she has won two Grammy Awards and has become the only guitarist to record with New York Philharmonic Orchestra (concertos by Rodrigo, Villa-Lobos and Ponce – Warner Classics), she was the featured soloist on the soundtrack to Martin Scorsese's Academy Award-winning film *The Departed*, and her latest release *Journey to the New World* (Sony) featured guest artists Joan Baez and Mark O'Connor. This is Joan Baez's first collaboration with a classical artist. Isbin's previous collaborations also include work with Laurindo Almeida and

---

[11]   Sharon Isbin, Paul Winer and Thiago de Mello, *Journey to the Amazon*, Teldec 0630-19899-2 (1997). For a useful and lavishly illustrated overview of how the guitar and its antecedents took root in the New World see 'Guitar Trek: Guitar in the New World' at: www.performances.org/education/pdf/guitar1.pdf. Victor Coelho (2003:7) mentions Craig Russell's two volumes on the music of Murcia, the King of Spain's guitarist, who in the 1720s travelled to Mexico, where he took inspiration from local musical sources (see Russell, 1995).

[12]   The YouTube video has the title 'Sharon Isbin': www.youtube.com.

[13]   Sharon Isbin 'plays Augustin Barrios Vals Op.8 No4', www.youtube.com.

Figure 1.4   Sharon Isbin performing with the New York Philharmonic Orchestra, Avery Fisher Hall, June 2004

Larry Coryell in the 'bossa nova/classical/jazz fusion trio', Guitarjam.[14] The Spanish classical nylon-string guitar has had music written for it by composers from countries as far apart as Paraguay and Japan. Indeed, Isbin's back catalogue reflects this as she continues to explore the world of the guitar, in recordings such as *Dreams of a World: Folk-Inspired Music for the Guitar* (Teldec, 1999).[15] She continues to direct the Juilliard School of Music's first guitar department, which she created (see Figure 1.4).

The history of the classical guitar includes several virtuoso women performers, all of whom have played a role in its musical, social and cultural development. From Sharon Isbin (b.1956) one can trace a line back through time to Alice Artz (b.1943), Ida Presti (1924–1967), Luise Walker (b.1910), Maria Luisa Anido (1907–1996), Vahda Olcott Bickford (1885–1980) and Madame Sydney Pratten (1821–1895). But one can also find extant classical guitar virtuosi across the world, for example Lily Afshar (Iran), Xuefei Yang (China), Ana Vidović (Croatia), Nicola Hall (England), Amanda Cook (England), María Esther Guzmán (Spain), Sonja Prunnbauer (Germany), Eleftheria Kotzia (Greece), Badi Assad (Brazil), Christina Azuma (Brazil), Berta Rojas (Paraguay) and Tali Roth (USA).

Hasan Cihat Örter is a multi-instrumentalist, playing not only traditional Turkish art and folk music but also music across a range of (more obviously) globally mobile genres (from jazz to classical, from hard rock to metal). He is surely one of the most versatile guitarists alive. I first discovered him when I came across one of his classical guitar CDs in Tower Records, London.[16] In one of his many video clips to be found on YouTube, he is to be seen in his recording studio playing a fretless electric six-string guitar with an E-Bow. This is an intimate and relaxed encounter with Örter. He is a genial host. As he smokes a Sherlock Holmes-style pipe he sits playing his fretless guitar against a backdrop of computers, recording equipment and keyboards.

I switch between several other video clips to remind myself of Örter's extraordinary virtuosity on a range of traditional Turkish instruments, as well as piano and violin. I hear a range of influences in his playing. With the E-Bow (producing a constant and uninterrupted note) on a fretless electric guitar (with reverb) he produces the sound of what might be described as a cosmic violin. More than this, on the fretless guitar he is easily able to produce glissandi and microtones, which are impossible on a normal guitar but very much in keeping with the phrasing and microtones found in the melodies and modes of Turkish music. The three YouTube video clips which completely capture my attention are

---

[14]   Liner notes, Sharon Isbin et al., *Journey to the Amazon*.

[15]   *Dreams of a World: Folk-Inspired Music for the Guitar*, Teldec 3984-25736-2 (1999).

[16]   Hasan Cihat Örter, *Inspiration. Turkey: Anatolian Folk Music for Classical Guitar*, EMI Records Ltd. 724356588226 (1996). The liner notes state: 'The Inspiration series aims to encompass a broad spectrum of music from within the worldwide "classical" tradition, displaying its diversity and its many colourful facets.'

of Örter improvising on three *makam* or modes. These are: 'Hasan Cihat Örter-Hüseynî Taksim', 'Hasan Cihat Örter-Segâh Taksim' and 'Hasan Cihat Örter-Hicaz Taksim'. Each improvisation (*taksim*) slowly builds to explore the subtleties of the pitch relations of each mode as well as the tonal range of the fretless electric guitar and the sustaining qualities of the E-Bow.

I was also able to access an Örter composition entitled 'Buse', a slow ballad with two main sections (minor to major), a short improvisation in between the sections and a return to the opening melody.[17] The strings and harp on the backing tape provide a lush and one might say sentimental musical framework for his soulful melodic workout. I flick between video clips of him playing in classical, jazz and rock guitar styles. He can play the standard repertoires and displays a virtuosic technique as a classical, jazz and rock guitarist, and not always with a fretless guitar. Then he is to be seen in concert on the piano and playing the *cura* (small Turkish long-necked lute) in both traditional and non-traditional style (that is, a blend of Turkish traditional music and guitar techniques involving rock-style showmanship).

The presenters of the French-Canadian television show introduce Montreal-based guitarist ***Erik Mongrain***, who is, one is told, about to play his own composition. Seated and hunched over the acoustic guitar which is laid flat on his lap, Mongrain begins to play 'Air Tap'. This seems to be Mongrain's showpiece, where one can see unique facets of his approach on display. 'Air Tap' is not just a technical exercise; the interjections of cheers and applause from the audience suggest that they, like me, not only find Mongrain's technical prowess exhilarating but also are moved by his music. The carefully spun melody lines are created out of a web of arm, hand and finger movements. He taps with both hands all over the fretboard and soundboard of the guitar as they are laid out in front of him. Melodic, harmonic and percussive material is carried by both hands, although there is some specialization. Indeed, the piece is opened by a march-like rhythm and a repeated chordal figure in the left hand. The left hand tends to sustain harmonic and thematic material in the lower registers of the fretboard, coming together with the right hand to co-produce quickly tapped-out melodic phrases and fills in syncopation. The right hand is the lead vocalist and percussionist in the Erik Mongrain guitar ensemble.

I am amazed by Mongrain's ability to pick out harmonics by tapping his right-hand index finger onto the strings high up over the fretboard (with the guitar on his lap). These chime-like harmonics also help make up the melody and make it distinct. The role taken by the right hand involves several techniques: flamenco-like strums (*rasguedo*), string slapping, a clenched fist banging on the soundboard, the side of the palm of the hand hitting the bridge and tapped notes and harmonics at the higher end of the fretboard. The performance ends as Mongrain depresses

---

Figure 1.5   Erik Mongrain

the strings between the nut and tuning peg, creating a glissando to the tonic (see Figure 1.5).

I have not seen a guitar style quite like this before, although it most obviously seems connected to the work of acoustic guitarists Michael Hedges, Don Ross, Preston Reed, Andy McKee and Kaki King, but also Stanley Jordan's electric guitar work. Mongrain's 'Air Tap' has popular appeal, but it seems unlikely that his instrumental works will reach the top of the album charts. Mongrain is a self-taught musician who does not just play in the lap tap style (of which the piece 'Air Tap' is an example) but is also able to employ a variety of fingerstyle and flat-picking techniques to produce music with different shades of colour for acoustic guitar.[18]

Steve Vai, the former 'Devil's guitarist', enters stage right, to loud cheers and applause.[19] Tall, thin, long-haired and dressed in black, he is wearing purple shades and sporting a goatee. The crowd at this Denver concert is ecstatic, and the atmosphere is electric. The look of awe on the face of one of the guitarist's many fans reflects the general sense of fervour and expectation one gets from the crowd. The fan turns round to a fellow audience member and then back to face the stage again, as the charismatic guitarist moves centre-stage just in front of him. The camera catches this well. Can he believe it? I feel that I am being drawn into some kind of ritual for which the initiated are getting prepared. Vai waves to the crowd, just before the instrument of transformation is handed over to him by his assistant. He sits down. The monster triple-necked white solid-body Ibanez guitar is at last back in the hands of its master.[20] In the hands of its master, the instrument becomes the means of conveyance for the journey ahead.

Vai begins to play. He has an unmistakable sound. It *is* him! The surroundings begin to change. The stage is set. A spell is cast as sonic waves emerge out of cone-shaped mouths and spread among the crowd. In this way, it seems, the crowd has actually been touched by his power. In other words, the speakers do their job well. And so does Vai. He begins with an unaccompanied melodic improvisation (with chord interjections) on the middle neck of the guitar. He then employs a

---

[18]　See videos of 'Air Tap' at YouTube.com and www.erikmongrain.com. This piece features on Mongrain's album *Fates*, Alter Ego/Prophase Music MVDA4585 (2007). See also Erik Mongrain, *Equilibrium*, Alter Ego/Prophase Music MVDA4821 (2008).

[19]　Steve Vai played the role of Jack Butler (the Devil's guitarist) in the film *Crossroads* (Columbia Pictures, 1986).

[20]　Ray Hitchins notes: 'I am not sure how to best define this instrument(s) or if you need to. Referring to it as a 'triple-neck' is accurate but you should perhaps note that each neck has its own set of pick-ups and outputs with individual amplifiers and processing. It's therefore closer to three independent guitars than a typical multi-neck instrument that employs a single output and a switch that moves between necks, only one of which can be heard at any time. The piece he plays, with the looping etc., is dependent on that separation of necks, each with an independent output, amplifier (etc.)' (Ray Hitchins, personal communication).

foot-controlled looping mechanism to select and record, and then infinitely repeat, part of his performance, thus providing an accompaniment. Vai begins to call up the ancestral spirits, and we are pulled into his magic circle. Using his left hand he slides tones out of the fretless fingerboard, without plucking the strings (his right hand is held up in the air). The camera moves in. It seems as if the instrument is being plucked by a hand from another world. He uses the middle neck to advance his project: 'The talk with the sun and the moon and stars'.[21] Playing with incredible invention, he rings a dazzling array of notes and tones out of the instrument using a variety of fast picking, legato, tapping and whammy bar techniques. His playing quickens. Is he possessed? A ghostly orchestra suddenly comes to life through a chord plucked from the twelve strings of the third neck. The possession is complete! We are in his hands.[22]

I Wayan Balawan plays a red double-neck Stephallen thirteen-string guitar in several of his YouTube clips. Six strings in the upper neck, and seven strings in the lower neck. The upper neck has normal frets whilst the lower one has frets that slant left and right, at angles from mid-neck position (providing different intonation for each string). The two necks are joined at the top of the headstock. The appropriateness of this unusual-looking guitar becomes immediately obvious as Balawan begins to play. To my mind he plays in an inimitable jazz-oriental guitar style. I am amazed not only at the speed of his jazz inspired runs, but also at how well they seem to complement the music of the other Balinese musicians featured. Balawan was born in Bali, Indonesia, in September 1973. His website states:

> He grew up amongst Balinese gamelan music. At age of 8 he began to play guitar and start[ed] his first band [at] the age of 14. [He has been playing] rock guitar virtuoso style like Yngwie Malmsteen since he was 10 years old. In 1993 he went to Sydney and got a scholarship to study jazz at the Australian Institute of Music for two years. He went back to Bali in 1997 and form[ed] Batuan Ethnic Fusion (A mix of Balinese Gamelan and Jazz).[23]

---

[21]   Lyrics by Steve Vai, from 'I'm Your Secrets' on the album *Real Illusions: Reflections*, Epic/Red Ink, Sony BMG EPC5170792 (2005).

[22]   Steve Vai, Joe Satriani and Yngwie Malmsteen, *G3 Live in Denver*, Sony Music Video SNY57319 (2004). YouTube title: 'Steve Vai's 3 Necked Guitar Solo!', www. youtube.com.

[23]   See www.wayanbalawan.com. According to his website, Balawan uses the following instruments: Blueberry double-neck acoustic guitar, Stephallen thirteen-string GuiBass guitar with Midi and acoustic pick-up, Stephallen 66 twin-neck guitars (two models, with Midi Piezo pick-up and Standard), Stephallen six-string Dual Sound (with Piezo and electric pick-up), Ibanez SA 420 XDR, Ibanez RG 550, Ibanez Rhoadstar 1986, Fender Stratocaster. All the guitars use Dimarzio, Paf, Evolution and Tone Zone pick-ups.

Figure 1.6   I Wayan Balawan (guitar) with other Balinese musicians

One video clip of Balawan's work above all others captures my imagination. It is a clip of him playing with the Balinese ensemble Made Agus Wardana in Brussels in May 2007 (see also Figure 1.6). The ensemble is made up of Balawan on double-neck guitar and vocals, a bass guitarist, a drummer, and two players on a single metallophone (the instrument consisting of a row of bronze slab-like keys suspended above a wooden box containing bamboo resonators). The drummer plays the double-headed drum used in Balinese gamelan ensembles. The two metallophone players sit opposite each other and strike the keys of the same instrument with wooden hammers. This instrument is the lead metallophone found in Balinese gamelan orchestras. Each player plays one note at a time and contributes, in turn, to the construction of a swiftly moving, interlocking melody (*kotekan*). Balawan plays along with the two metallophone players, mirroring the unison of the two players with his own two hands on the guitar. The ensemble is extremely tight, involving lightning switches between sections, which are episodes involving changes of both musical material and tempo. The metallic sound of the gamelan instruments complements Balawan's guitar tones, which are at one minute clean and unprocessed, the next sounding like a keyboard (via a midi pick-up). Although one hears his jazz-inflected runs and chord voicings played with the fingers of both hands (he also uses a plectrum), the music clearly has local roots also in terms of its changing tempos, interlocking parts and modality.[24]

Before moving on to the next chapter, the reader may find it useful to explore the Internet links given in the footnotes in order to see and hear the actual performances described above.

---

[24]   I refer to the following YouTube video clips here: 'balawan and made agus wardana', 'Balawan – gloBALIsm', and 'Balawan and Chris Hinze'.

Chapter 2
Taking Stock of the Guitar Phenomenon

Many years ago I knew the guitar was going to be the number-one instrument in the world. (Les Paul, in Gibson, 2008:11)

The inventors of the modern electric guitar and the frozen food industry are among this year's thirteen inductees into the National Inventors Hall of Fame. Musician Les Paul, already a member of the Rock and Roll Hall of Fame, and Clarence Birdseye, a household name that still appears in kitchens around the country, head this year's class. (Bob Sullivan, Technology Correspondent, NBC News, at www. msnbc.msn.com/id/6947927, 10 February 2005)

The ten guitarists featured in Chapter 1 were among the many musicians who inspired me to write this book. Their performances also gave me the courage to suggest that, to date, a study of the contemporary world of the guitar had been, at best, limited. Not that the present can be discussed without reference to the past, or without reference to a great deal of useful literature on the guitar.[1] This book

---

[1]   One writes a book about the guitar with some trepidation. It is one of those 'everybody claims to be an authority' books. But more than that, the standard of scholarly writing on the instrument, such as it is, is generally very high indeed. A shortlist of well-known and exceptional highlights might include: Coelho (1997), Grunfeld (1969), Pinnell (1980, 1993), Turnbull (1974, 1984), Waksman (1999), Noonan (2008). The extraordinary work of John Gavall, Angelo Gilardino, Thomas Heck, Brian Jeffery, Ivor Mairants, David Tannenbaum and Graham Wade is usefully acknowledged in Summerfield (1996). But see also Andy Bennett and Kevin Dawe (2001), Graham Wade (1980, 1983) and James Tyler and Paul Sparks (2002). Those writers on the guitar who could perform several if not all of the following roles as author-editor-journalist-performer-composer-broadcaster include George Clinton (*Guitar, Guitar International*), Colin Cooper (*Classical Guitar*), John Duarte (associations and output too numerous to mention) and Banning Eyre (*Guitar Player*). These four polymaths, in particular, provide a very reassuring but almost frightening level of expertise in all areas of their work. Figures who stand out among a legion of guitar writers and journalists, but who also display a vast knowledge of the guitar world and its players, styles and technologies, include Tony Bacon, Paul Day, Dave Hunter and David Mead. Many of these talented writers are also exceptionally good musicians. For instance, Ivor Mairants played, composed, wrote and taught across the worlds of jazz, classical and flamenco guitar. Several of the writers mentioned here are also concert performers or, at least, very good amateur players. But most serious writers on the guitar tend to specialize (as is the way with research) and become world authorities (for instance, Brian Jeffrey, Richard Pinnell, Graham Wade and Steve Waksman).

could not function without a mooring, tethered at the juncture of its diachronic and synchronic axes, demonstrating, I hope, an awareness of the high standards set by previous studies but also a willingness to engage with some of the issues and challenges currently faced by musical instrument studies (and guitarists). Although my study of the guitar reaches back into the past, I try to stay firmly in the present (although the pull of the guitar's past is strong), whilst moving sideways (synchronically) across a range of literature, musical styles, cultures and technologies.

I have often heard people say that the guitar is the most popular instrument in the world – the 'number-one' instrument according to Les Paul as noted above – but how can one test such a claim? (Not that one has any real reason to doubt Les Paul!). However, it is certainly worth pondering such a claim, given its potential significance. Manufacturers' replies to my emails, as well as numerous comments found in guitar magazines, indicate a boom time in terms of guitar sales (but not everywhere in the world or the high street). But how is one to break down sales figures to reveal exactly *why* the guitar sells? Throughout this book I note a great many reasons as to why the guitar is economically viable. But the guitar's *popularity* could also be gauged by the extent to which it features in people's everyday lives, and also by the way it features as a part of what we might call some people's extraordinary lives (especially if the individuals involved are professional performers). So some people will have a greater awareness of the guitar than others, and their engagement with it may hold much greater significance for them and other people. Thus the guitar will be the basis of a wide range of investment (beyond directly economic considerations) for some, but much less so for others. Yet even if one studies the guitar phenomenon for a short time one soon comes across evidence to suggest that the guitar is not only popular, but is consistently so, and in evidence in the lives of very many different people (in one way or another).

Moreover, this popularity – and, indeed, the very idea of popularity itself – is also commercially driven, reaffirmed and shaped. The guitar is the object of a vast number of dedicated corporate industries and retail trades, is an icon of popular culture in sound and image, a part of global media and developments in advanced technology, and has wide appeal musically and culturally across the planet. Readily available and observable, this wide-ranging evidence supports the claim that the guitar is widely spread, even if there is a small but detailed number of ethnographic studies that are able to support such a claim, or are able to show the full *extent* (and meaning) of the guitar's role within very many different people's lives. The guitar is clearly much more than a trivial pursuit or casual leisure-time interest for the very many people who make it or play it, but also for those who do neither but appreciate its value in numerous ways.

To be clear, in gauging the guitar's popularity, one needs to know not only the *extent* to which the guitar is present in music, culture and society, but also the extent to which it is the object of *investment* (in terms of time, money, usage, status, meaning and power). Of course, a musical instrument, or various other things for that matter, can be phenomenal without necessarily being extensive, widespread, economically viable or particularly meaningful. Yet evidence readily confirms the fact that the guitar is more extensively distributed and has greater utility than most other musical instruments currently in use. The guitar is the instrument of choice for a great many different kinds of people from multifarious backgrounds. It is in high profile in an enormous range of music genres; it is a feature of a vast number of Internet sites, educational establishments, promotional culture, advertising, video games, toys and art; and it is the focus for a growing body of written studies (academic and otherwise). Perhaps a preliminary list of reasons why the guitar can be considered phenomenally popular (or a popular phenomenon), in terms of its utility, use-value or creative potential might be helpful at this stage; the reasons for its use-value also point to reasons why it is extensively available or widespread.[2]

- Portability
- Versatility (which may be defined in several ways)
- Affordability (there is a wide-ranging price scale)
- Expressivity, potential for communication (of emotions, in particular)
- Playability, responsiveness
- Tuning facility, tuneability, potential for altered tuning, range of tunings
- Distinct sound, tone, volume, sustain, potential for a wide range of playing techniques, amplification, add-on effects
- Durability, malleability, high level of user and professional customization, reproduce-ability (copies can be made, cheap copies can be made, it can be scratch built), yet retaining the potential to be personalized

---

[2]   The reader may have noticed already that this book represents a serious attempt to understand the guitar phenomenon at the time of writing. However, I am keen to mention that guitar is also the subject, object and vehicle of much humour, and used by comedians to make people laugh as much as to make them cry. I do not intend to 'lighten up' at any point in my analysis as it proceeds through this book, but it is important to mention that the guitar is also the object and vehicle of fun and frivolity, which, I claim from experience, is another reason for its phenomenal popularity. Two important examples of comedians using guitars in their act (or musicians being funny, according to one's perspective and taste) are Tenacious D (Jack Black and Kyle Gass) from North America and Bill Bailey from England. Bailey, for instance, is able to find much to comment on in the fields of both popular and classical music: often his humour is conveyed or emphasized via sound (vocals, guitar and keyboards). He uses what is called a 'guitar-banjo' in one YouTube video (an unaccompanied acoustic guitar through a modelling effects processor to create a banjo sound) to play Led Zeppelin's classic heavy rock piece 'Stairway to Heaven', in what he calls a 'hillbilly style'. Moreover it is important to note the various shades of humour that one regularly finds in guitar magazines, for instance, from tongue-in-cheek remarks by editors to advertisements designed also for comic effect. There is much comic relief to be had in the new guitarscape, especially when performers poke fun at themselves in the role of guitar heroes. And as noted in Bill Bailey's case, even he is able to make use of new guitar technologies in his act. But in terms of the corporations that invest heavily in the world of the guitar, it is a very serious business indeed.

- Iconicity, from sexual object to art object, representative of 'attitude', the guitar as gun, air guitar, photogenic (part of advertising and promotional culture)
- Ability to retain identity across a wide variety of media
- Feel, touch, closeness to body, fit with the body, optimally designed for comfort
- Mentally and physically demanding, yielding to minimum effort but requiring enormous dedication for mastery
- Self-contained (harmony, melody, drone, percussion) but potential for ensemble work
- Wide-ranging dedicated repertoire and wide-ranging application in music
- Offers a range of opportunities in terms of performance
- The object of research, from sound design and composition to cultural studies and iconography
- Historically important to the field of music and in musical instrument studies
- Well-established and growing pantheon of great and master guitarists (providing role models, benchmarks, standards, repertoires, techniques, sounds)
- For all the reasons above and more, the guitar sells (it is economically viable), as does a range of musical equipment, recordings, software and publications related to the guitar

In terms of the guitar's versatility, but also its potential for universal musical application, it may be more accurate (without being too reductionist) to suggest a model based on a three-line simple-to-complex continuum:

Line 1 (technique): how the guitar is played, the activation and stopping of the strings and other parts of the guitar by the performer (as well as the manipulation of a range of devices now found in guitar rigs, patched in but also controlled in performance);

Line 2 (technology): the guitar and its equipment, the setting of the controls and string height or action, for instance, including the strings used, amplification potential and settings, as well as further adjustments and modifications (all of the performers mentioned in Chapter 1 use custom-built or customized instruments as well as, in some cases, amplification, effects and computer patches, tailored to a specific set of performance and musical demands); and

Line 3 (repertoire): the variety of music that is played upon the guitar by guitarists of numerous musical orientations, and the musical ideas sustaining but also driving the instrument's development.

The three lines on this continuum run parallel – in and out of phase and intensity – in intriguing but also identifiable ways, performers' musical choices and decisions making up the guitar's multifaceted sonic identity in response to social and cultural contexts (aesthetics, ideas, the role of music, genre ideals), resulting in a mosaic of culturally based musical approaches, scenes and styles. Not that this is the only such model of how technique, technology and repertoire interact guitaristically in a world full of music and musicians. With regard to the role of the guitar as an instrument of global performance, and with specific reference to the comments of slide guitarist Bob Brozman, Christopher J. Smith notes: 'the cross-cultural impact of the guitar results from the contact between the instrument's diatonic applications (specifically, the use of chords) in the West, and the non-diatonic ideas (specifically, an orientation towards modes and drones) of indigenous music from around the world' (Smith, 2003:33).

The Extent of the Guitar Phenomenon

In Érik Orsenna's novelette *History of the World in Nine Guitars* (published in French in 1996), guitarists from different nations, generations and musical persuasions hear about the plans for a celebration of the instrument via the guitar grapevine, a grapevine that includes, among its various networking devices, the Internet. Orsenna takes the reader on a journey through time and space, connecting up many historical periods and places, building upon the stuff of guitar lore and legend. In this book, I engage indirectly with time-travel, largely because, as noted already, several important and authoritative books have been written on the history of the guitar.

The World Wide Web, invented by Tim Berners-Lee and available from the early 1990s, has changed the world of the guitar. Although hard-copy music sales continue to decline because of their availability over the Internet, there is evidence to suggest that live performances have increased as a response to that loss of income. But many of the events described here are dependent on promotion, sales, upgrades and support from online sources. User groups, blogs, specialist interest pages (for example, Wikipedia, premierguitars.com, guitar-channel.com, guitargeek.com, newmillguitar.com), tuition, instrument manufacturers, artists' websites, guitar magazines (which also feature reviews of new acts and provide links to their MySpace or other web pages), Guitar Idol (the yearly search for a winner via YouTube video re-postings on the Guitar Idol site), musical instrument trade fairs and shows, YouTube itself, MySpace, Music Player Network, online music networks supporting new acts, all promote, disseminate and share every aspect of the guitarscape to bring it to anyone with access to a computer. It might be claimed that the World Wide Web has also pumped new life into old media, for instance in increasing the availability of offline and online guitar magazines, which can elaborate on items and add more features not only in print, but via DVD, CD and now Internet pages and links. This is what Henry Jenkins has called elsewhere 'convergence culture', a catchphrase that makes reference to the view that 'new media' has not displaced 'old media' *per se*, but has forced old media to engage with it (after Jenkins, 2006). In connection with this idea, Robert Shaw also notes the effect of the Internet on the well established occupation of guitar building:

> The advent of the World Wide Web in the mid-1990s helped fuel the expansion of guitar building. The Internet levelled the playing field for small entrepreneurs by making it far easier for consumers, builders and retailers to find each other and by helping advance the careers of many luthiers, dealers and consultants. (Shaw, 2008:11)

World Music recordings, now readily available and promoted online, continue to reveal the many guitar styles that exist across the planet and something (if not much) about the many different cultures in which the guitar has taken root. Monthly guitar magazines proliferate, if not expand exponentially, on the shelves of news agencies (but now also via Internet links as noted above). The North America-based monthly magazine *Guitar Player* celebrated its fortieth birthday in 2007. Tom Wheeler, one-time editor-in-chief of the magazine, notes that beyond the team of journalists and the printing press, the magazine's 'greater heritage' lies in:

> print, photos and graphics, in thousands of stories, columns and departments, and ads stretching over forty years. These collected works are not merely the legacy of employees; they are part of the literature of the broader guitar community – artists who inspired us, advertisers who supported us, and you, the readers who told us what you wanted and needed and who let us hear from you when we got it wrong. (Molenda, 2007:x).

Based in Britain, *Guitarist* magazine celebrated its twenty-fifth anniversary in 2009, recalling that the cover of the first issue in 1984 featured George Benson, Ted Nugent and 'the none-more-modernistic SynthAxe', even if 'Leo Fender's rudimentary Telecaster would gloriously outrun the SynthAxe for the rest of time: probably good news all round' (Taylor, 2009:3). At the time of writing, the Fender Telecaster guitar is still very much in high profile and is the main guitar of artists as musically different as John 5, Sue Foley, Bill Frisell and Brad Paisley. However, whilst it may have 'outrun' the SynthAxe, it now faces a possible challenge from guitars using advanced technologies, from Gibson's Robot Guitar to the Moog Guitar (even if some people – who shall remain anonymous – doubt if there is a potential market for these instruments, given their high prices and requirements for use). It must also be noted that, although the Telecaster, like many other guitars still in existence (but created in the 1950s), retains many of its original design features, the Telecasters of today also reflect and feature the latest developments in a range of technologies, from tools of manufacture to pick-ups. Such developments are charted in a great many books on the history of the guitar (and several of them are referenced in this book).

As noted elsewhere in this book, the guitar is the basis for a worldwide manufacturing industry, from cottage industry to corporate culture. Teje Gerken writes of 'Global Lutherie' in a recent edition of *Acoustic Guitar* (see Gerken, 2003),[3] and Robert Shaw, whose richly illustrated book contains more than 300 examples of the work of contemporary guitar makers, notes:

> Whatever the future holds, the present is a moment without precedent in the history of the guitar. … Both the quality of the workmanship and materials are at an all-time high as creative luthiers explore the use of every conceivable type of tonewood and go to extraordinary lengths to find rare and exotic timber. … The entire history of the guitar is at the disposal of today's builders, and both the guitar's history and future can be told through the amazing instruments they are creating. (Shaw, 2008:17)

The National Association of Music Merchants (NAMM, at Anaheim, California), Music Live at the Birmingham National Exhibition Centre, the London Guitar Show (part of the London International Music Show), the Dundee International Guitar Festival, and the Bath International Guitar Festival (organized and hosted by the International Guitar Foundation and Festivals, and Bath Spa University) exist among many guitar (as well as many other musical instrument/ equipment) fests attracting huge crowds every year via their own Internet sites and ticket hotlines. Moreover, the first World Guitar Congress was held in Baltimore, Maryland, in June 2004, and the thirtieth annual Dallas International Guitar Festival was held in April 2009 (see premierguitar.com, guitarshow.com).

The ninth New York Guitar Seminar at Mannes College was held in July 2009, with the theme of 'New York/New World: Guitar in the Americas'. With a focus on the Spanish six-string or classical guitar, the seminar aimed to highlight the 'rich and diverse heritage of the guitar in music throughout North, Central and South America'.[4] Moreover, the world of the classical guitar is also represented by the website www.worldguitarist.com. Despite the fact that the classical guitar

---

[3]   Wikipedia's 'List of Classical Guitar Makers', for example, includes makers from twenty countries, including Brazil, Finland, Indonesia, Japan, Peru, South Africa, Turkey, Venezuela and Paraguay. See: www.en.wikipedia.org/wiki/List_of_classical_guitar_makers. Studies of guitar making and manufacture outside the USA include: Romanillos, 1987; Ramírez III, 1993; Dawe with Dawe, 2001. See also Thomas Kies's ethnographic study of guitar makers in Mexico (Kies, 2006). Moreover, it must be noted that guitars by the same company (but, perhaps, different models) may be made in various countries. For example, Ovation guitars make particular models in the USA, Korea and China. See www. ovationguitars.com. See also a useful article on Ovation guitars in *Gear*, 17 (2005):34–6.

[4]   See http://216.71.55.88/gi/index.php?option=com_content&view=article&id=13& Itemid=28.

is played around the world (as noted in Chapter 1), it might be seen to inhabit one of the less high-profile areas of new guitarscape. However, Richard Corr sees hope 'in the re-emergence of the guitarist/composer, for example, Roland Dyens (France), Gary Ryan (England), Dusan Bogdanović (Serbia), Andrew York (North America). This harps back to the nineteenth century tradition where players such as Sor and Aguado were also prolific composers for their instrument' (Richard Corr, personal communication).

African guitarists recently played the 'Guitars for Africa' concert in New York.[5] Since 2000 the International Guitar Night has featured guitarists such as D'Gary (Madagascar), Clive Carroll (UK), Miguel de la Bastide (Trinidad) and Brian Gore (USA) on stage together.[6] An earlier model of 'world guitar' could be seen in the concerts and recordings (1980, 1982 and 1996) made by John McLaughlin (UK), Al Di Meola (USA) and Paco de Lucía (Spain) as a guitar trio.[7] John McLaughlin's collaborations with musicians from India were, perhaps, at their most intense in the group Shakti. This group seems to represent what I have heard musicians around the world describe as the 'first and last world music group'.[8] Moreover, John McLaughlin, Al Di Meola and Paco de Lucía, together and apart, remain a driving force in the world of the guitar, connecting up musicians around the world as three of the instrument's foremost virtuosi, innovators and champions. Their significance remains clear as they continue to nurture and encourage new musical talent, and continue to endorse new musical products.

---

[5]   See Guitars for Africa: http://www.3rdearmusic.com/gallery/ggfa.html.

[6]   See internationalguitarnight.com. The web page states that the International Guitar Night 'is the longest-running "mobile guitar festival" in North America. Each year, the IGN founder Brian Gore of San Francisco is joined by three of the world's foremost acoustic guitarists to perform their latest original compositions and exchange musical ideas in a public concert setting.' Artists listed as having featured in concerts between 2000 and 2007 include: Badi Assad ('Brazilian Guitar/Vocal Innovator'), Vishwa Mohan Bhatt ('Indian Slide Guitarist, inventor of mohan veena'), Clive Carroll ('Brilliant English Fingerstyle Guitarist'), Alex de Grassi ('New Acoustic Legend'), Peppino D'Agostino ('Italian Guitar Wizard'), Mimi Fox ('Female Jazz Guitarist'), Gerardo Nuñez ('Nuevo Flamenco Visionary'), Don Ross ('Canada's "Heavy Wood" Guitarist'), Ralph Towner ('Influential Jazz/Classical Innovator'), Andrew White ('Dynamic New Zealand singer/songwriter/ guitarist') and Andrew York ('America's Classical Guitarist/Composer').

[7]   See the following albums: Al Di Meola, John McLaughlin and Paco de Lucía, *Friday Night in San Francisco*, Columbia FC37152 (1980); John McLaughlin, Al Di Meola and Paco de Lucía, *Passion, Grace and Fire*, Columbia FC 38645 (1983); Paco de Lucía, Al Di Meola and John McLaughlin, *The Guitar Trio*, Verve 533215-2 (1996). The trio became a quartet when it was joined by guitarist Steve Morse on its second world tour in 1982.

[8]   The recordings from the 1970s are noted here: *Shakti with John McLaughlin*, Columbia PC34162 (1975); Shakti with John McLaughlin, *A Handful of Beauty*, Columbia PC 34372; Shakti with John McLaughlin, *Natural Elements*, Columbia JC 34980 (1977).

One can learn to build a guitar, set up a guitar and repair it, and even if one is reluctant to do so, there are many specialists offering such services.[9] Guitar technicians, especially those who tour with well-known bands or solo artists, are highly prized for their skills by musicians, journalists and audiences, and may be seen to be revered in a similar way to many guitar heroes (see, for example, Frost, 2008; Vines, 2008).[10] Some established players are also guitar makers.[11] Likewise, one can learn to play the guitar in a wide range of styles with monthly lessons in guitar magazines (they may also come with assorted 'free' items or 'gifts', such as collector's cards, plectrum tins and posters wrapped up with the magazine in a plastic bag), in DVD series, from Internet sites,[12] through tutorial books which may have CDs attached, from printed sheet music or in face-to-face lessons (a large array of levels and styles is available),[13] perhaps involving clinics, weekend breaks, camps or guitar holidays, often marketed as 'Getaways' and 'Awaydays'.[14]

Various guitar institutes offering tuition by virtuosi and professionals alike exist as far apart as London and Los Angeles. Moreover, out of 3,800 musicians attending the Berklee College of Music in Boston in 2004 – the largest music

---

[9] See the advertisement in *Vintage Guitar* (September 2008):71 or visit www.specimenguitars.com.

[10] In fact, guitar technicians are often drawn into the frame when guitarists are interviewed talking about their on-stage rigs or gear set-ups. See, for example, the DVD to *Guitarist* magazine, 303 (July 2008), which features glimpses of both Steve Lukather's and Alter Bridge's guitar technicians (as well as front- and backstage gear layout). The guitarists featured take the viewer on a guided tour of their rigs (guitars, amplification, effects, etc.).

[11] See the article 'Building to Play' by Ron Forbes-Roberts in *Acoustic Guitar* (March 2009):54–9.

[12] See, for example, the following *very small* selection of guitar-related websites: www.guitarworld.com, www.guitarteachermagazine.com, www.playguitarmagazine.com, www.guitarsessions.com, www.GuitarPlayertv, www.acousticguitar.com, www.modernguitars.com, www.premierguitar.com, www.guitar-channel.com, www.ultimate-guitar.tv, www.guitarmasterclass.net, www.gibson.com, www.guitarcenter.com, www.guitarfoundation.org, www.laguitarre.com, www.guitarkulture.com, www.booksforguitar.com, www.fretsonly.com.

[13] See also the online Registry of Guitar Tutors: registryofguitartutors.com. The patrons of the registry give some indication of the esteem in which it is held as well as its musical eclecticism. They include Sir Paul McCartney, Carlos Bonnell, John Etheridge and Suzi Quatro.

[14] See, for example, guitargetaways.com and a recent advertisement in *Guitarist*, 309 (November 2008):173. The Ministry of the Guitar offers rock camps for young musicians (guitar, bass, drums, voice). The Internet links given are: www.igf.org.uk; www.oracle@ministryofguitar.org.uk. See also the National Guitar Workshop: www.guitarworkshop.com.

conservatoire in the world – 1,100 were guitarists.[15] Not only has the college fifty guitar teachers in its guitar faculty (five of them women), but it has also another 2,000 students registered online (see berklee.com). On the other side of the Atlantic Ocean, the Academy of Contemporary Music in Guildford, Surrey, has drawn upon and developed the talents of a wide variety of teachers and students, from the late Eric Roche to Newton Faulkner and Guthrie Govan. Such places generate an interest in the guitar, nurturing talent whilst helping to maintain a consensus and standard of excellence in performance and teaching.[16]

Yet even when the guitar is not played, it is well able to attract the interest of an audience of admirers and collectors. Vintage guitars, or guitars with special associations and historical significance, fetch high prices among the collectors who buy them (see Ryan and Peterson, 2001). The first guitar that Jimi Hendrix set aflame with lighter fuel in 1967 – a 1965 Fender Stratocaster – had at the time of writing sold for £280,000.[17] Similarly, Maybelle Carter's 1928 Gibson L-5 arch-top changed hands for $500,000 and Roy Roger's Martin OM-45 Deluxe acoustic reached an auction price of $460,000.[18] Moreover, in keeping with the subject of the ways in which the guitar-as-object is valued, the guitar as art is a concept explored by Frederic Grunfeld in his 1969 publication, *The Art and Times of the Guitar*, and explored in passing in various parts of this book (also in terms of photography, advertising and promotional culture). As André Millard comments, in the caption to a photograph of a guitar by Hawaii-based guitar maker Steve Grimes: 'Guitar as art. A stunning blue guitar from the Chinery Collection that was featured in the "Blue Guitars" exhibit at the Smithsonian … It is called Jazz Laureate and looks so good you might think twice before playing it' (Millard, 2004:117). Robert Shaw's book on contemporary guitars also shows off designs that one might consider as artworks as much as fully functional musical instruments (Shaw, 2008), involving experiments with new construction materials and electronic technologies, ideally uniting scientific knowledge and aesthetic considerations through the skills and imaginations of both makers and performers. The guitar is clearly valued, appreciated, sold and consumed in many diverse and, to my mind, rather unexpected and extraordinary ways.

---

[15]   See 'A Professor of Guitar from the School of Rock', www.npr.org/templates/story/story.php?storyId=4123589 (2004).

[16]   Whilst lecturing at the Open University in 2001 I was fortunate to be involved in the making of a BBC video documentary on the heavy metal guitar. The Guildford Academy of Contemporary Music features prominently in the programme. Perspectives and insights gained at the time also inform this book. I continue to be grateful for the participation and input of Dave Kilminster and Jamie Humphries (teachers at the academy at that time), and also Yngwie Malmsteen, Phil Hilborne and David Mead.

[17]   *Guitar and Bass Magazine* takes up the story in a short news item entitled: 'Hendrix Strat Fetches Big Bucks' (issue 19/12, December 2008:6).

[18]   See the short news item in 'The Roy Done Good: The Most Expensive Acoustic Ever?', *Guitarist*, 316 (June 2009):18.

It must also be noted that several biographies of guitarists have emerged. For example, see those of Robert Fripp, B.B. King, Les Paul, Memphis Minnie, Eric Clapton, Jeff Beck, Danny Gatton, Charlie Christian, Suzi Quatro, Stevie Ray Vaughan, Wes Montgomery, Andrés Segovia, Djelimady Tounkara, John McLaughlin, Martin Taylor, Franco (Luambo Makiadi), Joni Mitchell, Fernando Sor, Roy Buchanan and Julian Bream, all available via the Internet. These biographies show up the complex and multifaceted role of the guitar in individual lives. Moreover, they show the demands made upon professional performers and the extent of their dedication to the guitar in the intensity of various musical scenes and local cultural contexts, tours and recordings, over long periods of time.

Moreover, in various ways, LGBT (lesbian, gay, bisexual and transgender/transsexual) guitarists are also exploring the opportunities of the new guitarscape as seen, for one thing, in the great diversity of musical styles in which they play. Robert Urban, a musician, producer and writer who is also founder and moderator of the website 'Gay Guitarists Worldwide', notes:

> LGBT guitarists and bassists, and/or rock acts, that are very popular with LGBT audiences, who I personally think are awesome and who I've also featured on Gay Guitarists Worldwide, include: Connecticut-based lesbian guitarist Vange Durst, formerly of the all lesbian funk rock band Sister Funk and now fronting her own trio – EV3; the U.K.-based rock project Zerocrop (consisting of gay songwriter Parker and straight guitarist Marlon Banjo; England's transgender singer/songwriter/guitarist Jenny Slater; NYC's African-American lesbian blues/funk guitarist/singer/songwriter Nedra Johnson; Holland's new age/classical acoustic gay guitarist Gerard Slooven; American transgender 80s Glam-influenced guitarist and pop star Lisa Jackson; dual transgender guitarists Marylin and Sarafina of the all transgender San Francisco based rock band Lipstick Conspiracy; and gay icon, punk guitarist/singer/songwriter Scott Free of Chicago, USA; and British Columbia, Canada transgender 'surf-guitar' virtuoso Suzy Wedge of Suzy Wedge and the Waves. (Robert Urban, personal communication)[19]

Yet, as already noted, it is my claim that studies of the contemporary world of the guitar, beyond a handful of academic and scholarly works, have been, at best, limited in scope. To my mind, the BBC's *The Story of the Guitar* (October 2008, televised on Sunday evenings at 10.00 pm) demonstrates this point well. It follows a predictable and well-worn formula.[20] It mobilizes a canon of masterworks and guitar heroics that makes for a well-known celebrity-based history. Although the documentary touches on themes taken up in this book, such as the importance

---

[19] Robert Urban comments: 'meet and read reviews/interviews of all the above at: http://www.roberturban.com/gayguitaristsworldwide.html'.

[20] See 'The Story of the Guitar', http://www.bbc.co.uk/musictv/guitars/.

of the look, feel and sonic versatility of the guitar, as well as its role in musical, technological and social developments, it represents a great opportunity missed.

Moreover, recent developments which make for the contemporary field of the guitar are hardly explored, such as the variety of extended techniques, and the more prominent role or greater exposure gained by women (even though women guitarists are featured). The story of the guitar is cut short, its role as an instrument of global and intergenerational performance – an instrument of men, women and children, from a wide variety of cultures – is hardly acknowledged (even if the series touches briefly on the role of the guitar in Africa and China in rather esoteric terms). The enormous range of approaches to performance, use of technologies and playing techniques still remains largely undocumented and scattered for a general audience. The strength of *The Story of the Guitar* lies in its ability to document audiences' reactions to the guitar and its reception and assimilation into certain north European and North American contexts, times and places, using precious documentary film (which actually demonstrates that a great deal more is going on than the programme makers suggest). Given the theoretical trajectory of this book, I cannot claim to have solved the problem of how to go into any great detail about various aspects of the guitar phenomenon either, and certainly do not try to do everything in one publication (nor a short television series for that matter). But there are models which aid a more in-depth exploration of the guitar phenomenon.

To my mind, Steve Waksman's *Instruments of Desire* (1999) represents a new epoch in guitar research. (This seminal publication on the electric guitar has been inspirational in my own work in several respects.) Not only does Waksman chart the history of the electric guitar in a largely North American context throughout the twentieth century, but he expands upon issues of identity and ethnicity and how these can be seen to have been carried in sound and image by the guitarist (and the guitar). Waksman explores issues of 'the aesthetics of sound and the politics of sonority' in the work of such guitar luminaries as Charlie Christian, Les Paul, Chet Atkins and Jimi Hendrix (Waksman, 1999:290). It is clear that all of these guitarists have had a major and lasting impact on the soundscape of North American popular music, but also on the musical landscape of the wider world. I draw on Waksman's insights at various points in this book, but also note what seems like an invitation from him to elaborate on more recent developments in the world of the guitar (in the light of its complex history).

In his final chapter, Waksman seems to invite a study of a range of aspects of the guitar phenomenon, from the use of the body in guitar performance to the apparently radical designs of guitar makers (for example, Hans Reichel), who, in their search for new sounds, also employ a wide range of playing techniques and musical technologies. Such processes of musical creativity transform the guitar in a cycle that also transforms the music that is played upon it. Clearly, the transformations of the guitar have come about in a nexus of musical, technical, technological, social and cultural developments. Importantly, Waksman signs off his book with a statement that certainly attracts my interest: he says that the electric guitar is 'a device used to explore, challenge, and compose the systems of order and disorder, sameness and difference that have constituted popular music in this century' (Waksman, 1999:294). As he notes, writing of the twentieth century and popular music, and as I wish to emphasize here (focusing on early-twenty-first-century music), the evidence also suggests that the guitar is a device that continues to uphold as many values and beliefs, legends and myths as it continues to challenge in music and beyond music. Moreover, order and disorder, sameness and difference are negotiated and contested guitaristically on a worldwide scale, as is clearly observable via a range of sources (from archives and ethnographies of guitar-based music to live performances now disseminated on the Internet).

I found myself pondering upon how elements of Waksman's work (but likewise that of André Millard, whose book is also based ostensibly in a North American context) might be applied not only in a wider contemporary setting but also cross-culturally or, rather, how ethnographic research in various parts of the world might usefully continue to put a critical plough into what has already been written about the guitar, particularly in the light of comments from Waksman about the connections and coincidences 'in markedly different musical settings' which are 'the stuff out of which the history of the electric guitar has been made' (Waksman, 1999:293). One now has access to some scholarly material on how the electric guitar, but also the acoustic guitar, took root and has been used in sub-Saharan Africa, for example (see Waterman, 1990; Schmidt, 1994; Eyre, 2000 and 2003; Charry, 2000). I note the efforts made by Bennett and Dawe (2001) and Coelho (2003) not only to try and rectify the dearth of writing on the guitar as an object of global performance, but also to review what research there is comparatively. It is clear that, although there is a small but well-written pool of literature on the guitar phenomenon, this has primarily concentrated on North America and Europe. Moreover, given the complex and multifaceted world of the guitar as revealed in a handful of studies on the instrument inside and outside North America and Europe, there is much work still left to be done.

A great deal of ethnographic research is still required, and this book soon began to take the shape of an ideas book, literature review, survey and research companion in the hope that more ethnographic research might be forthcoming. However, I try to draw on my own fieldwork experiences as much as on those of other individuals. My own long and short fieldwork trips and micro-studies have taken me to a range of countries, to places as far apart as Papua New Guinea and Spain, where I encountered many different types of guitarists making music, as well as a wide range of guitar-based music and types of guitar. I agree wholeheartedly with Richard Chapman when he states that 'For many years, I have felt strongly that something needed to be written about a phenomenon that plays a part in almost every musical genre and musical culture throughout the world' (Chapman, 2000:7). I was also encouraged by André Millard's edited collection, *The Electric Guitar: A History of an American Icon* (2004), which concludes with the optimistic chapter 'The Electric Guitar at the New Millennium'. Millard's collection usefully connects up the past with the present whilst outlining a few more recent trends in guitar-based music and guitar manufacture.

Ralph Gibson's photographic collection entitled *State of the Axe: Guitar Masters in Photographs and Words* (2008) also encouraged me to continue the pursuit of my own goal of a study of the guitar in contemporary perspective, keeping in mind the powerful and empowering images evoked by the guitar and guitarist. Gibson's book features the work of eighty-one guitarists, including Dominic Frasca and Fred Frith, whom one might consider contemporary (some of whom I mention in this book, and most of whom I would have liked to mention). My intention is to offer a publication that extends the academic terms by which the guitar might be studied. But it is the guitar phenomenon as it currently stands that has provided both the stimulus and the test bed for my critical, analytical and theoretical approach. In turn, I hope that this book will also provide a useful survey of the guitar phenomenon. The ten examples in Chapter 1 are included because, to my mind, they reflect something of that current state, both contemporary and cross-cultural, whilst hinting at the various routes of enquiry developed in this book.

Therefore, the choice of who and what to include and who and what to leave out has to a great extent been decided by the availability of reliable scholarly research, documentary evidence and my own experience. And, moreover, the intention is not to create an encyclopaedia of guitar players but rather to give a theoretical exposition of the study of the guitar in its current state, also suggesting areas for further research. There is clearly a set of broad questions that I ask of my selection of ten guitarists (and those featured elsewhere in the book), those whom I can only mention in passing, and those whose names may not be found in this book but feature within the references given.

Who to Include, Who to Leave Out?

When discussing the guitar phenomenon, one quickly finds oneself referring to the work of individual guitarists, whether part of supergroups (such as The Edge of U2, Djelimady Tounkara of the Rail Band, John Petrucci of Dream Theater) or solo artists who sometimes work with small ensembles (Bob Brozman, D'Gary, Martin Simpson, Martin Taylor). I think there is a well-established and logical precedence for introducing this book, even with its theoretical focus, through a description of guitarists in performance (describing the music and the guitars that they play, and their amplification and effects). Perhaps such an approach makes connections between theory and practice clearer, and acknowledges the relevance of theorizing up in the light of the complexity of the performances described.

Moreover, although the ten guitarists in Chapter 1 play a pivotal role in introducing some of the book's themes, they all play music that grabs my attention and alerts me to the relevance and potential of the topics I am investigating (as discussed in the next chapter and found as core questions at the heart of the remaining chapters). Indeed, I have been a follower of the work of Fripp, Isbin, Frith and Vai for some time. But, clearly, if this is not to turn into another fan book I need to be able to justify their inclusion in a book that might have introduced its core ideas through the work of a host of other guitarists.[21] There is, of course, room for more focused studies of the acoustic, electric guitar and bass guitar (in its acoustic and electric forms) that could run to several volumes. The omissions in this book – in terms of players, styles, instruments – will be obvious to most guitarists, especially to bass players. But I am hopeful that bass players and scholars of the bass guitar, for instance, will find material of interest to them here. I argue that the ideas in this book are applicable to a wide variety of instruments coming within a broad definition of 'guitar', even if they can only be mentioned in passing (or lie outside the author's knowledge and experience), such as the pedal steel, lap steel, Touch and Stick guitars.

It was my intention all along to include a mixture of well-known and well-established guitarists alongside those less known and not as well established (at least with an international audience).[22] I want to feature both electric and acoustic guitarists, crossing as many fields of music making as possible in ten key examples. And I want to show off the guitarists' technique, their use of technology (including types of guitar) and their approach to performance. It is crucial to include both men and women, and guitarists from a range of cultures, not just to be politically correct but to reflect my observations, that is, the evidence before my eyes and ears. In the end, I limit myself to ten guitarists in Chapter 1, in the spirit of Érik Orsenna's *History of the World of Nine Guitars* (1999). My ten guitar players and nine chapters would reflect his world of nines and zeroes at the turn of the millennium, but with my own publication date of 2010. It must also be noted that Orsenna's book was originally published in France as *Histoire du monde en*

---

[21]   Not that each and every reader will agree on my choice of guitarists. I have the same problem here as any writer on the guitar: who to include and who to leave out? In their 'Publisher's Note', the publishers of *Guitar Heroes* (2008) comment: 'One thing that we can all agree on is a book like this will never be complete. No doubt we will continue to revise and update it, so if we've missed out any of your personal favourites, please e-mail us with your suggestions at guitarheroes@flametreepublishing.com. We can't promise to agree with you, but we would love to hear from you. Let the debate rage on!' I am also aware that the guitarists I have featured are not going to be to everyone's taste. Indeed, Robert Fripp kindly sent me two very revealing but also markedly contrasting reviews of his own more recent recordings. See a summary of reviews of Fripp's *At the End of Time* (DGM, 2007) at www.robertfripp.comarchive.htm?artist+14&show=1202. See also recordcollectormag. comreviews/review-detail/34.

[22]   See also www.listverse.com/2008/04/27/top 10-guitarists-you-don't-know/.

neuf guitares in 1996 (see Orsenna, 1996). Too often one writes with glee and abandonment about the guitar in the English language, forgetting that there are many books and articles written in other languages on the subject, including, for example, the many guitar magazines and websites in French, Spanish, German, Japanese and Arabic. I cannot claim to have included many of them in this book.

In one way or another, each and every guitarist of the ten is involved in pushing musical boundaries. Some are more able than others to challenge the guitar canon, and some are a part of it, but all are able to demonstrate performance ability at the highest level as judged not just by me but through an emerging consensus of opinion as observed in a range of sources (from the legions of popular or light reading books on the guitar to more academic tomes, from YouTube blogs to album reviews in the popular press). All ten guitarists have close links with guitar makers and have been involved in the design or the promotion of new models of guitars, amplification and effects, from fretless instruments to advanced looping systems. Moreover, all have videos on YouTube or MySpace (at least at the time of writing), all have web pages, all are potentially contactable, and all have recordings that are obtainable via the Internet (at the time of writing). Most are well known among the guitar-playing fraternity. But I aim to include a few surprises.

But if I could have included one or more solo performances in my ten that might be seen to complement Robert Fripp's soundscapes, it would have been a solo piece by Bill Frissel or David Torn, or perhaps by a younger musician, such as Otso Lähdeoja or Santiago Quintans (whom I had the privilege to meet and work with in Paris in 2009). And there are several solo artists and groups who have emerged out of Robert Fripp's Guitar Craft courses, including the California Guitar Trio.

Kamala Shankar, along with Brij Bhushan Kabra, Debashish Bhattacharya and Vishwa Mohan Bhatt, is among the leading lights of Indian slide guitar playing. But, of course, there are slide guitar traditions elsewhere in the world, most obviously in Hawaii, and the blues slide guitar seems also to have taken root among guitar players across the world. North Americans Bob Brozman and Ry Cooder are internationally respected for their slide or bottleneck guitar playing, whether on acoustic, resophonic or lap-style guitar. Both musicians have collaborated with musicians worldwide, including North Indian slide guitarists Debashish Bhattacharya and Vishwa Mohan Bhatt.

I tend to link Fred Frith's approach with that of Keith Rowe, Hans Reichel, Glenn Branca, Rhys Chatham, Janet Feder, Paolo Angeli, Ava Mendoza, Alessio Monti, Mike Cooper and Thurston Moore of Sonic Youth, taking in a broad sweep of musical ideas and experiments with the musical, technological and ensemble potential of the guitar. I also see as connected the work of Bill Frisell, Nels Cline, Phil Keaggy, Marc Ribot, David Torn and the late Derek Bailey (among many others), who improvise across a wide range of styles and genres, including jazz, rock, ambient, country, world and classical music.

Banning Eyre notes that 'African guitarists with manifestly individual sounds are gaining worldwide reputations' (Eyre, 2003:44). However, alongside Lionel

Loueke there are several guitarists from sub-Saharan Africa, for example, whose work I am not able to feature (including D'Gary and Djelimady Tounkara), not to mention the vast number of jazz guitar players whose representation is lamentably small in this book (except for Lionel Loueke and Pat Metheny). But besides Lionel Loueke, the other African guitarists mentioned above are indeed present on the Internet in one form or another – in their recordings, pictures, reviews – but there are no reliable video recordings of their performances, particularly solo performances, immediately accessible to me at the time of writing. Nor did they necessarily demonstrate the confluence of technique, technology and repertoire in their work that I needed to try and get across in the opening chapter. It was only when I was in the last stages of writing up this book that I found video performances by Lionel Loueke on YouTube.

Hasan Cihat Örter displays an extraordinary command of the music of his homeland and music from well beyond it. Almost beyond belief, I discovered that there are many, many more musicians in Turkey whose video clips on YouTube show up the ways in which they use the guitar in their work. Erkan Oğur can be found in concert singing and playing the *cura* (small long-necked lute) in one clip, then playing fretless electric guitar with an E-Bow in the next. I only recently discovered the recordings that he has made featuring the fretless classical guitar, an instrument which he has championed since the 1970s.[23] Younger Turkish musicians, for example Cenk Erdoğan and Uğur Varol, are also playing the fretless electric guitar (also in fretted and unfretted double-neck form). As featured in an article in *Guitar Player*, composer Erdem Helvacioğlu uses an Ovation electro-acoustic guitar plugged into a laptop computer, through which he draws on contemporary sounds from both inside and outside Turkey (see Cleveland, 2007).

The fretless guitar is also played by such musical luminaries as Steve Vai, Pat Metheny, Ron Thal, Tim Donahue, David Fiuczynski, Michelle Webb, Simon Yu, Elliot Sharp and Edward Powell. These players draw attention to the wider world of fretless guitar playing that now exists, experimenting with microtones and the modal systems found in the music of the Middle East, but also within the *raga* systems of India. Simon Yu explores a range of styles, including the musical systems and traditional repertoires of China. Dedicated Internet sites exist to promote the instrument and the playing styles that are being developed (essential starting points include: fretlessguitar.com, unfretted.com), there is also the annual Fretless Guitar Festival held in New York City (organized by Michael Vick). Two seminal compilation albums must be mentioned here: *Fretless Guitar Masters* and *Village of the Unfretted*.[24]

---

[23] Erkan Oğur: *Fretless*, Feuer und Ice FUEC 714 (1994); *Bir Ömürlük Misafir* (A Guest for his Life), Kalan CD184 (1996).

[24] These recordings appear to be independent productions. *Village of the Unfretted* was masterminded by Jeff Berg and recorded in 2005 with the number 634479130182. See again links to CD suppliers on fretlessguitar.com and unfretted.com.

I have already mentioned the various guitar techniques employed by Newton Faulkner and Vicki Genfan in Chapter 1. But if I could have featured three more acoustic guitarists alongside Erik Mongrain among my ten they would have been Tommy Emmanuel, Adrian Legg and Richard Thompson, their different but internationally acclaimed pyrotechnical playing on acoustic guitar (a mix of both electric and acoustic playing techniques, but including virtuosic ability on electric guitar) typifying the eclectic approach and wide-ranging ability of several virtuosi who may be seen as leaders within the new guitarscape. On reading a draft of Chapter 1, David Mead commented:

> No mention of Andy McKee among the new glitterati on acoustic guitar? His video 'Drifting' on You Tube has been viewed many millions of times (more than Erik Mongrain) and, as far as I am aware, he now leads the post Michael Hedges generation of 'new age acoustic players'. He employs the percussive style, too – something I heard recently referred to as the 'Acoustic Guitar Martial Arts Squad'. I would also have been tempted to include reference to Pierre Bensusan as well as his unique fusion of jazz, classical and modern day compositions powered by the acknowledged hallmark tuning of the 'new generation' – DADGAD – clearly takes the baton from Davy Graham and the experiments he did with that tuning back in the 1960s. (David Mead, personal communication)

Then again, not only would the driving percussive sounds of Mexican acoustic guitar duo Rodrigo y Gabriela have served to show up the current state of acoustic guitar playing (they play with fingers and plectrums, use effects pedals, and are influenced by thrash metal), but such an example would also have drawn attention to the guitar skills of yet another female musician, Gabriela Quintero.[25]

Steve Vai is surely a highly individualistic player, but he may also be considered as a member of the generation of heavy rock and metal virtuosi who came to the fore in the 1980s (what David Mead calls the '1980s Guitar Gymnastics Display Team'). Eddie Van Halen, Joe Satriani, Yngwie Malmsteen and the late Randy Rhodes are among the most celebrated of a legion of players in this field, but within a field of sublime musicianship that must also include the eclecticism and sheer stylistic panache of Eric Johnson, as well as the speed of Rusty Cooley and Michael Angelo and the very broad talent of the late Shawn Lane. Vai's music not only has links back to his time working with the similarly eclectic Frank Zappa; it still exerts a big influence on up and coming rock guitar virtuosi. If I could have featured yet another electric guitar player in the ten performances (besides Joe Satriani, Steve Morse, John McLaughlin, Allan Holdsworth, Frank Gambale, Guthrie Govan or Pat Metheny, of course), whilst perhaps demonstrating the influence of the above-mentioned virtuosi), it might have been one of several

---

[25]   See *Rodrigo y Gabriela*, Rubyworks RWXCD37L (2006), and *Rodrigo y Gabriela: Live in Japan*, Rubyworks RWXCD66 (2008).

younger guitarists currently playing metal music (Black Metal, Doom Metal and so on).

Perhaps John 5 (Marilyn Manson's guitarist), who plays metal at speed but moves into country and bluegrass?[26] Zakk Wylde and the late Dimebag Darrel spring to mind as heavy metal generalists, but so did Mark Morton and Willie Adler of Lamb of God. In fact, such a choice is so hard to make that I would have probably had to write about a band: Slipknot? Children of Bodom? Opeth? Alter Bridge? In the end, I probably would have included the band Trivium, guitaristically composed of Matt Heafy (guitar), Corey Beaulieu (guitar) and Paulo Gregoletto (bass), to set out some of the parameters of the current, widespread and highly influential (heavy) metal sound which is a big part of the new guitarscape.

There is but little mention herein, for example, of the blues players (including individuals of varying ethnicity who play it) and flamenco players, whose presence is clearly felt in the new guitarscape. But clearly, the work of blues, Cajun blues and flamenco players such as Keb' Mo, Corey Harris, Tab Benoît, Vincente Amigo and Gerardo Nuñez deserves the in-depth treatment that space does not allow here. Joe Bonamassa, John Mayer and Derek Trucks are among the most celebrated of a new generation of white guitarists who not only acquired a highly developed playing technique at a very early age but show more than a passing allegiance to the blues. Joe Bonamassa starred at the BB King Blues Club in Memphis at the age of sixteen. (He had his thirty-second birthday in May 2009.)

Moreover, flat-pickers such as Brad Davis, and electric country players such as Vince Gill, Brad Paisley and Johnny Hiland, as well as Fender Telecaster 'pedal steel' master Jim Campilongo and Fender guitar master Jerry Donahue (see his albums *Telecasting*, Spindrift, 1986, and *Telecasting Recast*, Pharoah, 1999) clearly do not get the attention they deserve. Furthermore, one must also mention British guitarists who have been heavily influenced by North American country electric guitar styles, including Albert Lee and Ray Flack, both of whom are well able to hold their own on the Nashville music scene. The legacy of Telecaster players such as the late Jimmy Bryant, Roy Buchanan and Danny Gatton lives on. So too does the legacy of fingerpicking styles left by Merle Travis, Chet Atkins and Jerry Reed in the work of Australian Tommy Emmanuel and North American Pat Donohue, for example.

There is also little mention of gypsy jazz or 'Manouche swing' as embodied by the work of Django Reinhardt, now not just in Belgium and France, but emulated by guitarists across the world among a network of players which includes Biréli Lagrène, Sylvain Luc, John Jorgensen and the Rosenberg Trio. British guitarists such as Martin Taylor and John Etheridge also, at times, turn their hand to this style. Gypsy jazz is included in jazz festivals in Belgium, France and elsewhere (the Django Reinhardt Jazz Festival in Liberchies, Belgium, and Django Fests in Colorado, Los Angeles and San Francisco, for instance). I was also surprised

---

[26]   John 5, *The Devil Knows my Name*, Mascot Records M72172 (2007).

to learn of specialist performance venues supporting gypsy jazz, such as the Le Quecum Bar in London.[27]

I Wayan Balawan is my third featured guitarist from the continent of Asia, from south-east Asia to be more exact. However, the Balinese guitarist is among several Indonesian guitarists who are not only becoming well known among the guitar playing community of Indonesia, but are also building an international reputation and profile. Besides Balawan, Kamala Shankar and Hassan Cihat Örter, if I had had more space I would have discussed in some detail the work of a range of guitarists based on (or with roots in) the Asian continent, including Erkan Oğur, Debashish Bhattacharya, Vishwa Mohan Bhatt, Nguyên Lê (born in Paris of Vietnamese parents), Chit San Mung (Myanmar), Tak Matsumoto (Japan), Enver İsmaylov (originally from Crimea) and Khaled-el-Dwady from Bahrain (more accurately the Middle East) among many others.[28]

Joe Satriani is famous in guitar circles for his ability to capture the electric guitar sounds of the moment, as demonstrated on his album *Professor Satchafunkilus and the Musterion of Rock* (2008).[29] I must note here that charting the twists and turns of Satriani's album and DVD releases, the influences reflected in them and his own influence in the world of the guitar since the 1980s has been both highly inspirational and instructive during the writing of this book (as most guitar aficionados would expect). I refer to aspects of Satriani's work throughout this book, but his albums released just before and during 2000, for example *The Crystal Planet* (1998) and *The Engines of Creation* (2000), seemed to indicate that Satriani, as one of the best-known popularizers of the electric guitar, is determined to pull the instrument into the twenty-first century, exploring current sonic and technological trends and possibilities and reminding a worldwide audience of the instrument's musical (and thus social and cultural) potential in both electric

---

[27]   There is a wide-ranging literature on the life, music and guitar style of Django Reinhardt. Reliable starting points include Nygaard (2008), Jorgensen (1996); Delaunay (1961); Givan (2003), whilst focusing on Django's guitar technique, also includes references to research on the current state of gypsy jazz in France, Belgium, the Netherlands and elsewhere. Se also Paul Vernon's important and extremely useful *Jean 'Django' Reinhardt: A Contextual Bio-Discography 1910–1953* (2003). See also www.django.montreal.com.

[28]   There is a dearth of literature on the guitar traditions of Asia. However, Philip Yampolsky's field recordings of the guitar in Indonesia (Smithsonian Folkways, 1999) and Martin Clayton's chapter on the guitar in India (2001) provide clear evidence of a significant and diverse engagement with the instrument throughout the continent in folk, popular and art music traditions. It must be noted that: (1) there are major centres of guitar production and consumption in Asia; (2) the guitar has a multifarious role in Asian musical traditions (from Vietnamese street music to Turkish classical and folk music, from North Indian classical music to Taiwanese rock); (3) Asia now has its own nationally and internationally recognized guitarists playing across a range of local and non-local genres and styles. For these reasons, I am currently working on an edited book with the title *The Guitar in Asia*.

[29]   Joe Satriani, *Professor Satchafunkilus and the Musterion of Rock*, Sony Music Entertainment, Epic 88697278862 (2008).

and acoustic form (see also, for example, the acoustic track 'Andalusia' on the *Professor Satchafunkilus* album).[30]

From the Crystal Planet to the Crystal Guitar

In my own mind, during the writing of this book, the guitar began to transform itself into a kind of prism. It became the Ampeg Dan Armstrong 'See Through' guitar (original 1969 or reissue), its body made of clear acrylic resin material (Perspex, Lucite or Plexiglas).[31] In its prism-like state, the guitar became a means of refracting and reflecting information and ideas. Using the academic literature as my main source of illumination, I held the guitar up to the light, and turned it this way and that. Not that one can always look straight through a prism (or an apparently see-through guitar). The light passing through comes from many sources, is split, and is also reflected in several directions.

My crystal guitar is at times clear and in focus, at other times opaque, distorted or fractured. The sources of light vary in their strength. However, it is significant that even in crystal or virtual form, solid or liquid state, in particles or waves, the guitar remains *clearly* in my field of view, as I look into it to find a trace of an 'embedded human agency' (Miller, 2005:13). At times, in parts, the guitar is clear enough to see through – that is, through to the people on the other side, those who hold the instrument in their hands and against their body. The guitar might also be seen to function as a lens for the musical oculist, a window onto the world of musicians and guitar makers. But the guitar not only invites panopticism; it seems thoroughly to demand it as a sound-producing object of music, culture and society. Moreover, the guitar is not just an instrument to be viewed but one to be thoroughly listened to, heard, felt, touched and, importantly, as I argue later, tasted and smelt.

Ultimately, a broad range of disciplines will need to be involved in any long-term study of the guitar. In this respect, it soon became clear to me that I would need to refer to a wider range of literature than I first envisaged, including publications in science and technology, design theory, material culture, cognition, sensual culture, ethnography (real and virtual), gender and sexuality, power and agency, globalization, and genre and style. These areas of study inform the critical-theoretical approach and argument developed in the remaining chapters of this book.

---

[30] Joe Satriani, *The Crystal Planet*, Sony Music Entertainment Inc., Epic 489473-2 (1998) and *The Engines of Creation*, Sony Music Entertainment Inc., Epic 497665-2 (2000).

[31] The 'See Through' guitar (1969–71) features in a recent 'Used Gear' article in *Guitarist* (April 2009):146–7. See also Bacon (1991:95) for a revealing picture of this guitar in the context of a discussion on 'new materials' used in guitar construction (and in its bass form on p. 169). See Bacon (1991:109) for more see-through guitars, including the 1975 Ibanez 2364 and the 1978 Clearsound 'Strat'.

Whilst researching this book, I have been both captivated but also tantalized by the ways in which the guitar appeared to be shaping up and revealing itself as an instrument of global performance, a social and cultural phenomenon, part of a wide range of musical traditions, the hallmark of expressive culture, revealing of links between music, culture and technology but also of the role of the body in musical performance. My research questions would, of course, have to test the validity and integrity of such observations and links. Preliminary questions included: Why and how has the guitar achieved such a high profile and multifaceted role? Does this mean that the guitar has achieved some new level of significance? If so, what kind of significance does it have, and if it is influential, how is this influence maintained? Moreover, what kind of approach would be needed not only to model the guitar phenomenon but also to broach such basic questions as those above? Dare one try to assume a 'one size fits all' model, emphasizing cultural diversity on one hand whilst suggesting common ground on the other? Why have there been so few attempts to try and pull together observations made, but also to synthesize the extant literature on the guitar?

There is, of course, a resoundingly obvious reason why the bigger picture has received limited attention. Given the sheer scale and complexity of the guitar phenomenon, it is difficult to know where to begin. One sees the canvas outstretched, but it is very hard to imagine a frame for the composition as a whole (or any part thereof). Any study of the current state of the guitar would need to find ways of limiting its scope, as well as providing an adequate framework for discussion and analysis. I set out my approach to the problem in the next chapter, where I develop further the line of reasoning and discussion presented so far.

Chapter 3
The New Guitarscape and Musical Instrument Studies

A complete unified theory is only the first step: our goal is a complete *understanding* of the events around us, and of our own existence. (Hawking, 1990:169)

The guitar is an instrument that distils ideas, and I love the results – sometimes – of that distillation. (Julian Bream, in Stearns, 1993:18)

It was clear to me at the outset of this project that there is no adequate term of reference in general circulation for the guitar phenomenon. There certainly is no term in use that emphasizes more recent developments within the phenomenon. But if I was to proceed with my discussion and analysis, I needed a term that would enable me to encapsulate readily the phenomenal popularity of the guitar (or the popular phenomenon that is the guitar) *and* flag up the theoretical dimension of my book. I needed to create a term of reference that would give an indication of the size and complexity of the guitar phenomenon as it currently stands (2009) *and* show that the guitar is a large-scale musical-cultural-social occurrence that merits serious and ongoing academic study. Such a term would have to convey an attempt to model the guitar anew, providing a framework for the ideas I wished to interrogate in the context of a guitar study, ideas that were, to my mind, crucial in a study of the instrument and its performers, music, cultures and technologies. After some deliberation, I coined the term 'new guitarscape'. The term seemed to be a handy one, reasonably short and easy to use; it had some practical application, and it has stuck.

The New Guitarscape

The term 'guitarscape' is somewhat in accord (or in resonance) with a range of concepts used by writers from varying disciplinary backgrounds, as is its newness. The claim here is that any attempt to model the guitar phenomenon as it stands at the time of writing might usefully draw on theories of 'scapes' (some of which I discuss below). What I call 'scape theory' tends to be used to model a range of phenomena at the time of writing (but with long-established roots)[1]. Most

---

[1] According to the *Oxford English Dictionary* (10th edn), the word 'landscape' (probably the commonest associated term) has origins in the sixteenth century from the

obvious, in any discussion of current trends and developments in globalization, are Appadurai's 'scapes' (ethnoscapes, mediascapes, technoscapes, financescapes, ideoscapes), which, according to his model, flow together as components in the global cultural economy (Appadurai, 1990). I argue that the guitar is firmly placed as an agent of the global cultural economy. But it soon became clear to me that the subject of musical globalization would need to be kept in check if it was not going to eclipse other guitar-related matters in this book.

Hardly unrelated to the topic of globalization (or, at least, urbanization studies) was the need to include mention of the lasting influence of research into acoustic ecology and 'soundscapes' (particularly R. Murray Schafer's *The New Soundscape*), now also applied in the analysis and study of music cultures worldwide (see Keil et al., 2002; Shelemay, 2006). Such a model helps to throw into relief the extraordinary variety of sounds that take on meaning and significance in particular contexts and through particular means, usefully connecting up music, culture, technology and physical environment (manufactured or otherwise).

Important also in any theory of 'scapes' is research into what David Howes calls 'sensescapes', described as 'local ways of sensing ... the experience of the environment, and of other persons and things which inhabit that environment, is produced by a particular mode of distinguishing, valuing and combining the senses in the culture under study' (Howes, 2005:143). In this book, I apply aspects of this research in a discussion of the use of the body in guitar performance, learning and teaching. I detect facets of a sensual culture of the guitar, often articulated in the most simplistic terms, such as 'feel' and 'touch' (see also Classen, 2005), the guitar phenomenon also representing a particular form of sensescape.

Of course, a discussion of how musical instruments interface with the human sensorium as a whole is well beyond the scope of my discussion here, and I focus on the positioning and functioning of the body, arms, hands and fingers in relation to guitar performance. Yet I consider it vitally important to include a chapter on the body and senses in this book. After all, the guitar is still an instrument that makes demands on the body as much as the mind, remaining in solid form whilst existing in virtual states. The new guitarscape is also, of course, heavily reliant on teaching and learning practices to sustain and disseminate practical knowledge of the guitar (and the music which is played upon it). Any discussion of the new guitarscape must include not only the ways in which the guitar travels around the world but also, quite literally, the ways in which it is held in place by those who design it, make it, play it, touch it, feel it, photograph it, paint it, varnish it, polish it, and so on.

More recent research in social history has included the use of term 'timescapes', usually involving qualitative longitudinal studies of certain individuals and groups over the course of their life, or for a specified or limited period of time therein. I note a timescapes study in progress at the University of Leeds, with its focus on 'relationships with significant others' using the method of 'walking alongside'

Middle Dutch *lantscap*, formed from *land* 'land' plus *scap* (the equivalent of 'ship').

people to document their familial and other relationships as they move through life.[2] In this book, I reflect on the role and effect that the guitar has had in my own life, on those people I have known, come across and talked to, and make reference to various guitarists' biographies and interviews in the popular press. Moreover, musicians who have literally carried and lived with the guitar throughout a great part of the twentieth century and into the twenty-first century, for example Les Paul and BB King, are now in their ninth and eighth decades, respectively, upon this planet. It might be said that their lifetime has also been the lifetime of the electric guitar. Les Paul died on August 12, 2009.

To a great extent then, in the 'new guitarscape' I intend to make connections to the literature and across various social and cultural domains (to other 'scapes', as noted above) which, I claim, contribute to the make-up of the guitar phenomenon. The aim is to not only demonstrate the applicability of the various ideas I include in this book, but also keep the guitar firmly rooted in the world as an instrument of musical, cultural, social, economic and political interaction, investment and exchange. The guitar is an instrument of material culture as much as a technology of globalization: that is, as much as the Internet carries the guitar further afield, so the guitar globalizes the Internet still further. So although I have already cautioned that this book must be seen as much more than a study of musical globalization, it seems prudent to begin with some kind of mapping-out of the involvement of the guitar in what, in general terms, is known as the 'global order' (see, for example, Hurrell, 2007).

In an effort to do just that, I make reference here to tried and tested models, the global cultural economy (after Appadurai, 1990) and the global political economy (after Hall, 1991), although at this stage the subtle and not-so-subtle differences contained in such models are not clear to me in the context of a guitar study, except for the emphasis laid upon culture, economics and politics in each, perspectives which, I claim, are completely necessary in a guitar-based book. However, this study at least emphasizes the importance of musical instruments in the cultural flows and interactions that are said to sustain economic and political activity on a global scale. How else does the guitar get to travel?

The newness of the guitarscape model will, of course, be partially superseded as this book goes to print (2010). But the phrases 'the latest guitarscape' and 'the current guitarscape' hardly had the makings of a book title, nor were they suggestive of a strong and rigorous analytical approach (the approach I have tried to adopt here). The term 'new guitarscape' – as shaped and driven by a range of new media (for example, the Internet) which impact upon music business practices, in particular – implies a complex and intense realm of experience in which everyone who plays the guitar or has ever played the guitar is implicated. This is a new phenomenon.

Moreover, 'guitarscape' is not meant to suggest a monoculture of the guitar. The new guitarscape is made up of the myriad and changing cultures of the guitar:

---

[2]   The University of Leeds Timescapes project: www.timescapes.leeds.ac.uk.

cultures of the new guitarscape that merge and diverge as part of broader musical, social and cultural developments (especially as a part of ethnoscapes, mediacapes, technoscapes, financescapes and ideoscapes, the usefully designated areas of the global cultural economy as proposed by Arjun Appadurai, as already noted). With reference to a model of the global cultural economy, I am keen to emphasize not only Appadurai's points about heterogeneity over homogeneity, but also economic and political disjuncture and difference. Clearly, one must temper any idealization that might be read into the concept of the new guitarscape as 'one world, one guitar', especially when built up from a series of fragments, as on the Internet. Of course, the Internet cannot be accessed by everyone, everywhere, let alone by every guitar player in the world, even if mobile telephones appear throughout the world, and also impact on musical and business practices, including the posting of videos of guitarists in concert on YouTube.[3] Moreover, given the resoundingly obvious fact of life that some people are more empowered economically and politically than others, one does not always find the finest Gibson, Fender or Paul Reed Smith guitar in the hands of amateur guitarists in North America or Europe, let alone parts of Asia, Africa or South America. Economic and political maps of the world are reflected in the new guitarscape.

The new guitarscape is widely based, but I do not suggest that it is happening everywhere at all times, as if it were some kind of new sonic carapace for the world (or even the human body). It connects up musics and cultures, individuals and communities, economics and politics, in various ways, sometimes in harmonious synchrony, sometimes not, and if anything it underlines the complexity, challenges and problems of any theory of musical globalization. Indeed, the location of culture (after Bhabha, 1994) is negotiated and contested not just in spaces defined as local and global, but also in spaces variously defined or theorized as, for instance, hybrid, third space, diasporic, transnational, refugee and displaced, cultures not necessarily tied to national boundaries but involving people intent on crossing them, putting roots down somewhere else, or even eluding national boundaries altogether (see, for example, Diehl, 2002). There can be little doubt that the guitar, like many other forms of material culture, remains 'entangled' as an object of music, culture and society (after Thomas, 1991).

The study of musical instruments as sound-producing objects caught up in the cultural politics, the socio-economics and, ultimately, the power struggles of the 'global order' – whose global order? whose model of global order? – has only just begun (see also Stokes, 2004). But a study of the guitar must eventually reflect the way in which it is also caught up in various locations of culture and reveal the facets of its power and agency as a locus for, or locus of, culture. Even if one can see the roots of such a study very clearly embedded in histories of imperialism and colonialism, such frameworks for enquiry alone, though still potent, are inadequate in any analysis that seeks to understand the extent of, wider role, meaning, power

---

[3]   See Tara Brabazon's engaging critique of Internet practices, including YouTube, MySpace and Wikipedia (Brabazon, 2008).

and agency of the world-travelling guitar in the musical cultures of the early twenty-first century. In fact, a historiography of musical instruments – from Curt Sachs in 1942 to Margaret Kartomi in 1990 – tends to reveal and insist that a broader perspective be adopted in any attempt to understand their *raison d'être*.

The Broader Picture

This study would also hint at the wider significance of musical instruments as part of the human story, emphasizing the continued significance of sounds and sound-producing objects in human cultures and societies. I also make reference to the fact that the guitar is an instrument of global performance, if not pre-eminent as an instrument of human musical creativity. As such, the predicament of the guitar demands that a very broad approach be adopted in any study of its role and potential significance in human cultures and societies. The following seminal texts were particularly helpful in this respect: Margaret Kartomi's *On Concepts and Classifications of Musical Instruments* (1990), wherein the author shows the various ways in which cultures' understanding and organization of musical instruments are tied into cognitive schemes fundamental to the organization of human societies; Paul Théberge's *Any Sound You Can Imagine: Making Music/ Consuming Technology* (1997), in which the author puts forward the view that musical instruments, scales and tuning systems 'are only the material and conceptual infrastructure onto which musical style is built' (Théberge, 1997:166) – but it is a very important infrastructure nevertheless; the anthropologist Alfred Gell's *Art and Agency* (1998) which demonstrates the power and influence of material culture and art objects in human society; and David Howes's *Empire of the Senses* (2005), which draws attention to developments in the anthropology and sociology of the senses. The influence of this timely body of work is clearly observable in a range of academic studies.

These four books are not always in agreement, and I take issue myself with some of the points the authors make. But there are significant areas of convergence (some of which emerge in the writing that follows). Or, rather, coming to this *oeuvre* as a guitarist and ethnomusicologist I can see patterns and overlaps, useful connections to my own work but also elements of useful debate. Moreover, the above studies not only draw attention to areas of an ongoing polemic in terms of the relationships between musical thought, music making, material culture, and science and technology (for example, the real and the virtual, materiality and immateriality, the mind and the body, acoustic and electric, musical style and cultural meaning, tradition and modernity), but also convince me of the complete necessity of including such material in a book such as this, a book that endeavours to extend the academic terms of reference by which the guitar might be studied.

The above books happen to span the decades which interest me in terms of the new guitarscape, as I conceive it, and encourage me to consider: (i) how the guitar has been written about, thought about and talked about; (ii) the power and agency of the guitar in culture and society; and (iii) what kind of experience it is to play the guitar (an experience involving both the mind *and* the body). Along with the work of Arjun Appadurai and James Clifford (as cited in various places in this book), the above-mentioned scholars not only provide me with new views on how aspects of human cultures and societies in the late twentieth century and early twenty-first century are organized, but suggest, in their approaches, the ways in which I might try to provide a broader approach to the study of the guitar (without losing sight and sound of the instrument or its musicians and makers).

In this respect, the work of Raymond Tallis has also been inspirational, his wide-ranging and typically challenging books providing the perspectives of both the medical researcher and the philosopher. Moreover, in his revealing discussion of the importance of the hand in human physical evolution and cultural development, Tallis talks of the 'toolscape' – 'the world became filled with artefacts and the landscape became a toolscape' (Tallis, 2003:152). More than anything, a notion of the toolscape draws attention to those tools manifest today, a world inhabited by a technology that is able to create virtual worlds and, it is claimed, augmented realities. Despite the seemingly infinite variety of sounds that it is now possible to produce and manipulate with electronic and digital technology, musical instruments are, nevertheless, in their numerous forms still all around us in abundance. The guitar, for instance, is now linked inextricably to a range of other tools of production (from chainsaws to bandsaws) and consumption (from print media and the Internet to audio recordings and guitar shops). Arguably, as a form of musical technology, musical instruments have been readily used in the past to conjure up virtual worlds and augmented realities, known otherwise as altered states of consciousness or altered states of reality, though these are qualitatively different from those offered by early twenty-first-century technologies (see, for example, Diamond et al., 1994; Olsen, 2002).

There are, of course, links here to a broader study of the definition, specifics, subtleties, deeper meanings and links between tools and technology in human life, links that are only touched upon in various parts of this book (see, especially, Chapter 6). In *Hand's End: Technology and the Limits of Nature*, David Rothenberg makes the point that:

> Technology is the totality of the artifacts and methods humankind has created to shape our relations to the world that surrounds us, modifying it into something that can be used and manipulated to submit to our needs and our desires. The World changes as we learn to see it in new ways. And the way we see the world depends on how we use it. (Rothenberg, 1993:xxi)

That the guitar is an 'instrument of desire' is well noted by Steve Waksman in his focused study of the development of the electric guitar in North America (Waksman, 1999). But the main point here is that the world has changed (especially in the 1990s and 2000s) and so has the guitar, especially in terms of how it is linked to our needs, desires and aspirations. To my mind, Tallis and Rothenberg suggest ways of extending such an analysis in several directions, providing for what one might call the 'broad picture' (after Kartomi, 1990) in musical instrument studies.

Music, Culture and Technology

A growing field of studies draws attention to the relationship between music, technology and culture as found in societies around the world. However, given its scope and pronouncements, this research touches lightly on the study of musical instruments as worldwide social and cultural phenomena. Yet for Kai Fikentscher, for example, the set-up of a modern DJ represents a new musical instrument requiring a 'new performance mode', all part of developments in the production and consumption of music that is 'redefining' of the role of music technologies (Fikentscher, 2003:290). 'New performance modes', such as the DJ set-up, have been affecting musical performance around the world for some time.

The editors of *Music and Technoculture*, in which Fikentscher's article appears, try to 'make sense of the new uses and meanings that various communities find for existing technologies – and how such technologies may change in meanings as they cross national, linguistic, and cultural boundaries' (Lysloff and Gay, 2003:8). The aim is to bring ethnomusicology into contact with twenty-first-century issues and concerns. The editors stress the fact that new technologies 'are developed for explicit reasons by people living in specific historical moments and social contexts' where 'technologies also become saturated with social meaning as they acquire a history of use' (Lysloff and Gay, 2003:8).

Similar themes find expression in *Strange Sounds: Music, Technology and Culture* by Timothy Taylor, where the author notes:

> Whatever music technology is, it is not one thing alone. It is not separate from social groups that use it, it is not separate from the individuals who use it; it is not separate from the social groups and individuals who invented it, tested it, marketed it, distributed it, sold it, repaired it, listened to it, bought it, or revived it. In short, music technology – any technology – is not simply an artefact or a collection of artefacts; it is rather, always bound up in a social system, a 'seamless web' as is often described. (Taylor, 2001:7)

Taylor refers to 'any technology', and among his examples includes the clarinet, the theremin and the Moog synthesizer alongside various digital technologies, noting how technology in all its forms generally becomes absorbed into the normality of human daily and social life.

According to Paul Théberge, recording technologies not only provide a means of capturing and manipulating sounds, but also have given them a new materiality (Théberge, 1997:191), a new reality based on electronics and digital logic. Engaging with Théberge's ideas, Steve Waksman states that the electric guitar, in contrast to recording technologies, 'retains too many of the features of traditional instruments' to be drawn entirely into such a world, its sound activated by a player whose body and techniques of playing are physically (and I might add, universally) contingent upon the instrument itself (Waksman, 1999:8). The extent to which developments in new technologies are being applied to the design of the guitar – its shape and sound processing – suggests that many inventors, manufacturers and musicians are more keen than ever to explore the interface between new technology and guitar design. Moreover, the numbers of features of the traditional guitar that are retained seems to vary enormously between designs.

Some guitars now come with in-built robotic tuning systems, infinite sustain controls, computer interface software, mp3 players and built-in recording systems, for example the Gibson Les Paul Robot Guitar and Gibson Les Paul Dark Fire solid-body electric guitars, the Moog guitar, the Ovation iDea electro-acoustic guitar and the Ambrosonics MP3 Recording Guitar. A BBC news report featuring Gibson guitars reveals further the aspirations of certain guitar manufacturers to 'tune into digital sounds'.[4] The report contains the comments of Jeffrey Vallier, a senior engineer at Gibson Laboratories, who says: 'It is not a synthesizer, it's not a special computer program ... we're trying to capture the real character and sound of a normal guitar but give you more control and ability to express yourself'.[5] In this regard, the article reports that: 'The instrument has an Ethernet connection like those found in the back of computers, using a standard network cable connection.' Jeffrey Vallier is quoted again:

> You can send each string on a separate sound channel and you can do all kinds of modifications on that sound individually to make it big or full, something which you cannot get with current guitar technology ... it opens a new page in what you can do with guitars, expanding the creativity and expressiveness for musicians anywhere[6].

The Gibson Robot and Dark Fire guitars are but the tip of a very large iceberg in terms of the application of advanced technologies to guitar design. Moreover, advances and innovations in the field of technology have led to a wide variety of guitar-related and guitar-driven developments, from sound modelling – 'People can download recommended sound cells from the internet in order to change or manipulate their guitar sounds'[7] – to audio production systems that can be used to enhance the 'comfort' of one's home:

---

[4] 'Guitars Tune into Digital Sounds' (11 February 2003), www.news.bbc.co.uk/2/hi/technology/2737331.stm.

[5] Ibid.

[6] Ibid.

[7] Quoted from the website of the sound designer Amit Zoran. The article continues: 'There are guitars then there are awesome guitars and this Zoran guitar concept looks the best, not only the looks makes this stand out but the fact you can customize your very own sounds that are unique for acoustic instruments. All guitar players will be able to customize

SoundTech Professional Audio has announced the SoundTech Guitar Home Theater Interface, a new device that enables musicians to plug their guitar directly into their home theater stereo system. The Guitar Home Theater Interface offers customizable features that make it easy for anyone to plug-in, tune up and enjoy their guitar in the comfort of their living room.[8]

Clearly, the study of the guitar must locate its significance in wider social and cultural contexts, including the acoustics laboratory as a continuing site of importance in guitar history but also going well beyond it. Indeed, some key studies in the history of the guitar have tended to adopt this approach.

Guitar Studies

There are several foundation stones in guitar studies which are mentioned in this book. But in order to provide an overview of the approaches adopted, I will discuss a few key examples in greater depth in this section. Harvey Turnbull's *The Guitar from the Renaissance to the Present Day* (1974) remains one of the most widely read and significant publications on the historical development of the guitar. Turnbull not only covers developments in construction, design and innovation that led up to the appearance of the modern six-string guitar; he also provides rich insights into the guitar cultures of each historical period. The chapter on Baroque guitar features not only guitar makers, performers and composers, but analysis of the music played, playing techniques and musical concepts associated with various guitar schools. One acquires a sense of how time and place shape the development of the guitar as Turnbull skilfully reveals a human, as much as a musical, story. Turnbull's book has a very clear idea of what constitutes 'the guitar'. In his model of guitar history it is the classical six-string guitar. Flamenco and electric guitar are seen as 'offshoots' (Turnbull, 1974:125).

Evidence suggests to Turnbull that the development of right-hand techniques on the classical guitar made possible an exploration of ever more complex music

---

their own unique sound by using CAD, CAM process. The stunning conceptual acoustic sound box will allow you budding musicians to custom choose your very own sound cells which in return will create a true and unique tone. Each of the Amit Zoran designed guitar strings has its own bridge which will allow each bridge to be linked to different custom sound cells. Guess all in all the best feature I really love, has to be the fact you can print out your very own cell designs using a very cool 3D printer, oh yeah and download other recommended sound cells from the internet.' (www.product-reviews.net/2008/01/16/amit-zoran-guitar-concept-looks-the-best-customize-your-own-sounds/). See also: http://architectradure.blogspot.com/2008/01/structural-innovation.html.

[8]   Quoted from the article: 'SoundTech's Guitar Home Theater Interface by Premier Guitar: New device plugs guitarists into their existing home speakers', Chicago, IL (9 January 2008), www.premierguitar.com/Magazine/Issue/Daily/News/SoundTechs_Guitar_Home_Theater_Interface.aspx.

that broke with a past that still relied, to a certain extent, on lute technique. He proposes that the use of the plectrum (one assumes he means on the electric guitar) limits 'musical possibilities' (Turnbull, 1974:126). His words seem almost prophetic. Guitarists are still trying to overcome the limitations it might impose on the right hand, by developing advanced picking techniques, by discarding the pick, by playing on the fingerboard with both hands, or by using new technology to provide looped accompaniments which enable the player to concentrate on more limited tasks with the picking hand.

The critical historical perspectives on the guitar contained in Turnbull's book, find expression to a more limited extent in Tom and Mary Evans, *Guitars: Music, History, Construction and Players from the Renaissance to Rock* (1977). The Evans' book is path finding in terms of its breadth of subject matter, including classical, electric and steel-strung guitars, the guitar in flamenco and a short section on 'The Guitar in Latin America' (see also, Waksman et al., 2003; Tanenbaum, 2003). There is significant historical and musical detail, with a richly illustrated section on the stages and methods of guitar manufacture, and an important chapter on the social history of the guitar which attends to such subjects as class, art, fashion, sentiment, and virtuosity as they found expression in the guitar cultures of the Baroque period up to the 1970s.

Steve Waksman's *Instruments of Desire: The Electric Guitar and the Shaping of Musical Experience* (1999), is a groundbreaking cultural history of the guitar in North America which explores why the instrument has such a broad musical and cultural impact. It might be said that where Turnbull leaves off, Waksman takes over – but the links are now obviously made to Jeffrey Noonan's book *The Guitar in America: Victorian Era to Jazz Age* (2008). However, quite different approaches (between Turnbull and Waksman) emerge as the history of the same but different musical instrument is interrogated. In *Instruments of Desire*, Waksman reveals how different approaches to sound (pop acceptability and radical distortion) challenge popular ideas about what was and what was not musically acceptable in North America. These different approaches to sound production also entail different ideas about the body in musical performance, the ways in which music articulates racial and gendered identities, and the position of popular music in American social and political life. It clearly shows up the agency of the guitar in social and cultural life, a powerful sonic marker of identity with Waksman writing about the guitar at the intersection of race, gender and sexuality.

Whilst Harvey Turnbull writes about a range of guitar maestros from the past (from Aguado to Sanz), Waksman writes about the guitar in the comparatively recent past. The guitar work, in particular, of Charlie Christian, Les Paul, Chet Atkins, Muddy Waters, Chuck Berry and Jimi Hendrix are included in a thoroughly critical examination of the cultural and social contexts which not only play a hand in shaping their music but also its meaning. Waksman writes with the insight of both a cultural historian and guitarist. He comes up with a tight and convincing argument that demonstrates the need to explain the guitar not just in technical terms but as a social and cultural phenomenon reflecting complex social issues of the time. In taking forward into my own study the influence of the texts mentioned above, it must be said that it is Waksman's book that has blown the door wide open in guitar studies as it draws on major texts in musicology, cultural history, and gender studies. In adopting such an approach to the history of the guitar in twentieth century North America, Waksman is able to elaborate on the crucial links that exists between developments in music, culture and technology. His study also demands a reassessment of the field of musical instrument studies.

Studying Musical Instruments

> Even in the music disciplines we find there is little agreement on the meaning and scope of organology ... its true scope is sorely neglected. (DeVale, 1990:4)

Organology has been variously defined as 'the study of musical instruments' and 'the study of music instruments' (or 'the instruments of music'). It has also been defined as the study of 'sound-producing objects' (see Fischer, 1986), the 'cultural study of musical instruments' (Dawe, 2003) and 'the science of sound instruments' (DeVale, 1990:4). Each one of these definitions informs my own approach to the study of the guitar, although my own focus lies with the cultural study of musical instruments (rather than their science) in this book. But there are also many 'sound-producing objects' under discussion here: from various kinds of guitars to the various chains and filters that affect sound production, for example, plectra and slides, the use of pre-selected objects, amplifiers, and effects pedals, and so on. Moreover, in terms of classification (the crucial factor being the means of sound activation), the guitar in the new guitarscape is at one minute a plucked chordophone and a box lute, the next an idiophone and an electronic device (or part of some other electronic device, such as a sampling keyboard or a video games system).

Organologists have tended to focus largely upon the investigation of the material and acoustic properties of musical instruments, the description of probable methods of construction, tuning systems, timbre, the techniques required to produce sounds from them, and an analysis of their repertoire (where available). The organological investigation has required centuries of work using scientific techniques of measurement, classification, preservation, conservation, restoration and reference to historic musical treatises, public records and private letters.[9]

The methodologies and techniques of acoustics, wood studies, materials conservation, museum studies, and biological systematics for the purposes of preserving, classifying, cataloguing, and display have all been applied in the study of musical instruments. In most cases, the musical instruments studied have ended up in display cases in private or public collections – though they may be taken out for research and other educational purposes, and even played on special occasions.

---

[9]   Useful overviews of this work appear in DeVale, 1990; Kartomi, 1990.

Indeed, musical instrument collections provide a handy educational resource and bank of information for research.

Given the scope of organology, the study of musical instruments from all times and all places, it is hardly surprising that its project must proceed by drawing on the perspectives and techniques of enquiry offered by a wide range of scholarly fields, from materials conservation to ethnomusicology. The contents of both the *Journal of the American Musical Instrument Society* and the *Galpin Society Journal*, the two leading musical instrument journals, reveal a wide range of approaches, topics and examples of musical instruments from many different times and places. Some scholars study musical instruments in the field, through deep immersion in a music culture, others study the material and acoustic properties of musical instruments in the laboratory, still others focus on the history of musical instruments, the changes in the way that they were built and the musical developments played out upon them. This book champions the combined and continued efforts of scholars of every type of disciplinary orientation in terms of the study of musical instruments, although I do not claim to include each and every perspective possible in this book.

However, core to my approach here is ethnomusicology, which might be defined as the study of music in or as culture, includes a detailed study of musical instrument's *raison d'être*, as explained by those who make them and play them, focusing on detailed observations of the role of musical instruments in their cultural setting, from the contexts in which they are made to the ways in which they feature as part of performance practices. In Titon and Slobin's model of a music culture, musical instruments feature as a part of the 'material culture of music' which also includes printed music, music notation, and electronic media (radio, record player, television, etc.) (Titon and Slobin, 1996:13–14).[10] Moreover, ethnomusicologists may also learn to perform on the musical instruments that form the basis of their study of a particular music culture.[11]

Both ethnomusicology and organology provide a global vision of music making, the latter considering comparatively the ways in which sound is further humanly organized through musical instruments (involving detailed classification into types), the former considering sound-producing objects as a part of the cultures which shape musically organized humanity (after John Blacking). Clearly, there is a great deal of overlap between these two disciplines, and, to some extent, one is reliant upon the other. Ethnomusicology is inextricably linked to the study of anthropology, with both ethnomusicology and anthropology often claimed to be deeply humanitarian in terms of their aims and objectives, presenting detailed, fine-grained studies of human cultures and societies gained from fieldwork, but also from comparative study. As an ethnomusicologist and organologist, I am myself in debt to anthropological studies, as will be clear in this book.

---

[10]   See also Théberge, 1997.

[11]   See John Baily (2001): 'Learning to Perform as a Research Technique in Ethnomusicology'.

Organology must also include and account for the multidimensionality of the guitar phenomena as it is carried across the realms and domains of material culture even when digitised and pixelated, with sound coming not only from the soundhole of the instrument but also from the speakers of a home computer. Moreover, there can be little doubt that the guitar exists on the cusp of what one might call the 'new organology',[12] an all-inclusive study of musical instruments that incorporates all the sound producing devices ever devised, an acoustic guitar, a gamelan, a loudspeaker, a Neolithic bone flute, a deejay's turntable, or music software: all ways in which the physical world has been taken in hand, all examples of our material culture, our humanised technology and our attempts at 'humanly organised sound' (after John Blacking).

Space and Place in a Study of the Guitar

I develop the model of a guitarscape in this book, well beyond the context in which I originally applied it. Although the exact co-ordinates of the guitar phenomenon in time and space are difficult to plot, there are, of course, models which usefully enable some mapping-out to be done. Arjun Appadurai's much quoted theory of scapes is now rather well worn, but to my mind that also means that it has been thoroughly tried and tested as an analytical model and, moreover, has yet to be abandoned or completely replaced (see Appadurai, 1990). In an earlier publication on guitar making in Spain, I note:

> Clearly, within the dimensions of Arjun Appadurai's 'global cultural economy' a set of fluid and overlapping landscapes – ethnoscapes, mediascapes, technoscapes, financescapes and ideoscapes – converge upon and interact with the guitarscape of the workshop in quite specific and subtle ways. This merging of scapes comes in many forms, from the rising prices of timber to the fluctuating interest in the classical guitar, from the ways in which global tourism enters into the workshop to the dialogue between small workshop owners and internationally acclaimed guitarists. (Dawe with Dawe, 2001:63)

At the time of writing, I now suggest that the guitar workshops of southern Spain are but one locus of a much broader phenomenon where ethnicity, media, technology, finance and ideology *guitaristically* converge and diverge, within and across national boundaries, revealing new social and musical formations which are to a great extent registered in the form of *something like* the new guitarscape.

If one takes Appudurai's model of 'scapes' further into a study of the new guitarscape, the phenomenon itself can be seen to emerge partly out of the interaction of 'scapes', their overlap and interaction, and to be somewhat composed

---

[12] A term I first came across when used by Martin Stokes in a personal communication.

of and shaped by them. Certainly the guitar might be seen to be extending the intentions and influence of a range of social, cultural, political and economic activity, and that this is happening on a worldwide (if not global) scale indicates that it is more than likely caught up with the processes and forces of musical globalization. As much as the guitar provides a vehicle for the aspirations and vested interests of very many different types of individuals and groups, it is also the product of corporate culture and, ultimately, the ongoing project of all of the above-mentioned agencies.

Focusing on a single musical instrument, I am interested in the ways in which it is featured in what Mark Slobin – testing the musical applicability of Appadurai's model – referred to as the 'global industrial interculture of commodified music' (Slobin, 1993:61) and what Lysloff and Gay call 'illustrations' of this global industrial interculture, 'its use of media and information technologies and its overlapping, often colliding domains that reflect both local traditions and international conventions' (Lysloff and Gay, 2003:11). Indeed, aspects of the broader musical and cultural dimensions of more recent developments in technology (from the Internet to public address systems) are illustrated in Lysloff and Gay's seminal collection, *Music and Technoculture* (2003).

The business of the guitar provides a pertinent example of this musical interculture, operating on a worldwide scale and rooted in many different economic contexts (and economies of scale), but part of an international network that connects timber merchants, forestry commissioners, guitar makers (as well as amplifier, pick-up and string makers, for example), designers, electrical and mechanical engineers, physicists, health and safety officials, transport companies (shipping, aviation, road), retailers, advertisers, promoters, musicians, guitar technicians, the music industry, the recording industry and the media. My claim is that all this activity around the guitar (or in which the guitar is caught up) is happening on a new level, encouraged and accommodated by the World Wide Web in particular. As Ray Hitchins notes:

> Guitarists are becoming product endorsees, boutique pickup winders, instrument builders using preexisting parts, refinishers etc. with a level of detail never seen before. Do you use 42awg or 43awg wire wound to 5.6k or 5.65k for the 'classic' Telecaster sound? There is a growing cottage industry of these player/bedroom manufacturers who are trying to make a living via E-bay, Amazon and their own personal web pages. (Ray Hitchins, personal communication)

These features are an important illustration of the directions in which the expansion and growth of the guitarscape has gone; they are also aspects of its 'newness'.

Although advertisements involving the guitar may not necessarily be designed to mislead or deceive (compared with those for counterfeit guitars), they are often shamelessly evocative and even provocative in their attempts to attract their target audience. Perhaps the following examples will serve to provide a sense of the scale of ambition and sales drive among some of those concerned. Moreover, these examples not only reveal something of the sales pitch of the advertisers and companies, but also show the kinds of themes that are appropriated for the cause.

I note both the caption and the image used in an advertisement by Taylor guitars: a huge acoustic guitar stands as tall as the skyscrapers and building cranes that surround it: 'big sound for a big world' reads the caption.[13] The new guitarscape embodies this 'big sound' and also alludes to the role of the guitar in the construction of modern cultures and societies; its significance in our everyday lives goes far beyond the sounds it is capable of making. The guitar as presented as a part of the landscape of a modern city is a common theme seen, for example, on the cover of the air guitar compilation album *The Very Best of While My Guitar Gently Weeps* (Universal Music TV, 2008).[14] Here guitar necks and headstocks point skywards amid the skyscrapers of a modern cityscape.

Conversely, take for example an advertisement for Larrivée guitars (almost exclusively made in Oxnard, California) that shows the master luthier Jean Larrivée perched on the top of log booms in British Columbia whilst 'personally' selecting wood from which to build his guitars.[15] The guitar maker becomes a traveller, an explorer of the world of wood, on a quest for the perfect materials for guitar making. I have written about the Madrid-based Contreras family's quest for the perfect guitar elsewhere (see Dawe with Dawe, 2001) and the rhetoric that champions the sonorities provided by local woods over those from some other place. A sense of place is important, it seems, for the marketing of guitars in a business saturated with providers; it also provides an authenticating reference point in terms of the identity of a guitar and its firm.

Guitars made in certain places must be better than those made in places that may not be so conducive to guitar making, and, in terms of construction, hands-on or handmade must be better than hands-off or not handmade (Dawe with Dawe, 2001). There are many examples of this rhetoric at work. Brook Guitars, based in Devon, England, are described in *Acoustic* magazine as 'surrounded by traditional woodland and rolling green hills' (Welton, 2008:66–8), as if such a setting *really mattered* to the success of guitar making. In fact, Brook Guitars name their instruments after the rivers of Devon: among the many models of the Brook guitar are the Tamar, Dart, Teign and Exe. Such is the attempt to place and market these guitars solidly as part of the rural landscape in which they are made, and thus provide a distinct identity for Brook guitars, which are highly regarded as musical instruments, but are not the only ones which are highly regarded.

Other advertisements try to straddle the rustic and the up-to-date, 'rurban' guitars, if you will, where the rural and the urban, but also the traditional and the modern, come together, distilled, in the form of a guitar. Competing notions of

[13] See the six-page advertisement in *Acoustic Guitar* (March 2007):20–25. See, especially, pp. 24–5.

[14] *The Very Best of While My Guitar Gently Weeps*, Universal Music TV 5309421 (2008).

[15] Advertisement in *Guitar and Bass Magazine*, 19/11 (November 2008):79.

identity might also reflect strategies of presentation, promotion and competition in the marketplace. Norman Guitars advertise the fact that their acoustic instruments are 'made in the village of La Patrie, Quebec, using only premium tonewoods and state-of-the-art technology', a fact which they claim makes their guitars 'truly world class' whilst remaining rooted in a particular place. The advertisement concludes: 'Play a little piece of Canada.'[16] The advertisement also highlights the importance of attention given to 'tonewoods', woods selected for their potential to provide 'tone' (usually described as 'warm'), whose resonance provides for the distinctive voice of a guitar (see Hunter, 2008).

Increasingly, guitars are attached to places, as part of regional and national cultures, where the claim might also be that they are internationally relevant but also upholding of local values, 'homegrown' if you will, as epitomized by the craft of guitar making, which may be seen to be dependent on the land and its timber production, as if rooted in an often imaginary rural landscape. Of course, this does not just happen in a North American or European context. I note, for example, the advertisement for Afri-Can Guitars on the manufacturer's website which reads:

> AFRI-CAN Guitars are different and uniquely African instruments capturing the history and heritage of handmade guitars, but they play like professional instruments. The AFRI-CAN Guitar uses 20 per cent 'maximum' of the wood of a conventional guitar. Therefore in our own little way we are helping to promote sustainable development. They utilize recycled oil cans as body and pickup covers and bottle tops as volume and tone controls. The guitars are intended to look like the original authentic African hand built guitars, and so some dents and bashes add to the character of the instrument. AFRI-CAN Guitars is now the largest manufacturer of guitars in Africa and also the largest individual monthly seller of guitars in South Africa.[17]

Some manufacturers claim to be inspired by a combination of the culture and environment around them. Take, for instance, Maingard, maker of acoustic guitars in South Africa (Scarborough). Marc Maingard writes:

> As a South African, I am very fortunate to live in a country that has as its heritage, ancient rock paintings. From my walks in the mountains, to study these paintings close up, I have been astonished at, and fascinated by, the form and style of them. Unbeknown to many, I've discovered that the forms, shapes distances and sizes in this bushman art all conform to dimensions found in the golden mean, and Fibonacci dimensional progressions. As an artist and designer, I'm always looking for interesting, eye-catching icons for my guitars.[18]

---

[16]   Advertisement in *Acoustic*, 22 (June/July 2008):79.
[17]   www.africanguitars.com.
[18]   www.maingardguitars.com

Others manufacturers make the case for a rather broadly based claim to excellence and uniqueness in their guitars. I note the introductory information for Coura guitars, made in Kenya but managed from Germany:

> Almost all the music played today on electric guitar or electric bass would be unimaginable without the influence of African culture. Africa is not only the cradle of humankind, but also of handicrafts and the first musical instruments. A large percentage of the wood necessary for building guitars grows here. In the woodworking business, the proportion of manual craftsmanship is greater than in most other countries. African tonal sensitivity and responsiveness to sound is much closer to Western contemporary tastes. … We did not go there because of any weaknesses (low wages, low social standards), but because of its strengths. … With the high proportion of skilled craftsmanship available in Africa it would be possible to guarantee 'Mojo' [soul] for every guitar or bass without artificial ageing.[19]

The claim to ownership of the guitar as well as a distinct niche in the marketplace is fiercely pursued by guitar makers and manufacturers. Sometimes manufacturers display a competitiveness and desire to succeed that stretches credulity. As Ray Hitchins notes when discussing technical descriptions of an instrument's attributes: 'PRS's use of "Rare Mexican rosewood veneer" or Eddie Van Halen's use of "Bourne's low friction potentiometers", "The vintage sound", "the classic PAF sound", etc, etc. Many of these descriptions are simply misleading' (Ray Hitchins, personal communication).

Not in any way related to the guitar manufacturers mentioned above is the growing trade in counterfeit guitars. The rather disturbing world of guitar counterfeiting is discussed in some detail in an article in the online magazine vintagerock.com:

> From the solid body, single-cutaway styling of a Gibson Les Paul to the sleek contours of the Fender Stratocaster and Telecaster guitars, the instruments and many of their top-level rivals are being cloned in massive Chinese guitar factories and sold through web sites and eBay for as low as 10 cents on the dollar compared to the genuine guitars. The instruments are all stamped with trademarked U.S. company names and styled after their American counterparts, complete with logos, stickers and cases. Only guitar experts and very savvy guitar buyers can identify the knock-off guitars as fakes, with younger or more inexperienced buyers in danger of committing a felony while buying what they think is their dream guitar. Even though they are stamped 'Made in USA', that once-revered product label doesn't necessarily mean something was indeed made in America; not in the age of the twenty-first century global marketplace where clandestine factories are as plentiful as American convenience stores,

---

[19]   www.kenyaguitars.com.

and where copyrights, patents and trademarks are as respected as Paris Hilton's privacy.[20]

As much as guitar manufacturers are concerned with the protection of the patents and copyrights pertaining to their products, they are also concerned with meeting demands made of industry in all its forms to be more eco-friendly (as noted already in the reference to Afri-Can guitars above). Mentioned in advertisements by guitar manufacturers are instruments labelled as 'ecological guitars' constructed using woods approved and sanctioned by the FSC (Forest Sustainability Commission). According to a recent Rodriguez classical guitar advertisement, this means that the 'afforestation of woods involved in the production of these guitars has been subject to "cut controls" in the respective forests, meaning that each tree which has been cut must be replaced with a new sapling'.[21] Is this responsible guitar making, an attempt to gain an edge over rivals, or both? Potential rivals have also adopted such schemes. A recent advertisement for Laguna guitars has the headline 'One Guitar, One Tree', with a guitar on one page and a tree sapling that has been just planted on the opposite. A double-page spread, it shows Laguna's awareness of the fact that 'great wood makes great guitars' but reports that Laguna 'proudly plant one tree for every guitar we make'. The advertisement ends with the claim: 'Laguna players: Reforesting the earth, one great guitar at a time'.[22] A leading manufacturer of guitar strings also makes the claim that it is acting responsibly towards the environment by 'utilising "clean" wire' and avoiding '97,000LBs of air pollution'.[23]

The promotional culture surrounding the guitar is, as I have tried to demonstrate, highly complex and ideologically driven, drawing on a range of past and present themes and topics in its advertising. It is also true that the guitar's claim to rootedness in various places around the world is not a new thing. For instance, on the islands of the Azores, the name of the *viola da terra* (a small twelve-string guitar) translates as 'the guitar of our land' (Abreu and Oliveira, 1988).[24] Then again, virtual rootedness is also part of the new guitarscape. For

---

[20]   Carl Cunningham, 'Counterfeit Guitars: Real or Real Good Knock-Off? *Vintage Rock* (1997–2008), http://www.vintagerock.com/fakeguitars.aspx. See also Ellen Mallernee, 'Gibson Leads Industry Fight against Counterfeit Gibsons' (6 June 2007), http://www.gibson.com/en-us/Lifestyle/Features/CounterfeitGibsons/.

[21]   Advertisement in *Gear* magazine, 22 (2008):11. See also www.guitars-m-r-sons.com.

[22]   Advertisement in *Guitar Player* (Holiday 2008):8–9. See also www.environment@playlaguna.com; www.AmericanForests.org.

[23]   See, for example, a recent D'Addario strings advertisement in *Guitar Player* magazine (April 2009):33. See also www.DADDARIO.COM/SAVES.

[24]   See the official website of the guitarist Luis Baptis, where the 'terra' guitar (alongside many other guitars from the Portuguese world) is featured in sound samples and photographs: www.musiclbm.com/ed/index.html.

instance, one might care to take a trip to the Gibson Forest on Gibson's virtual 3-D island where one can (virtually) 'Walk the path and learn about the woods that make the extraordinary Gibson guitars …' (gibson.com).[25]

Guitar magazines, like the Internet or guitar shops, are a portal into the world of the guitar, also helping to shape the new guitarscape. However, the guitar shop or the guitar workshop (akin to the streets of Memphis or Nashville) is a place where one can literally step through to the other side of that portal, into a world whose landscape and even dimensions are largely created by the guitar (plus its amplification and accessories), as it hangs from the walls and takes up floor space, rests on a workshop bench or hangs in a factory rack. The shapes and colours of the instruments are as intoxicating to enthusiasts as the memories and images they conjure up in their minds. I speak from experience. One's senses pick up the sounds, scents and sights of these guitar-based worlds. One dares to reach out and touch a guitar to confirm it is really there. Similarly, one pinches oneself under the giant neon guitars that hang high above the streets of Memphis or Nashville.

I note a recent article in *Acoustic Guitar* magazine entitled: 'Great Guitar Towns: Acoustic Guitar Examines US Cities where the Guitar is King' (Joyner, 2008:59–70). Gibson GuitarTown projects have a variety of purposes, from the bringing together of musical and visual artists (Gibson GuitarTown Miami) to the raising of funds for charities (London GuitarTown) (see Gibson.com). I note elsewhere in this book the role of guitar festivals and shows in promoting towns and cities. Take, for example, the International Guitar Festival of Córdoba, southern Spain, which, as Marcos notes, 'has gone a long way to ensuring that the city achieves its goal of becoming the guitar capital of the world' (Marcos, 1991:13). The festival, founded by Paco Peña in 1981, is an attempt to bring together professional performers, teachers, composers, students and constructors of the guitar from around the world, and is ongoing at the time of writing.

Obviously the development of travel guitars extends the reach of the guitar, that is, its presence and utility around the world, ever further. It is, more than ever, *on the move*, *present*, *agential*. Moreover, there are several performers who use the travel guitar well beyond its means of providing a handy instrument for practice in situations and locations outside of the norm. (But perhaps the travel guitar *is* part of the norm for professionals in demand and also among musically dedicated explorers?). Some performers use the travel guitar on stage (and not necessarily at far-away-from-home venues): is it to make a statement, perhaps – identifying the performer as a global traveller or rambler – or is that the travel guitar (or particular models of it) is also a viable professional instrument with a distinct sound? Playawayguitars.com provides not only a wide selection of travel guitars, called variously 'Traveler' and 'Rambler' as electric, acoustic and bass guitars (now also provided in fretless form), but also portable amplifiers, headphones and gig bags among a range of accessories. Patrick Keating of Play Away Guitars notes:

---

[25]   www.gibson.com/en-us/Lifestyle/Features/enter-a-virtual-3d-world-with/.

Some are frankly quite amazing designs and whilst they are labeled 'travel guitars' (a job they do really well) this does not do them justice. We sell to professional performing musicians who take them on stage, to budding maestros who work in IT and out of hotels all week, to oil men stuck on a rig for a month at a time, to airline pilots who must travel really light, to dentists who keep them in the surgery for missed appointment opportunities, to firemen on night shifts and to people with injuries, disabilities and women with simply short arms! (I could go on ...). The 'travel guitar' makers can only get away with their 'radical' and 'lateral' designs on the pretext that they are for 'travel' and thus they are not to be taken too seriously. A strategy that in all honesty saves them from ridicule by the oh-so conservative 'modern' or 'contemporary' guitarist and the big makers (Gibson, Fender, Paul Reed Smith). (Patrick Keating, personal communication)[26]

In the new guitarscape, definitions of space and place, as much as the location of guitars and the dimensions of their travelling cultures, are subject to a politics and poetics of place. This is, of course, inextricably linked to marketing and advertising agendas in a highly competitive marketplace, as mentioned elsewhere in this book. One of the most important outcomes of the proliferation of guitar makers and manufacturers is that they provide jobs for local people, and contribute to the rich sonic and cultural identity of the new guitarscape. Moreover, such phenomena show that the identity of the guitar is constantly negotiated, contested, the subject of rhetoric and hyperbole, and even fabrication.

Limitations and Scope

In the end, this book is more about the opportunities that now exist for interdisciplinary study, than it is a search for a unified theory. The application of a wide range of ideas will, I hope, lead to an ever deeper analysis of the significance, meaning and potential of not just the guitar but also, perhaps, of other musical instruments as well in human cultures and societies. The aim is to throw into relief the role and agency of objects and their creative assemblage and use in music, culture and society, to reveal something of the intentionality behind the building and shaping of the new guitarscape.

I was clearly not going to have the space to feature in-depth musical analyses of all the guitar styles mentioned in this book (nor could I hope to provide any adequate audience responses to the musical works cited). There are several reliable sources available that feature transcriptions and analyses of guitar styles, including wide-ranging academic tomes (see, for example, Coelho, 2003), focused studies of guitar styles in context (see, for example, Waterman, 1990 on the guitar in the

---

[26]   See Playawayguitars.com. A useful one-page review and sample of travel guitars is provided in *Guitarist*, 316 (June 2009):16.

jùjú music of Nigeria; Schmidt, 1994, who includes an analysis of four African guitar styles; and Charry, 2000, on Mande guitar), guitar magazines (see the many excellent and reliable commentaries and transcriptions by leading professional guitarists in, for example, *Guitar Player, Guitar Techniques, Acoustic Guitar, Classical Guitarist*), on the Internet (although the reliability of transcriptions online is extremely variable), or as part of DVD and CD-Rom 'Learn to Play the Guitar' packages. There is, of course, a vast range of printed music for the guitar.

In this book, I argue that there is a necessity for scholars of the guitar to address a range of other concerns, as there is already material available that provide for the theory, method and practice of transcription and analysis on the guitar and its historical musicology, as well as how to play it. Moreover, in its synthesis of cultural theory, musical analysis and musicians' comments, Timothy Taylor's *Global Pop: World Music, World Markets* admirably addresses the question of 'How are we to talk about globalization (or any large-scale cultural occurrence), real people, and their music?' (Taylor, 1997:xix). So there is little point in reinventing that particular wheel here except to acknowledge Taylor's influence and provide reasons for focusing elsewhere.

In writing this book, I have been mindful of Victor Coelho's comment that not only is it 'impossible to cover all guitar styles in a single book': it is 'even more difficult to suggest that they would *all* share some common ground' (Coelho, 2003:xii). I think it is certainly 'difficult' but not *impossible* to suggest that *all* guitar styles share *some* common ground, as noted throughout this book, even if that common ground is not easily demonstrated with reference to facets of musical style. I am convinced that the themes discussed in this chapter are a further indication of 'common ground', involving specific music cultures but also cutting across cultures and considering the broader context in which we find musical styles (which may or may not be intimately connected). Indeed, further into his edited collection, Coelho points to the 'common ground that exists across guitar cultures' (Coelho, 2003:5), and I think his work makes extraordinary inroads into establishing the common ground that may exist across extant guitar *cultures* if not guitar *styles* with their extraordinary complex musical histories and interpretations that often rely on the individual musician or scholar. In a similar vein, Bennett and Dawe's *Guitar Cultures* (2001) not only helps to show up distinct cultural differences in how the guitar features in the music of various nations, but also suggests ways in which aspects of its study can be viewed as interconnected or as having characteristics in common. In my survey of the new guitarscape, I try to develop a wider theoretical model of what I believe is the common ground and interconnectivity found in the world of the guitar, celebrating cultural difference but also offering a point of departure into the world of ideas about the guitar. These are ideas which in themselves make possible and even demand comparative study without, that is, obscuring or undermining the complex histories attached to the formation of musical styles.

Chapter 4
Notes on Guitarscaping

My vocation is more in composition really than anything else – building up harmonies using the guitar, orchestrating the guitar like an army, a guitar army. (Jimmy Page, quoted on the cover of *Guitar Heroes*, 2008)

Well, we're a one-guitar band, so I don't like our records to sound like walls of guitar textures. I doubled all of the leads and rhythms, but that's it … If I layered guitars like crazy, all that air between the instruments would disappear, and I think the band would actually sound smaller. (Mick Murphy of My Ruin, in Molenda, 2009:38)

I'm into textures, dissonance, and anything that's hurtful to the ear. (Omar Rodríguez López of The Mars Volta, in Molenda, 2008b:56)

The piece shows off a broad spectrum of the techniques I use – finger-picking, harmonic tapping, slide, and guitar percussion. (Vicki Genfan, in Molenda, 2008a:17)

To my surprise, I find that the term 'guitarscape' already has some musical currency, consensus and debate surrounding it, as many of the examples in this chapter demonstrate. It is clearly a term that could mean different things to different people (whether musicians or journalists) and, as such, must be considered something of a contested or polysemic term. However, when the term is not directly used, evidence suggests that it can be usefully deployed. Therefore, I include within the rubric of guitarscaping Jimmy Page's approach to composition and orchestration, Mick Murphy's limited layering and desire for space in his group's recordings, Omar Rodríguez López's textures, dissonances and sonic assaults, and Vicki Genfan's technical showpiece. But I also include, for example, Rhys Chatham's works for 100 hundred and 400 guitars, the soundscape created by Erik Mongrain's 'Air Tap', Pat Metheny's recording of Steve Reich's 'Electric Counterpoint', the interlocking guitar parts of the Rail Band from Mali and the musical eclecticism of Brazilian guitarist Egberto Gismonti where the guitar is noticeably a part of a widely based musical vision of both a Brazilian and a modernist soundscape.[1]

---

[1]   See Rhys Chatham, *A Crimson Grail: For 400 Electric Guitars*, Table of Elements, B000LMPELC (2008), and *An Angel Moves Too Fast to See: For 100 Electric Guitars, Electric Bass and Drums*, Table of Elements, B000FF022G (2008). See also Pat Metheny on Steve Reich, *Different Trains/Electric Counterpoint*, Nonesuch B0000051YU (1989),

The examples mentioned in this chapter demonstrate that a broad range of musical approaches have been taken to the use and application of the guitar in music (well beyond but also including strident solos and chord vamping, which also have their place). Moreover, the mostly guitar-based music mentioned in this book might usefully be distinguished or characterized by an appropriate term of reference: 'guitarscaping'. I discuss mostly studio recordings, but, of course, the challenges that beset the realization of musical ideas whilst playing live and/or recording live performances must also be seen to affect the reception of guitar music as much as any other form of music, and depend very much on whether the guitarist is playing solo or with an ensemble (a duo, string quartet, jazz combo, symphony orchestra, etc.), and is perhaps dependent on mixers and monitors, microphones and pick-ups, acoustic and social environments and the judgements of technicians and conductors. These are further critical elements shaping the sonic aspect of the new guitarscape and inclusive to the guitarscaping model (not seen as a world apart from other instruments, recording studios or stage acoustics but inextricably linked to them).

I am certainly not alone in my subscription to the notion of the term 'guitarscape' and by extension, 'guitarscaping'. In the examples below, the term is used as a musical descriptor of texture and timbre and of an approach to musical composition and arranging, and is used in album titles but also reviews of albums from North America to Australia. Clearly, such a discussion covers a broad sweep of genres and styles, where the issue of the guitar and its sounds as markers of genre (with broader social and cultural implications) can only be discussed in a short section below (but see also Chapter 8). The scaping of the guitar, of course, includes much more than just the manipulation of sounds and the realization of musical ideas (as noted in Chapter 5, as it spreads widely across a number of media). But I do wish to emphasize Paul Théberge's comment that 'Indeed, the manner in which you play an instrument can transform both the instrument itself and the nature of the musical sounds produced' (Théberge, 1997:166).

What follows, then, is a brief introduction to some of the ways in which the new guitarscape may be identified in terms of its sonic markers and acoustic parameters, as evidenced in a range of examples, from the guitarscape of the film *August Rush*[2] to the guitarscape that is a large component of a Pat Metheny concert, from Malian guitarists' adherence to a largely local musical aesthetic to the poetics and politics surrounding hybrid guitars.

Egberto Gismonti, *Selected Recordings* (1977–95), ECM Records/rarum XI 014199-2 (2004).

  [2] *August Rush*, Warner Brothers Pictures (2007).

Guitarscaping – in and across Genres and Styles

I was surprised to find that Guitarscape.com is the web link for the Guitar Foundation of America, an organization that is focused upon the Spanish classical guitar. The term is not only employed by that prestigious organization but by equally well-established musicians, such as Canadian classical guitarist Muriel Anderson, who released a DVD in 2006 with the title *A Guitarscape Planet*. The cover notes state that the film 'weaves a tapestry of beautiful concert footage with spectacular scenery and exotic wildlife'.[3] On this album Anderson plays Spanish classical guitar with added bass strings running parallel to the neck of the guitar (these bass strings are free-hanging, attached to the body of the main guitar at either end, without an extra neck), a harp-guitar in fact.[4] Moving to the southern hemisphere (from my UK perspective), Australian guitarist Graham Greene's album *Leap of Face* (2006) is described as a 'stunning album of solid rock guitarscapes', typically featuring Greene on multi-tracked electric guitars.[5]

I am mindful of Mick Murphy's comments above: although he layers his guitar parts, he does so in a limited way. However, there are other guitarists who not only fill out and pad the sound of their records and bands, but positively rely on such a process to create dense musical settings and backings, heterophony, rich multi-layered harmonies and varied chord voicings, as well as rich and dynamic rhythmic grooves. It happens that these musicians are among some of the most influential guitarists playing at the time of writing. To my mind, Guthrie Govan's *Erotic Cakes* (Cornford Records, 2006) is a more recent and masterful example of exactly this type of approach. The album is certainly indicative of Govan's extraordinary and (in guitar circles) widely known ability to play across a rich variety of guitar styles, –from country rock chicken pickin' to progressive metal, sometimes bursting into experimental sections (see the track 'Erotic Cakes') whilst retaining an overall sense of Govan's own musical identity. Govan is hardly a one-man band: he multi-tracks his guitars to the accompaniment of bass guitar (Seth Govan) and drum kit (Pete Riley), and there are guest guitar solos from Bumblefoot (Ron Thal) and Richie Kotzen.[6]

---

[3]   Muriel Anderson, *A Guitarscape Planet*, Concert Hot Spot/WEA 00108 (2006).

[4]   See also the CD recording *Beyond Six Strings: Harp Guitar Music* B000QZVU8A (2006). This is a compilation album featuring the work of thirteen guitarists, including Muriel Anderson and Andy McKee.

[5]   Graham Greene, *Leap of Face*, Graham Greene 634479315756 (2006) (available on CD Bay).

[6]   Guthrie Govan, *Erotic Cakes*, Cornford Records CORN0001 (2006). See also the Winter 2005 edition of *Guitar Techniques* featuring the track 'Guthrie Govan plays Who's Best?', where, in his own composition, Govan plays in the instantly recognizable guitar styles of Eric Johnson, James Taylor, Pete Townshend, The Edge, BB King, David Gilmour, Mark Knopfler, Albert Lee, Eddie Van Halen, Al Di Meola, Yngwie Malmsteen, Paul Gilbert, Zakk Wylde, Tom Morello, Joe Satriani, Steve Vai, Sonny Landreth, Jeff

However, given Govan's technical prowess it is hardly surprising that he should wish to record the guitar parts himself (apart from two short guest guitar solos). There are obvious technical, aesthetic and economic advantages and considerations at play here. It is clear, though, that Govan is one of several virtuosi who not only push at the boundaries of the technical and sonic possibilities of the guitar but also explore the combination of guitar and recording studio in some detail (see also the work of Dave Martone and Michael Romeo). I also note John 5's similarly eclectic though quite different-sounding guitar-based recording *The Devil Knows my Name* (Mascot, 2007), a work largely created by John 5 alone but with guest bassists and drummers (as well as guest guitar solos from Joe Satriani, Jim Root and Eric Johnson). Similarly well known in guitar circles is John 5's ability to move with apparent ease between high-speed metal guitar playing and country music-inspired tracks (see on *The Devil Knows my Name* his unique rendition of Chet Atkin's 'Young Thing'), his multi-layered guitars and use of feedback, distortion and other effects to create atmospheres, ambient textures and background/industrial noise throughout the album.[7]

Of course, guitarscaping often relies on the availability of multi-track recording devices. In guitar terms, such interdependency of musical and technological innovation goes back to Les Paul's guitar-based recordings of the late 1940s and 1950s (see 'Lover', 1948). Les Paul was, or course, largely responsible for inventing the multi-tracking recording techniques needed to realize his guitar-based arrangements (and the vocal harmonies of Mary Ford) during the 1950s.[8] From the 1980s to the 2000s, the works of Joe Satriani (see his seminal album *Surfing with the Alien*, Relativity, 1987) and Steve Vai (see his seminal album *Passion and Warfare*, Relativity, 1990) have continued to provide highly influential models of guitar virtuosity and multi-tracked guitar compositions (with both musicians recording either EPs or albums in the early 1980s).[9] Satriani is often credited with reviving the popularity of the instrumental album, given the success of *Surfing with the Alien* in 1987 and his ongoing career in the genre.

Clearly, Jimi Hendrix's recordings, especially *Electric Ladyland* (Track, 1968), Jimmy Page's work on the Led Zeppelin albums and Brian May's work with Queen

---

Beck, John Scofield and Jimi Hendrix. See also the YouTube posting that has pictures of all the guitarists mentioned set to Govan's recording. Among several other examples that demonstrate Govan's versatility is the '10 Essential Licks' recording made for the January 2003 issue of *Guitar Techniques*. Govan plays in the style of Eric Clapton, BB King, Albert Collins, Stevie Ray Vaughan, Gary Moore, Larry Carlton, Robben Ford, Eric Johnson, Paul Gilbert and Ritchie Kotzen.

[7]   John 5, *The Devil Knows my Name*, Mascot Records M72172 (2007).

[8]   See, for example, Waksman, 1999 and the DVD *Les Paul: Chasing Sound! Musician, Inventor, Architect of Rock'n'Roll*, Paulson Productions, Icon Television Music, Koch Vision KOC-DV-6432 (2006).

[9]   See, for example, *Joe Satriani EP*, Rubina Records (1984), as included on *Time Machine*, Epic Records (1993) and Steve Vai, *Flexable*, Epic Records (1984).

throughout the 1970s and 1980s have also proved inspirational in terms of defining and advancing multi-tracked guitar sounds, guitar orchestrations and what we now might call guitarscaping. To my mind, the works of British guitarists Jeff Beck and Mike Oldfield as well as North Americans Sonny Landreth and Eric Johnson also break new ground and add significantly to the history of guitarscaping (with musical references across genres, they do not rely on the layering of guitars alone, especially in Oldfield's case, and often draw a range of guitar-based texturings within one piece).[10] Guitarscaping also features sounds current and new in the work of Joe Satriani, Guthrie Govan, John 5, Dave Martone, Dominic Frasca, Andy McKee and Jeff Beck.[11] Perhaps the ultimate guitarscaper is Rhys Chatham, whose pieces for 100 and 400 guitars have already been mentioned, as has Robert Fripp's soundscapes (in Chapter 1). Fripp also records in churches, calling the results 'churchscapes'.

Album reviews also make use of the term 'guitarscape', usually referring to bands using the guitar as one of their sonic devices (if not their main one) for the realization of their compositions, particularly Radiohead, Sonic Youth, Rage Against the Machine, The Mars Volta, Verve, Muse, Red Hot Chilli Peppers, Kings of Leon and even Coldplay. These bands tend to concentrate on creating sound collages (of varying complexity) with the guitar within the framework of a song, experimenting with and exploiting the sonic colours of the guitar and its effects processors, its textures and timbres, and its ability to create an appropriate ambience. Andy Summers of The Police and The Edge of U2 might be seen as two of the best-known forerunners of the textural approach (along with producer-guitarists Michael Brook and Daniel Lanois with their 'infinite guitars'). Known for their *sound*, rather than extravagant or complex guitar solos, these musicians make creative use of effects processors and appropriate chord voicings which provide for depth and interest in the harmonic setting of a song, using chords in different inversions and with open strings and giving a rich palette of musical colours, textures and a sense of depth in bands that often make little use of keyboards. Various Indie bands have adopted such an approach. The work of the guitarist Peter Buck in REM springs to mind, with his simple but highly evocative chord figurations.

Johnny Marr, formerly of The Smiths, is, of course, well known for his multi-tracked guitar contributions to the group's albums, realizing relatively simple

---

[10]   The main exception to this rule is Mike Oldfield's album *Guitars*, Warner Music UK Ltd. 3984274012 (1999), an album on which all the sounds are made by guitars (multi-tracked or otherwise). Of course, guitars in various forms (from 'speed guitar' and 'mandolin-like guitar' to acoustic bass guitar) are to be found on Oldfield's early albums, for example, his first album, *Tubular Bells*, Virgin Records 724384938826 (1973).

[11]   Jeff Beck's albums *You Had it Coming* (2001) and *Jeff* (2003) are, to my mind, particularly outstanding in this respect. See Jeff Beck, *You Had it Coming*, Epic 5010182, Sony Music Entertainment Inc. (2001) and *Jeff*, Epic 5108202, Sony Music Entertainment Inc. (2003).

harmonic progressions in complex textural overlays and providing what appear to be highly appropriate settings for the lyrics of the songs and the tonality of Morrissey's voice (as noted, for example, by Bannister, 2006). I am reminded at this point of David Torn's concept of 'painting with a guitar' and his notion of 'sonic alternatives', a guitarscape that sonically emulates a visual landscape.[12] The contributions of Michael Brook and Kaki King to the soundtrack of the film *Into the Wild* (Lake Shore, 2007) are further examples of guitar-based scene setting in a sonic-visual medium.[13] A reviewer notes of Erdem Helvacıoğlu's *Altered Realities* (2006) – an album based on the computer-generated manipulations of a vibrating guitar string – 'There is absolutely no show of technique or odd musical acumen, but the amount of guitar being played is exactly the amount of paint a master needs to make a canvas. No more, no less is required.'[14]

To my ears, guitarscaping is also evident in the sound of Rush's *Snakes and Arrows* (Atlantic, 2007). In a recent *Guitar Player* magazine article, Rush guitarist Alex Lifeson is described as 'the glue that holds Rush together ... equal parts rock dude, sonic adventurer and texturalist. His huge washes of chorused power chords and clever arpeggios have been the mortar between Lee and Peart's bricks since the three first threw down together' (Blackett, 2007:80). The article details the ways in which Lifeson uses various guitars to timbral and textural effect throughout the *Snakes and Arrows* album (but, of course, Geddy Lee's contributions on bass guitar are also crucial here), and the interviewer once again makes the claim that the guitarist 'effortlessly cranks out unbelievable expansive soundscapes with three-dimensional richness, crystalline highs, and subterranean lows' (Blackett, 2007:82).[15]

Tom Morello's guitar sounds (see *Rage Against the Machine, Audioslave*) inspired by deejay gangsta rappers show also the guitar's potential to be used as a vehicle for more radical musical explorations and politically pointed statements at the music/noise interface. In Morello's case, this involves innovative use of such things as foot pedals and manipulations of the guitar's pick-up toggle switch.[16] YouTube video postings of guitarist Herman Li (Dragonforce) show Li demonstrating how he manually re-creates a range of extra-musical sounds on his

---

[12]   David Torn, *Painting with Guitar*, Homespun Tapes (VDTORGT01/2)/Hal Leonard (#HL00641065) (1993). See the YouTube videos 'David Torn – Painting with Guitar' (consisting of *Painting with Guitar* broken up into fourteen parts).

[13]   The soundtrack of the film *Into the Wild* features two tracks – 'Frame' and 'Doing the Wrong Thing' – from Kaki King's album *Legs to Make us Longer*, Red Ink/Epic WK92426 (2004).

[14]   See the article 'Erdem Helvacıoğlu from Turkey, Hardly Performs the Guitar on his New Albion Release, Altered Realities', New Millennium Guitar Publishing (2006), http://newmillguitar.com/erdem.html. See also Cleveland, 2007.

[15]   Rush, *Snakes and Arrows*, Atlantic 7567-89986-8 (2007).

[16]   However, Tom Morello's 2008 album *The Fabled City* more than suggests that he has now turned his attention to the acoustic guitar.

electric guitar, including 'The Pac-Man Noise', 'The Dive-Bomb Noise', 'The Elephant Noise', 'The Motorbike Noise' and 'The Break Your Guitar String Noise' (www.youtube.com),[17] again providing examples of the rich palette of sounds now available, as well as advanced playing techniques which are disseminated to a wide audience.

I have already mentioned the importance of metal music to the new guitarscape, with its distorted, thick-textured guitar sounds (the guitars often with dropped tuning and/or with seven or more strings). The guitar's multifarious distorted sounds and especially designed guitars and amplification, combined with a variety of tunings, facilitate the texture, timbre and dynamic range of the metal sub-genres, for example, the 'heaviness' (Berger and Fales, 2005) and the 'hot' sounds (Walser, 1993:43) of heavy metal. Such facts remind one of the importance of guitarscaping in the context of genre and notions of subcultural style (see Hebdige, 1979; Walser, 1993; Bannister, 2006), from 'one chord wonders' (after Laing, 1986) and three-chord tricks to complex cadenza workouts, from basic to highly sophisticated guitar rigs (not to mention the differing approaches held by other instrumentalists and singers in various ensembles that are clearly genre-linked) to the potency of textures and timbres as genre markers.

In his book *Guitar Rigs*, Dave Hunter provides the reader with equipment itineraries and settings for the recreation of the sounds of twelve examples of guitar and guitar equipment set-ups, including 'Early Jazz', 'Surf's Up', 'Club Jazz', 'Country Twang' and 'Brit Rock to Classic Metal' (after Hunter, 2005). In a similar vein, a recent edition of *Guitar Player* magazine also featured details (photographs of stage set-ups and equipment lists) of fifteen 'awesome guitar rigs', including those of Slipknot, The Mars Volta, Jeff Beck, Steve Vai, The Edge, Alex Lifeson, Lamb of God, Joe Satriani and Zakk Wylde (see Molenda, 2008b).

I have already mentioned the percussive and tapped acoustic guitar sounds of what has been dubbed as the 'new acoustic movement' as practised by Andy McKee, Vicki Genfen, Kaki King, Erik Mongrain, Antoine Dufour and Craig D'Andrea among others. These musicians tend to make use of microphones and contact pick-ups in strategic places on and off their guitar in order to emphasize and amplify the tonal qualities of the guitar as both a melodic and percussive instrument. Careful mixing of the guitar's amplification units are required to achieve an appropriate balance for the piece and venue at hand. In an interview with *Vintage Guitar*, Tommy Emmanuel reveals how he sets up his acoustic guitar for one of his own compositions, 'Initiation', a piece said to have been inspired by an Australian aboriginal ritual. Emmanuel's account of the piece is worth quoting in some detail here:

> The song is a piece of musical drama; it's supposed to be telling the story of the ritual where a boy proves himself to be a man. It takes time, and he has to go through all sorts of tests; they circumcise him with a rock, cut him, burn him,

---

[17]   www.youtube.com: 'Herman Li Video Game Guitar Effects'.

and leave him out where he has to survive. I try to create an atmosphere using the body of the guitar, and I try to create sound effects that add to the storyline. I use extreme EQ [equalization] on it; exaggerated midrange and bottom-end. That's the way you get those sounds, but if you bang on (the guitar) too hard, you'll break speakers, so I have to be real careful at the same time. I use digital delay, and the sound man at the front puts some long reverb on it; about four seconds. And I crank everything up until it's almost in the red. While that's going on with all of those noises that are supposed sound like wind, rain, thunder, and animal sounds, I've got this groove going, kind of like a pulse. The way I play the melody with the digital delay, it sounds like there's at least two things going on at the same time. In fact, people are always looking around to see who else is playing! Or they're at least looking around for a lot more equipment, and there isn't any.[18]

In relation to Tommy Emmanuel's careful setting up and monitoring of his stage equipment – see also Figure 4.1 below, which features four other guitarists – I note the importance of string use and guitar tunings to the scaping of a guitar piece. For example, a variety of guitar tunings is used on Erik Mongrain's most recent recording, *Equilibrium* (Alter Ego/Prophase, 2008),[19] including such unusual tuning series as A#A#DFGD and BF#DF#C#C# from low to high on a six-string guitar.[20] Such tunings not only facilitate the realization of certain musical ideas, perhaps melodic or chord-based, but also change the sound of the guitar. The use of open strings, open strings in combination with stopped strings, and 'slack key' or dropped tunings, as well as the type of strings used (often with gauge sequences and string actions dependent on individual choice), will also affect the overall timbre of the guitar. All of these nuances have been known by guitarists for some time but are now picked up and exploited by a new generation of acoustic players.

Guitarists are often identified by their tone, a marker of individuality that is clearly dependent not just on their technical playing ability but crucially on their choice of guitars (made from various 'tonewoods'), featuring particular makes of pick-ups and their amplification and effects, all of which affect the sonority of their musical instrument and the music made upon it. To varying degrees these are all linked in a vast chain of sound-producing, processing and filtering devices, from the soundboards of guitars to the baffle boards of speaker cabinets.

---

[18]   Willie G. Moseley, 'Tommy Emmanuel: Advocate of the Atkins Legacy' (posted 27 January 2009), http://www.vintageguitar.com/features/artists/details.asp?AID=2988.

[19]   Erik Mongrain, *Equilibrium*, Alter Ego Musique/Prophase Music MVDA4821 (2008).

[20]   See the *Guitar Player* article 'Web Exclusive: Erik Mongrain's Tunings' at http://www.guitarplayer.com/article/web-exclusive-erik/dec-08/91207. See also Weissman, 2006 for a comprehensive guide to guitar tunings.

One must also include discussion of some of the ways in which guitarists outside Europe and North America use their musical instruments and accessories in quite specific ways and in quite specific cultural contexts, from the street music of South Africa and Vietnam to the use of the guitar in both Turkish and Hindustani art music. I note four examples given in Chapter 1 where guitarists from Benin, Turkey, India and Bali (Indonesia) have developed or adopted particular guitar styles, guitars and means of sound production and projection to enable them to play in local musical traditions (and be heard). Lionel Loueke combines African musical styles within a jazz-based framework (and vice versa). Hassan Cihat Örter plays within and across a wide variety of local and globally mobile music genres, Kamala Shankar focuses on the performance of Hindustani art music whilst attending to local musical aesthetics (playing with tampura and tabla accompaniment on a guitar of her own design), I Wayan Balwan combines both local compositional techniques and instruments (gamelan) with jazz- and rock-inspired guitar sounds and improvisations. But there are many other contexts for performance, for instance performance for dance and drama, for which the guitar provides music, supports a musical ensemble or plays a leading role.

Of the very many examples I could have chosen to include here as representative of the guitar's role in global performance, the following example (my description and synopsis) is meant to demonstrate how guitarscaping in a West African context contributes to the sound and dynamic of music for dance, in this case Djelimady Tounkara with the (Super) Rail Band in Mali. A brief description of a Rail Band performance might be useful here.

> Djelimady Tounkara stands behind two dancers who are interlinked arm in arm, crouched down on the ground, they spin round and round in time to his hypnotic guitar patterns. He plays a mixture of repeated riffs, chord voicings and fast runs linked to short melodic hooks, behind and between the vocals. His style of playing is angular and idiosyncratic. As his cherry sunburst solid body electric guitar catches the spotlight, I am reminded that Tounkara is still at the time of writing a star of world guitar and that I am watching one of Africa's finest. The footage shows the Rail Band playing at the Buffet Hotel de la Gare in Bamako, in the mid 1980s. DT is the Rail Band's lead guitarist. The piece is called 'Sanakoro Moriba' (A praise song for three friends). The electric guitars (two six-strings and a bass) cut through the loud and dense mix of three vocalists (one lead and two backing singers), two saxophones, trumpet, congas, kit drums and additional hand percussion. DT seems to play an extraordinary cat and mouse game with the other guitarist as they share lead lines and literally bounce ideas off one another. Their duet, in and across the underlying timeline of the drums, adds a further rhythmic dimension to the performance. Throughout, DT keeps smiling. Despite the intensity and demands of the performance he takes it all in his stride. In the Rail Band he is part of a communal performance, where guitar playing melds with dancing, comedy, tight vocal harmonies, brass interjections, and a rich and vibrant percussion ensemble.

From this description, it is clear that the guitar parts, including Djelimady's improvised lead solo, are a core ingredient in the hypnotic sound of the Rail Band and one of its major driving forces.[21] This performance, among other extraordinary performances by the Rail Band, was captured by Mark Kidel, producer of the BBC television documentary film *Bamako Beat: Mali Music, Rhythms of the World* in 1989. Moreover, within that film, musicians discuss the various guitar techniques they use to produce the Mali guitar sound in terms of techniques applied and the influence of local instruments, discussing both *kora* (harp-lute) and *ngoni* (plucked lute) styles of guitar playing (a discussion taken much further in Charry, 2000). Having now provided examples of approaches to guitarscaping in a variety of contexts, it is necessary to discuss some of the ways in which guitars and their technologies relate to genre ideals (see also Chapter 8).

Genre and Guitarscaping

Genres are powerful and often empowering musical constructs, for musicians, audiences and the music industry. Having moved swiftly across genres in the last section, I think it may be useful here to anchor some of that discussion in relation to genre. I want to do this mainly by reference to guitar designs, guitar effects units and their sounds and images. When the Indie Guitar Company advertises its guitars as stalwarts of the independent music scene, this speaks volumes for its potential consumers. The Union Jack-influenced logo on some of its guitars is more than reminiscent of the Britpop-style guitars it also manufactures, slim-line, f-hole Gibsons with Union Jack decoration for Oasis-style Britpop.[22] The sound of the guitar in particular genres and styles has, in some circumstances, come to epitomize the underlying ideology of the musical subculture to which it belongs. For instance, Matthew Bannister talks about 'the white noise and wall of sound of punk standing for impersonality in contrast to the individuality of blues, jazz, and rock guitar' (Bannister, 2006:111), linking particular sounds of the guitar to the broader social and cultural dimensions of genre, but also presumably to the personality (or at least cultivated image) of particular guitarists.

Given the very many sound manipulators designed especially for use with the guitar, one needs to bear constantly in mind that the sound of the instrument is filtered and sculpted through an ever-growing chain of sound-altering devices. Guitar rigs are not just the linking together of various makes and models of guitars and amplification to define certain sounds and genre aesthetics, but also the chain-like links created between guitar and amplifier that include a variety of sound-

---

[21]   Djelimady Tounkara, *Bamako Beat: Mali Music, Rhythms of the World*, Mark Kidel (producer), BBC (1989).

[22]   See www.indieguitarcompany.com. Examples of Indie Guitar advertisements can be found in *Guitar and Bass Magazine*, 19/7 (July 2008):75; *Guitar Buyer*, 86 (October 2008:77).

manipulating devices (such as foot pedals and effects racks). As Dave Hunter notes, one has to be aware of how 'each link in the chain affects the sound as a whole' (Hunter, 2004:135). I note the potential of a flick of a switch or a turn of a knob to affect – that is, to sustain, corrupt or destroy – the sound and thus the musical meaning of a particular genre or sub-genre.

The development of a range of guitar equipment technologies enables the guitar player to have much more control over the guitar and its sound, even in performance. And now even his or her fingertips and palms may be used to control sound effects devices. Effects racks enable the player to switch between the sounds of different genres, with digital readouts for each of them with multiple variations now possible. There may be several variations of a particular genre, reading as 'metal #5' or 'indie #3', for example. The guitar player can, like his keyboard-playing counterpart, move sonically between genres at the flick of a switch, even if he or she remains outside the selected genre in terms of allegiance to its lifestyle and ideology and inhabits another. The sounds of guitars and their rigs are stored in effects processors and can be accessed with increasing ease to not only sonically emulate and re-create genres and styles, but also cross-reference and transform them.

As the guitar's technological resources grow in complexity, so they are increasingly designed to be user-friendly, with the manufacturer's aim of achieving optimal playing ability and responsiveness, adhering to ergonomic principles, and largely featuring straightforward controls operable by musicians who will, in the main, not be specialist technicians. Moreover, it has become clear to me that whilst the average guitarist may not be as knowledgeable about technical matters as specialist technicians, many guitarists demonstrate a keen interest in the equipment they use, how such equipment works and its musical potential. If one can afford to buy the right equipment, one can access a great many of the sounds which have come to mark out and define the guitar's history: and they are now all potentially musically operative in the new guitarscape, which has unlimited sonic range.

However, manufacturers also present a streamlining of the sonic resources now available for the musician, enabling players to focus on certain sounds and guitar styles (among an almost bewildering choice), usually bounded by notions of genre. Effects pedals are also, therefore, linked explicitly to the sounds and ideals of genre, and the vast choice of such effects also marks out the complexity of the field of music, a field made up of multiple genres and styles. A few examples among many should suffice here. Take, for instance, the genre known as 'metal'. One notes the variation in distortion pedal model descriptors linked explicitly to sub-genres and idealized stylistic variations: Digitech Death Metal, the Boss Metal Core and the Line 6 Uber Metal. Some distortion pedals (just like other effects pedals) are, however, designed in collaboration with or make reference to the sound of a particular guitar player. Examples include the Vox Satchurator (Joe Satriani, not specifically a metal guitarist) and the MXR Dime Distortion (the late Dimebag Darrell). Staying once more with the example of players who are (broadly speaking) metal guitarists, the Dean Magnetic Technologies (linked to Dean Guitars) also produce signature guitar pick-ups, such as the Dimebag Darrell Dimetime, Corey Beaulieu Ascension and Matt Heafy MKH86. Such a selection of options would seem to suggest that equipment-manufacturing industries are eager to keep their selling options open: one might buy a pedal because it is associated with a genre, a guitar player or both. And such a scenario also points to the interaction but also possible tensions between genre and individual style, as the manufacturers try to have it both ways.

Guitars and Technology in Performance and Composition

August Rush runs his fingers across the dusty surface of an acoustic guitar's soundboard. He plucks the lowest string of the Gibson guitar, and then strums outwards and away from his body with his thumb as he picks out the remaining five strings in turn. The guitar is lying on the floor of small room within a run down theatre. August is crouched on his haunches beside it. He slaps the strings over the higher frets, managing to produce harmonics, the notes ringing out across the small ante-room. The instrument has obvious sustaining power. He retunes the guitar's highest pitched string. The retuning, like the strums and slaps become part of August's sonic exploration of the guitar, but they are simultaneously ways in which he feels his way around the instrument and its workings within the confined acoustic space of the small room with its exposed concrete walls. The camera switches to a shot of the stage of the theatre, then its boxes and gallery, as the sounds of the guitar begin to travel upward. August Rush wastes little time in mastering some of the guitar's basic playing techniques, nor in finding the timbres and textures that inspire him ever onward as tries to externalise the music inside him. The sounds of the guitar ring out through the theatre, waking up his 'employer' and drawing the attention of his friends to his impromptu performance.

August inserts a jack plug into the acoustic guitar's input socket. The birdsong just before this, as well as the echo of the jack plug clicking into its socket, are not just a part of the soundscape of this scene, they seem to be a part of August's unfolding composition, part of 'the music in the wind and the sky' (according to the DVD cover notes). Moreover, they can be seen to emphasise the broader context of his discovery of self through music, now finding expression and taking its course through a dusty guitar in what seems to be the basement of a run down theatre. The guitar is connected to a small portable amplifier through a delay pedal. The delay pedal is held together with black masking tape. This particular guitar rig has a hard working life on the streets of New York City. August presses the pedal. The camera angle changes to a view looking down the neck of the guitar (towards the headstock). As August's hands bounce of the strings so too does a light cloud of dust, August's hand movements and the soundwaves coming out of the soundhole of the guitar appear to move the dust, like 'the music in the wind and the sky', now also filtered and delayed through the speakers of the small amplifier and lifted upwards and outwards into the auditorium of the theatre.

At a recent guitar workshop in York, England (15 March 2009), I was briefly reminded of the scene described above, taken from the film *August Rush*. However, I was at the time watching and listening to Jennifer Batten (see also Chapter 7), one of the foremost electric guitar virtuosi in the world. In her discussion of two-handed tapping, Jennifer Batten mentioned in passing that percussive techniques are actually quite basic to sound production on the guitar. 'Give a child a guitar and the first thing he or she will usually do is tap or slap the strings.' I think this is an important point. My description of a scene from the film *August Rush* above is intended to remind the reader of the agency of both technology (guitar, amplifier, effects pedal) and the musician (musical ideas, percussive playing and an almost instinctive understanding of the performance format at hand) in the creation of the new guitarscape, with August Rush's solo starting out from the most basic level, where there are elements of a rudimentary technique exposed, to become an effective musical composition. Moreover, the film showcases techniques of playing an acoustic guitar (even an amplified one) that have given the acoustic form of the guitar a seemingly new lease of life. August Rush's guitar pieces are played by Kaki King (and it is her hands playing the guitar that one sees in the film).

The extended techniques used in *August Rush* provide for what one can only describe as a showy virtuosic display whilst providing for rhythmic drive and melodic and harmonic compositional potential. Such a display is reminiscent of what has become commonplace in, but not exclusive to, rock and heavy metal electric guitar playing (at least in terms of the similar dynamic choreography created by August's arm and hand movements), but has more recently been exposed on acoustic guitar. Moreover, the apparent movement around the guitar (a choreography characteristic of acoustic playing in the new guitarscape), as well as the filmic or photogenic appeal of both the guitarist and the guitar itself, reminds one of the multifarious ways in which various individuals might be said to have designs on the guitar: from the composer to the manufacturer, from the journalist to the film-maker, scriptwriter and novelist (see, for example, Cezar, 2005). As noted before, the ten performances in Chapter 1 are intended to throw the world of guitar playing into relief, featuring distinct approaches to performance, uses of technology and methods of playing. Table 4.1 sets out these various approaches in a summary of the main technological and also musical components for four of the artists mentioned (those whom I was able to contact to find out exactly what they used or whose stage set-up featured in detailed interviews in reliable sources).

Figure 4.1   Kaki King

Figure 4.2   Jennifer Batten

Table 4.1   Techniques and technologies in performance

Guitarist	Techniques and technologies
Fred Frith	Fred Frith notes for both pre-selected objects and effects pedals: 'maybe half of the stuff actually get's used … and what it is used for is constantly under development' (Frith, personal communication). *Pre-selected objects*: string, piano tuning felt for string damping strings from below, large pieces of cloth for damping string from above, drumsticks, chopsticks/dowelling rods, two spindle rods from old industrial weaving machines, metal rods (some serrated), a bottleneck, a piece of stone with roughly sanded edges, an E-Bow (sometimes two), alligator clips, picks, a collection of tins and their lids (picked according to size), a small Chinese gong and a small cymbal, a child's 'cello bow, a small bag of rice, a small wooden finger massager, a larger wooden hand massager, a selection of various sizes of wooden balls. *Effects pedals*: two delays, two distortions, two tremolos, one noise gate used exclusively for triggering sound via a contact microphone, an octave divider, a reverb unit, and a ring modulator. *Additional*: microphones, two Fender amplifiers, Gibson semi-acoustic guitar with a pick-up mounted also at the nut and no whammy bar.
Sharon Isbin	1988 spruce-top Thomas Humphrey Millennium nylon acoustic guitar with hard-tension strings that are a mixture of a few brands, action set as low as possible. Amplification system Shure wireless SC system (no wires and no permanent electronics mounted on her guitar). The Shure system has a built-in microphone that is placed in the guitar's soundhole along with the unit's transmitter, which is wrapped in foam. The signal is transmitted to a box that houses the Shure receiver, an amplifier, a fifteen-band graphic equalizer and two Celestion speakers, and the whole system is powered by cell batteries rather than AC power to avoid ground hum. The box, which is placed about ten feet behind Isbin on stage, is ported to provide omnidirectional sound for orchestral performances and solo concerts in halls with more than 400 seats. One full symphony orchestra (www.acguitar.com/issues/ag103/gear103.shtml, Mark L. Small).
Steve Vai	Steve Vai Ibanez Signature Jem Guitars, Carvin Steve Vai Legacy amplification and speaker cabinets. *Rack-mounted*: Nady U-1000 wireless, TC Electronic G-Force, Eventide DSP 4000 Ultra-Harmonizer, Furman PL-Plus. *Pedalboard*: Digitech Whammy, Morley volume pedal, Boss DS-1, Peterson StroboStomp, Ibanex TS9 with Keely mo, a Dunlop Crybaby, and an MXR EVH Phase 90. *Techniques*: numerous string sounding, stopping and manipulation techniques including plectrum, tapping, use of whammy bar, looping.
I Wayan Balawan	Double-neck, solid body electric guitar, thirteen strings (6/7), one normal six-string guitar neck, one seven-string intonation guitar neck, with Midi guitar pick-up, amplification, also vocals, playing with a bass guitarist, a single double-headed drum, and two players on a single metallophone. *Balawan Batuan Ethnic Fusion*: one standard drum kit, two guitar amplifiers (Roland Jazz Chorus), two keyboard amplifiers (Peavey KB 300 or Roland 1 Bass Amp), eight or more microphones(five Shure SM 57 and three Shure SM 58 with stand (for the gamelan), three direct boxes, one digital piano (Fender Rhodes or similar type). *Small gamelan*: two Balinese kendang (drums), one metal gamelan, one wooden gamelan, one standard cengceng and four pairs of cengceng (cymbals), four flutes, one ten-piece reyong (gong set).

Guitarists and Gear

Guitarists, among many other instrumentalists, continue to exploit available musical instrument designs, amplification, effects and studio technologies, and the ways in which these might affect the sound of the guitar. And they are also increasingly involved with the design of the guitar. This ongoing engagement with technology in all its forms varies from tinkering with foot pedal effects (for example, equalizers, distortion boxes, delay and harmonizers) to the use of multiple effects racks and looping stations, and from the building of one's own guitar (even with a kit) to the development of a custom-built guitar rig, moving increasingly to software control. As mentioned before, discussion of the wide range of guitar technologies must also be related to extended playing techniques which currently feature in various guitar styles. Fingers or plectra on strings are still, after all, the primary means of sound activation, very much depending on how the guitar and its rig is able to respond as set up to the musician's individual needs and musical aspirations. Guitars are often custom-built especially to suit the playing techniques and desired sounds of an individual guitarist. For example, a guitarist may need a guitar with low string action and/or guitars made of wood with a high sustaining quality. Eddie Van Halen's various experiments with guitar set-ups led to his work on guitar design with some of the most respected guitar manufactures in North America (Kramer, Peavey, Music Man and Fender with the most recent EVH guitar) (see Walser, 1993, Waksman, 1999, 2003, Gill 2009).

In *Instruments of Desire*, Steve Waksman (1999) demonstrates how the musical needs of certain performers have affected the design of the electric guitar, from Charlie Christian's bar pick-up to Les Paul's solid-body Gibson guitars, and from Chet Atkin's Gretsch Countryman through to Eddie Van Halen's EVH guitars. Chris Gill proclaims that 'Eddie Van Halen not only changed the way the guitar is played he also affected the way it is made. Several guitar product innovations ... were directly influenced by Van Halen's playing style' (Gill, 1995:140). Not only do musicians perform and record with the musical equipment that they have had a hand in creating, but they also function as endorsees for prototypes and new models that they have not had a hand in designing. Once contact between a company and a musician has been made, musicians will be paid to use and endorse equipment (including guitars, pick-ups, strings, effects pedals, amplification and speaker cabinets, for example). They are in effect being paid to put prototypes and new models through their paces, not always on stage but also at clinics, demonstrations and workshops. As noted in a recent article in *Acoustic Guitar*:

> The key, from the manufacturer's point of view is that a potential endorser has all the career essentials in place – CDs out, publicity and management support, an active tour schedule, a dynamic presence online, a growing fan base, and, of course, top-shelf music. 'No product can make a so-so artist sound like a seasoned pro,' says Chris DeMaria, marketing director for Fishman Transducers.

'We all want our gear to sound great in the hands of great players.' (Pepper Rodgers, 2009:74)[23]

It is clear that the commercial and economic aspects of the instrument-building, equipment-building and technology industries now have a substantial impact on the way in which professional guitarists develop not only personalized sounds but also their playing styles. I tend to agree with Ray Hitchins, who notes:

> To my mind these players represent a new type of industrial virtuoso/designer 'guitar brand'. For example see Eddie Van Halen's EVH brand of guitars, amps and merchandise. Guitar and guitar equipment builders have increasingly integrated these players into the design, manufacture and sales of instruments on a scale not previously seen. Look at the range of Fender and Gibson's endorsement packages now compared to 1980. It seems that many players now have the ambition to become a top Fender endorser rather than a leading artist for a record company. My sense is that this area is very significant in the development of rock-derived guitar in particular. It represents a very different guitar world to the one that Jimmy Page and Ritchie Blackmore emerged out of, and based on your examples in Chapter 1 it has had a world wide impact. (Ray Hitchins, personal communication)

Moreover, a huge range of dedicated guitar equipment now exists. The gear that goes into the construction, setting up and maintenance of a guitar rig might include pick-ups, vibrato bars ('whammy bars'), onboard effects and tuners, amplifiers (tube and non-tube, analogue and digital), speaker cabinets, speakers, cables, cable-free transmission senders and receivers between guitar and amplification, effects pedals and racks, loopers (loop stations), plectra (picks), thumb picks, pick tins, false nails, slides (including bottlenecks), capos, half capos, mini capos, straps, footstools, tuners, nut fret files, adjustable guitar neck holders, bridgeplate assemblies, compensated saddles, pre-wired control plates, computer-aided fret dressing, guitar cases, amplifier and speaker cabinet cases and covers, flight cases, guitar stands, racks and display cabinets, and so on. Such a list is only the tip of a very large iceberg. But each and every item mentioned above can be seen to affect the sound of the guitarist directly or indirectly, through either producing and processing his or her sound or maintaining the means to do so intact.

---

[23]   See also www.eluthrie.org.: 'One of our new features, the Marketplace is a great place for readers to connect with vendors and for vendors to expose their products and services to a focused audience. Design & Technology Exchange – Our soon to be launched community will provide both professional stringed instrument builders and serious amateurs with a secure space to interact, collaborate and exchange ideas. Featured will be a number of eLUTHERIE.org co-founder Rick Toone's innovations which he will share under our terms of agreement.'

Despite the fact that certain guitarists, such as Steve Hillage (solo, System 7, Gong, and producer-guitarist for Rachid Taha), Ed Wynne (Ozric Tentacles) or Joe Satriani, for instance, engage variously with music technologies from programmed keyboard parts to synthesizers, as guitar players they retain what one might call the instantly recognizable sound of the guitar in performance. Often labelled Post Rock, the Irish group God is an Astronaut weaves guitar and keyboard lines (often long interlocking arpeggio sequences) to create not only atmospheric sounds but music that is highly programmatic (see, for example, the videos for the instrumental 'Fragile' on YouTube). Live, the Astronauts' lead guitarist Torsten Kinsella switches between guitar, keyboards and other electronic devices within the space of one piece (likewise Ed Wynne). Moreover, whether recorded live or in the studio, the guitar is clearly identifiable within the Astronauts' mix (as it is on Ozric Tentacles recordings).

Pat Metheny can often be seen using several different guitars of varying and distinctive design in his concerts, including arch-top electric-acoustic steel-string guitar, acoustic steel-string guitar, acoustic nylon-string guitar, fretless nylon-string acoustic guitar, guitar synthesizer, tenor guitar, and the multi-necked, forty-two-string Pikasso guitar. It is clear that Metheny has a particular sound in mind for a particular piece, and will go to the trouble of building a guitar to realize the sounds he has in mind for one piece on one album, as well as making use of it in concert. The ongoing symbiosis between musical ideas and aspirations and developments in musical technology is clear to see here, as Metheny notes:

There are three new instruments heard prominently on this album … The first of the new ones is something I've been working on for six or seven years, the fretless classical guitar. I've been trying to develop a fretless model since I was in high school; it's very difficult to get any sustain with strings as light as guitar strings normally are. Linda Manzer came up with an idea a few years back that really works out well, which is to have a fretless classical guitar with an almost cello-like bridge. Ironically, I wound up running it through a fuzz tone to get the sounds I like. It's featured on *Imaginary Day* and it offers me a set of new possibilities, in terms of phrasing and sonic colours. It ends up sounding a little like a slide guitar, but with me getting around the instrument a bit more than sliding technique would normally allow and trying not to play the usual blues phrases associated with the instrument.

Next, there's the 42-string pikasso guitar … Basically, it's a conventional guitar that's flanked by three other sets of multiple strings that cross underneath and over the main body of the instrument. So you can be playing a regular guitar but have these other areas on the same playing surface where you can have ringing notes, some of which are higher than the regular guitar and some of which are lower. It's really the closest I've come to something like a piano that's also a guitar; you can really have a lot of notes ringing and sustaining over other notes without using any kind of electronics.

Finally, there's the vg-8, a new kind of audio workstation made by Roland. It isn't a guitar synthesizer and it isn't an effect, its something in an entirely new category. It's a pick-up you can put on your guitar that allows you to make any guitar sound like other combinations of guitars, amps, microphones, speakers, rooms. The vg-8 is an incredible tool for manipulating the amplified sound of what your guitar delivers to the listener.[24]

There is now, of course, a bigger element of choice in terms of which sounds one will employ at any one time, whether in the recording studio or on stage. Pat Metheny relies on the help of his guitar technician, Carolyn Chrzan, to keep his many guitars in working order, but has also commissioned Linda Manzer to build some of the guitars mentioned above. However, few guitarists can afford to have built for them the fleet of guitars owned by Metheny, nor employ a guitar technician to tune them and set them up. But even when guitarists can afford to have such resources made available to them, some choose a different route. This is related to the question: What if one is the only guitar player in a band that requires both electric and acoustic guitar sounds in the space of *one* song?

Acoustic or Electric: Notes on the Politics and Poetics of Hybridity

The magazine *Total Guitar* included a double-sided poster with its December 2008 issue (issue 183) which, to my mind, was telling. Entitled 'Anatomy of an Axe', it features annotated diagrams of an electric guitar on one side and an acoustic guitar on the other. This double-sided model (the two sides of the guitar) is not only symbolic but very much in accord with the all-inclusive model I am proposing with the new guitarscape. In practice, the two sides of the guitar could not be closer together than they are at the beginning of the twenty-first century. Acoustics, like electrics, draw on advanced technologies in their making and may well be supported by a range of 'gear' in performance. The percussive acoustic guitar techniques already discussed sometimes rely upon quite complex performance set-ups, with sound sensor plates, contact microphones and pick-ups attached to various parts of the inside of the guitar (registering high- and low-frequency sounds that are then fed to the performer's mini mixing desk, sometimes through a multi-core cable).

Yet a recent advertisement in *Acoustic* magazine for a guitar/transducer/amplifier rig claims: 'Hear the guitar, not the gear: acoustic transducers that listen, acoustic amps that transmit, acoustic guitars that inspire'.[25] The gear is not

---

[24]   Pat Metheny Group, *Imaginary Day Live/Speaking of Now Live*, Collector's Edition box set (2 DVDs), Metheny Group Productions/Pioneer/Eagle Vision EREDV604 (2006, consisting of EREDV265, 1998, and EREDV367, 2002). See *Imaginary Day*, Special Features and Notes about the Instrumentation.

[25]   Advertisement in *Acoustic*, 24 (October/November 2008):85.

supposed to get in the way, but it is there. Peter Narvaez's essay on the 'Myth of Acousticity' (Narvaez, 2001) strikes at the heart of the matter, as if acoustic guitars are more 'natural', more in touch with one's musical soul. In terms of the acoustic guitar's claim to being the 'authentic' or 'natural' guitar, one is also reminded of outcry that ensued when Bob Dylan went electric in the 1960s. On the one hand the acoustic guitar is seen as the 'natural' relation to the electric guitar; they still share many fundamental features in common. On the other hand and in a roundabout way, the advertisement mentioned above also champions and advertises the role of the acoustic guitar's attendant technologies.

Acoustic guitars continue to be used as the physical and musical basis for extended playing techniques, but their players also engage with amplification, effects and sound-processing devices of many kinds. In a review of McPherson guitars, the author claims that they 'combine exquisite craftsmanship with cutting edge guitar design which features their signature Offset Soundhole Technology, state-of-the-art bracing and their unique "no touch" cantilevered neck design' (*Acoustic*, 24, 2008:10). In the same issue of *Acoustic* magazine, the internationally renowned guitarist and columnist Adrian Legg is described as bringing 'electric approaches to acoustic playing, creating a modern cross-over amalgamation in the tradition of eclectic folk playing that goes back to the 1960s' (*Acoustic*, 24, 2008:76). I have already mentioned the work of Tommy Emmanuel, Newton Faulkner, Vicki Genfan and Erik Mongrain, where the extended techniques that are now widely played out upon the acoustic guitar often involve driving percussive effects created on its strings and body.

Acoustic guitarists might also claim that at the flick of a switch they can make their instrument sound something like an electric guitar (and vice versa). Not that everyone is convinced, as it seems there will always be an element of compromise. For instance, Clive Osborn comments in *Performing Musician*: 'You can never achieve a true electric guitar sound from an acoustic, and the feel of an acoustic guitar (often with heavier gauge strings and a wound third string) is not the same as an electric' (Osborn, 2008:42). However, such a view has not stopped manufacturers searching and even competing for the best solution (or best possible compromise).

In an advertisement for their T5 Thinline Fiveway model, Taylor Guitars proclaim that 'The electric and acoustic worlds have merged'.[26] The advertisement goes on to say that 'After a rousing electric set, you turn a few knobs, and suddenly you become all sensitive', presumably as the acoustic sound of the T5 takes over. I note an advertisement for Crafter guitars which reads: 'Electric? Acoustic? A blend of both?' This is much more than clever advertising. There are practical considerations, as musicians may need to move quickly between electric and acoustic sounds in one song: now they can, without ever changing guitars.

---

[26]   Advertisement in *Acoustic Guitar*, 17/6, 168 (2007):16–17, 47. There is also a six-page advertisement for Taylor guitars in *Acoustic Guitar*, 17/9, 171 (2007):20–25. See also Taylorguitars.com.

The two kingdoms of the guitar (acoustic, electric) have regrouped, coming back together again in intriguing ways, for instance in the design of what are sometimes called 'hybrid' guitars. Hybrids can also be defined as combinations of electric guitar designs. A more recent example is Washburn W150 Pro E solid-body electric guitar, described as 'a bit of a hybrid beast. It looks like the neck of a Jackson's been stuck on the body of a Les Paul' (Scaramanga, 2008:138). Then there is the Steve Toon 'Montpelier' hybrid, described as 'unique jazz guitar, which attempts to produce the best of both D and oval soundhole styles, for rhythm and lead respectively' as a 'modern cohesion of concepts' (Wise, 2008:56). The article also asks the question: 'Is this the new age for Nuages?', referring to the fact that the guitar is based on the design of the Selmer guitars of the 1930s–1950s, thus connected to both maker Mario Maccaferri and guitarist Django Reinhardt (who recorded 'Nuages').

However, along with the Taylor T5 discussed above, there exists a range of acoustic-electric guitars that further exemplify the hybrid concept. These include the Crafter SAT Slim Arch Hybrid Electro,[27] the Ovation VXT,[28] the Gadotti electric nylon-string guitar,[29] the acoustic-electric steel-string Ibanez Montage (notable also for its onboard effects),[30] the acoustic-electric nylon-string guitar with dreadnought (or 'jumbo') body by Ibanez known as the EWN28 Bubinga (Francis, 2008:28–9) or the genre-bending acoustic guitar built for metal group Slipknot, the Ovation Mick Thomson MT37-5. According to one reviewer, 'the clipped clarity of the MT37-5 is ideal when your're shredding individual notes, as Thomson intended' (Yates, 2008a:26).[31]

In asking the question, 'What do you do when you need acoustic and electric guitar parts in the same song … and you're the only guitar player in the band?', Clive Osborn suggests, 'Well, how about a separate "fake acoustic" output from your electric, for a start'? (Osborn, 2008:42. To do this, he suggests using the X-Bridge, an integrated bridge and transducer pick-up combination to be fitted to an electric guitar, which also comes with a pre-amplifier and mixer. Recent developments include the Ovation iDea electro-acoustic guitar, which even has an mp3 recorder installed in its pre-amp.[32] The Godin Electro-Acoustic Multiac Spectrum SA also has a '13-pin output for computer and synth access'.[33]

Mention must also be made here of 'modelled' guitars. Such guitars can produce a wide variety of sounds through the setting and configuration of their

---

[27]   Advertisement in *Guitarist*, 306 (Summer 2008):153.See also www.crafterguitars. com.

[28]   www.thevxt.com.

[29]   Advertisement in *Vintage Guitar* (September 2008):166.

[30]   Round-Up/advertisement in *Guitar and Bass Magazine*, 19/5 (May 2008):8.

[31]   See also brief news report, *Acoustic*, 24 (October/November 2008):12.

[32]   Brief reviews in *Guitarist*, 309 (2008):22; and *Guitar and Bass Magazine*, 19/12 (December 2008):7.

[33]   Advertisement in *Acoustic*, 24 (October/November 2008):111.

pick-ups. For example, the Fender VG Stratocaster features a Roland GK pick-up. According to one review, this offers 'five guitar models (including a noise-free Strat), five tuning options, plus a 12 string mode'.[34] In the same report, the Line 6 Variax 700 and 300 guitars are also featured. There are no pick-ups *visible* on the guitars in the pictures accompanying the article, but one can, it is said, switch between twenty-five models, already patched into the integrated Workbench software. Moreover, there is an acoustic version of the Line 6 Variax guitar with patches available for a wide range of acoustic guitars (including acoustic twelve-string guitar) and other acoustic string instruments, such as the mandolin and banjo. Clearly, the identity of the guitar must now also make reference to a wide range of sonic transformations that include but also challenge the traditional divisions of the guitar (acoustic/electric), at once including current models as they interface with other electronic devices (such as computers) and an identity based on older augmentations of the guitar, for example, the harp-guitar, double-neck guitars with both six- and twelve-string necks, triple-neck guitars with six-string and twelve-string guitar necks and mandolin neck, as well as sitar-guitars, travel guitars, games controllers in the shape of guitars, guitars designed to be used as upgraded games controllers and even toy guitars.

---

[34] Brief review in *Total Guitar*, 181 (November 2008):20. See the detailed review in Harvey, 2009.

Chapter 5
Materiality and the Virtual Guitar

It's a Cyber World! Check our website! When in Houston drop by Rockin' Robin's Living Guitar and Drum Museum, 1000s of items in stock. (Rockin' Robin Guitars and Music, in *Vintage Guitar* (September 2008):93)

Culture is supposed to be about the molten liquidity of experience, whereas science aspires to the solid dimensionality of fact. But the empirical naming and knowing of the physical world is nothing if not a culturally expressive act with fully political meanings. (Ross, 2001:12)

When is a guitar not a guitar? Obvious! When the musical instrument in question is a trombone! Such an apparently null and void question – circular in motion, a tautology – would have seemed utter nonsense to me back in 1969 when I first picked up a 'proper' instrument and tried to play it. Perhaps the reader will permit a short autobiographical section at this stage, as a means of illustrating and developing my point. My first proper, near full-size or 'real' guitar was a nylon-string acoustic, a BM Spanish classical guitar. I eventually felt the effect of prolonged contact with that guitar, the instrument bearing down upon my body, in turn my fingers pressing down upon the strings, my body trying to hold the guitar in place (I did not fully adopt the classical guitar method or use a foot stool for some years to come). The combination of the prolonged contact of my fingers and the guitar's strings resulted in my having heavily grooved left-hand fingers after practice and, eventually, sores. The calluses that formed also became sore every once in a while too. This is, of course, quite a common experience for the beginner guitarist. I might have given another similarly flippant reply back in 1969 if I had been asked the question 'When is a guitar not a guitar?' Obvious! When it is not hurting my fingers or digging into my chest. This was no trombone.

The *solidity* of the guitar as an object which I held in my hands and which pressed against my body, hurt my fingers and other parts of my body and, at times, my ears never left me in any doubt of when a guitar was a guitar. Its form seemed as solid as a rock, its function very clear, and its sound unmistakable. But despite the difficulties in actually playing it, to my mind the instrument was clearly going to prepare me, eventually, for musical superstardom. I was mindful of its potential and of its effect upon me, even as I observed it standing in a corner of my bedroom (my fingers still smarting). As I grew up, my body seemed to grow into the guitar, as if moulded by it. That is, the fingers of my left and right hands seemed to grow into shape for playing the guitar as I practised daily for many hours, especially throughout my later pre-teen and teenage years. This was a case of both nurture and nature taking their course. Not that I turned out to be a technically gifted player or virtuoso (another common experience).

But there was little doubt then that the guitar to which I had grown so close to over all those years was the real thing, as it helped shape my music, mind and body, and became almost a part of me, or I a part of it. If I had ever made a claim to reality, the guitar would have certainly been included. Yet it was also an object which one could use to create a world of fantasy. As an only child, I also had it as my only constant companion, and it was actually of a similar age to me. It provided one very important way in which, eventually, this only child would grow up to make friends. But even so, most of us who grow up playing the guitar will never have the kind of journey through life with it that, for instance, Eric Clapton has had. Nevertheless, I think most guitarists would be able to empathize with Clapton when he says that 'it has become a friend' (Chapman, 2000:6). I might add that it is a hard-won friend at that.[1]

The Mutating Career of a Toy Guitar

However much the BM Spanish classical guitar was a *solid* friend to me, I also recall being aware of what might be called the *liquidity* of the guitar experience. I had another friend. It was plastic toy guitar, a 'Beatles guitar' coloured bright orange, which preceded the real thing.[2] However much that Beatles guitar was intended to be a toy, it still holds a special significance in my life and is included in my memories of childhood, which suggests it was much more than a plaything, trifle or mere amusement. The Beatles guitar had a different function from the proper guitar that I was given when I was a little older, but even so – as I noted later on – there was what one might describe as a significant degree of overlap.

Very clearly, by a consensus of producers and consumers (manufacturers and my parents, in particular), one sound-producing object was conceived of as a toy, the other as a musical instrument. Their difference lay in their intended use and, as a consequence, their design. The Beatles guitar had a picture of John, Paul, George and Ringo on its plastic 'soundboard', for instance, unlike the more 'serious' BM guitar, which was also played by grown-ups. But I could tune both, and tried to pick out a tune on the toy guitar as much as I tried a chord sequence on the proper grown-ups' guitar. I converted the four-string Beatles guitar – more like a ukulele – into a bass guitar. Well, at least in my mind I did. I put a clip-on pick-up across the soundhole of the Beatles guitar, which I eventually plugged into a Vox amplifier and a custom built speaker cabinet (made by my father and me) containing four

---

[1]   See also Will Hodgkinson's often hilarious, insightful and broadly-based accounts of his efforts to learn the guitar as an 'adult beginner' in *Guitar Man: A Six-String Odyssey* (2006).

[2]   The Beatles New Beat Toy Guitar was made in four-string and six-string versions between 1963 and 1964 by Selco in the UK.

nine-inch radio speakers, which was really meant for the arrival of what was the latest and soon to be my very best friend: a Hagstrom acoustic-electric six-string. I had progressed from a small solid-body Kay electric guitar to the Hagstrom, but the Kay catalogue guitar and the small amplifier that came with it were sold to finance the Hagstrom.

In recollecting my childhood experiences with my guitars, I find it difficult to draw a line between toy guitar and real guitar in several respects. The toy and the proper guitar could both function, more or less, as musical instruments. They were tuneable (the 'real' guitar more reliably so, it has to be said), and had similar informational surfaces and layouts for the young guitarist to orientate to (leaving aside the Beatles sticker). The Beatles guitar was for me easier to play than the proper guitar at the time. The two guitars were intended to play different roles, but did not always do so. I toyed with the grown-ups' guitar for some time. The toy was less expensive than the proper musical instrument, though. It was also made of plastic (some proper guitars have also been made of plastic, but not many). But now the toy guitar (which eventually got broken and ceremoniously deposited in the dustbin), in good condition, would be worth much more than the price that my parents paid for my first proper guitar. The toy guitar is, at the time of writing, a collector's item selling for up to $750 on e-Bay. This 'thing' that was my Beatles guitar might be said to have had a 'mutating career' (after Appadurai), moving from toy to a kind of real guitar and on to – in this case – the posthumous role of a collectable. At various stages in my life, then, both the toy and the later fully functional guitar were agential in introducing me to aspects of the popular culture but also the (so-called) 'high' culture of my childhood, an engagement which I was to take well beyond that time. Both guitars were devices of enculturation and socialization, inducting me into the ways of my elders and peers, shaping my mind and body as such instruments had also shaped other minds and bodies. Both were toyed with at some point. Now all the guitars mentioned above – whether or not designed as a toy – function as objects of nostalgia for me, a situation which, I assume, may be familiar to many readers of this book. I wish I had not sold any of them, nor put the broken Beatles guitar in the dustbin.[3] I still have the Hagstrom.

To my mind, on the basis of my own experience, the toy guitar and the fully functional guitars are different aspects of the same widely based musical, social and cultural phenomenon that is the guitar. But they are also representative of a young person's engagement with the overlapping worlds of music and material culture. They may also be seen as able to mark out and function within the stages of one's mental and physical growth, riding out periods of immaturity and maturation; the young person in turn responds to these culturally designed stimuli, which can also be used as creative vehicles and as the basis of play, fantasy and social exchanges. All of the aforementioned guitars are the externalization or extension of an idea: technology testing the limits of one's mind and body ('hand's end', after

---

[3] See, in particular, similar reflections by Ryan and Peterson (2001), 'The Guitar as Artifact and Icon: Identity Formation in the Babyboom Generation'.

David Rothenberg), providing for cognitive and physical tasks and the use of the imagination. Moreover, at times one responds creatively to these imposed systems of the technology of learning (or socialization into a particularly culturally based vision of what it is to be human). Guitars as learning vehicles or play stations open up some avenues of enquiry, but close off others. In his discussion of the development of wind instruments (which mirrors the way children usually start with simple instruments or basic approaches and move to more complex ones), David Rothenberg notes that the increase in fingering possibilities has provided for greater ease of playing. However, he notes: 'As each machine suggests more problems to be solved or features to be improved, those questions less susceptible to a technical answer become impossible to see' (Rothenberg, 1993:219). The guitar is an instrument that constantly seems to evolve around a standard design, whether developments are technology-based or technique-based or generally a combination of both.

Moreover, guitars such as the Fender Telecaster, Fender Stratocaster and Gibson Les Paul are still designed to be used by a wide variety of musicians playing all kinds of music. As is well documented, developments in guitar technique, particularly in the 1980s, hastened in the development of specialist guitars adapted for speed playing and increased sustain (for instance, the Ibanez series of heavy metal guitars and the 'superstrats'), reflecting an ongoing cycle of musical, technical and technological innovation in the world of the guitar (within recognizable boundaries, at least in terms of the basic design of the guitar). In the case of developments in heavy metal (as documented by Walser, 1993), both technical and musical 'answers' are found, within certain limits which require both mental and physical dexterity, as embodied to great effect in David Mead's '1980s Electric Guitar Gymnastics Display Team'.

As a child who banged and bashed away upon a toy guitar, I hardly imagined that professional musicians would be doing similar things to a fully functional, grown-ups' guitar in the first decade of this century, even if it is with far greater aplomb, organization and musical effect than what I could ever have mustered as a child. In the new guitarscape, so-called 'extended techniques' relate to some of the most basic techniques of exploration upon musical instruments: bash, bang, scratch, scrape, wallop! No wonder David Mead was moved to report that these players had been called the 'Acoustic Guitar Martial Arts Squad'. However, the extended development of certain techniques provides the basis for a virtuosic demonstration, involving a highly refined and co-ordinated technique that is also effective as a musical device. Yet at the same time advanced technologies are finding their way into guitar designs to enable players to interface with a host of digital technologies, expanding and extending the soundscape of the guitar to a potentially infinite degree. The reader may recall Tommy Emmanuel's creative use of both extended manual playing techniques and technology (microphones, equalizers) in the setting-up and sounding-out of his acoustic guitar in performance, described in the previous chapter.

However, research into what is often called the 'augmented' guitar at the Centre de Recherche Informatique et Création Musicale, University of Paris VIII, shows just how far the techniques and technologies of the new guitarscape have extended and intertwined to meet the musical desires, aspirations and needs of guitar-based composers and performers.[4] A range of augmentations to guitars of standard design (such as the Fender Stratocaster) enable the player to control digital technologies (sound samples, sound effects processors and pre-recorded patches, all of which can be looped) via physical contact with sensors on parts of the guitar. These patches can be stored and manipulated in a laptop computer.[5] Contact with sensors can be achieved through very basic means – tapping, knocking, scraping, and sliding – whilst also playing the guitar in the normal manner. Hardly a toy, but potentially playful, the augmented guitar is capable of providing the composer-performer-guitarist with ever greater choice and control over the sounds he or she produces. Moreover, as noted elsewhere, the augmented guitar may be extended further by devices that make the guitar (electric and acoustic) polyphonic. It is worth noting again here that each string of the guitar can now be linked to individual sound pre-sets. In the case of Dominic Frasca, as noted in Chapter 1, this now includes hexaphonic and decaphonic set-ups.

Within the new guitarscape, I claim that the gap between real guitars and virtual guitars, toys and virtual guitars, non-toys and real guitars, augmented guitars and non-augmented guitars has not only narrowed but exists on a continuum. They are all part of a guitarscape that is being extended and augmented, toy with non-toy, real with virtual, old with new, guitar designs linked to designs in other areas of technology (from computer software to furniture), in a complex web of interrelated and interacting influences. Such developments might be said to be part of the same experience that is *the guitar*.[6] Clearly, such notions require further critical analysis.

Encounters with Objects, Real and Virtual

In *Understanding Material Culture* (2007), Ian Woodward provides an extremely erudite and useful overview of the state of material culture studies, detailing the emergence of the discipline in a synthesis of Marxist thought, semiotics and cultural theory. Pertinent to my own discussion of the guitar as an object of some importance in the lives of all those who make it, play it or admire it is Woodward's reference

---

[4]   In May 2009 I was invited to give a paper at the Center as part of the conference 'Identités de la guitare électrique'. At the time of writing the conference website is still active. See www.guitarelectrique.fr.

[5]   See, for example, MySpace pages for Otso Lähdeoja and Santiago Quintans. See also: guitareelectrique.com: http://lib.tkk.fi/Diss/2008/isbn9789512292431/.

[6]   Augmented Reality (AR) is a field of computer research which deals with the combination of real-world and computer-generated data.

to the work of people–object relations within cultural anthropology, cultural studies, sociology and, to some extent, psychoanalytic theory. Woodward notes: 'There is a type of intersubjectivity – yet to be fully understood or investigated by researchers – between persons and objects that makes materiality a fundamental platform, and media of sociality' (Woodward, 2007:172). That he uses the term 'intersubjectivity' is, of course, crucial here as it refers to a subjectivity that exists between *conscious* minds.

Clearly, the guitar (as yet, anyhow) is not conscious. However, it is made in the image of its makers, has a beauty that lies in the eye of the beholder, and comes with a clear and intended range of uses circumscribed by materially configured directives from various conscious minds. The guitar can be said to invite a meeting of minds, conveying and exuding the influence of its makers and, at times, its players (famous or not). Clearly, my toy guitar and my real guitar carried the influence and intention of manufacturers, parents and me. Fundamental to a discussion of the intentionality behind art objects, but also their influence and power as social agents, is the work of Alfred Gell, whose notion of 'the extended mind' is discussed further in Chapter 7.

Ian Woodward also discusses the narrative power of objects in the lives of individuals and groups. He states: 'a material thing … has a range of different potential roles or "affordances" each dependent upon a different embedding narrative – its uses are not limited by its physical features or design' (Woodward, 2007:174).[7] This is a powerful and provocative statement in itself, for clearly the guitar fulfils a wide range of social and cultural roles which may or may not be ultimately limited by its physical features or design (the guitar tends to provide a fairly stable reference point in terms of its form if not its materiality or material state). The guitar can be a toy, a musical instrument, an art object and an item of nostalgia, all of which may retain, at a general level, distinguishing features but also similar design characteristics. He elaborates on how objects are embedded in social narratives to the extent that 'the question of whether this is the same or a different social object depends on whether and how this is the same or different story' (Woodward, 2007:174).

We have, of course, innumerable encounters with objects throughout our lives, some encounters lasting longer than others, but one also encounters objects in innumerable forms (the guitar being a particularly good example of the ubiquity and multiform character of some objects). Sometimes those objects, as noted above, are part of the same story and, are, perhaps, not as distinct as one might believe them to be at first, or are distinct because of the role they play in the story of an individual's life (where they take on particular meaning, make specific connections, recall special events, and so on). I am reminded yet again of Appadurai's notion that things can have 'mutating careers' and become meaningful only as they form part of a narrative thread in people's lives.

---

[7]   Woodard draws on James J. Gibson's theory of 'affordances' (see Gibson, 1986).

I believe the guitar's *materiality* is extensive, that is, its existence as a social object is broadly based, and that as a sound-producing object (but also as an iconic or art object) it is a multidimensional but also multimedia feature of music, culture and society. Take, for example, the presence of the guitar on the Internet and in other forms of digital media. Although I believe the guitar readily spills out of such media and, in fact, falls into others, it is worth mentioning again Henry Jenkins's ideas on the ways in which new media (narrowcast and grassroots) and old media (for example, broadcast and commercial media) can be seen to converge. Referring to a 'paradigm shift', Jenkins notes 'a move from medium-specific content toward content that flows across multiple media channels, towards the increased interdependence of communications systems, towards multiple ways of accessing media content, and toward ever more complex relations between top-down corporate media and bottom-up participatory culture' (Jenkins, 2006:126).

There are times when the guitar seems to disappear altogether, existing as an idea, its importance not exactly *immaterial* but its signature and potential influence carried in the sights and sounds of other media (from YouTube to advertising images, from the digital samples on home keyboards to video games). But the solid object that is or was the guitar also disappears in 'air guitar'. Or does it? The guitar in these cross-realm, inter-textual and interconnected states of existence also relates to what Daniel Miller describes as the 'somewhat unexpected capacity of objects to fade out of focus and remain peripheral to our vision and yet determinant of our behaviour and identity' (Miller, 2005:5) in the various contexts in which we find them. Does the guitar lose its potential for a meeting of minds – its intersubjectivity – when it appears as a part of a magazine advertisement (with no sound) or a pre-setting on a home keyboard (with the emphasis on its identity as part of a *keyboard* sample menu)? Although I find Miller's ideas useful, I believe the guitar demonstrates some resistance to 'fade out', as if it has taken on a momentum, energy or even life of its own, active, as it were, despite being re-embedded in a range of other forms of material culture which, by extension, can be seen to include the Internet, magazines, keyboard samples and air guitar. However, just as the solid guitar melts or dissolves into air guitar, so the instrument has (or has been given) the capacity to be transformed into other states – by the person who puts a mobile phone video clip of a guitar concert on YouTube, a video gamer who activates a guitar games controller or the child with a toy guitar.

Yet like other objects, but to a greater extent than many objects, the guitar touches upon the life of its owners and its audiences in multiple ways, and, perhaps, in unexpected ways. The guitar now *materializes* in many forms, manifesting in wood, carbon fibre and metal, in pixels and paper, on CD and DVD, on computer screens and games consoles (from *Guitar Freak* in 1998 to the *Guitar Hero* series from 2005 and on to *Guitar Hero World Tour* in 2008). In conversation about the video game *Guitar Hero III* (2007), guitarist Herman Li (Dragonforce) notes that 'to a certain degree' the game is responsible for popularizing the guitar, 'but some people only want to play games'. He goes on to say that the game is, of course, 'a fantasy' and that to play real guitar 'it's gonna take serious practice for many, many years' (www.youtube.com).[8] Known as a 'video game rock band', Dragonforce has made 'Through the Fire and Flames' the most popular song on *Guitar Hero III*, although it can be accessed only by those gamers who achieve advanced player status.

In a discussion of the numerous ways in which the guitar is spread widely throughout popular culture, mention must also be made of more recent cinema releases, including the film *School of Rock* (Paramount Pictures, 2003) which features a Gibson SG solid-body electric guitar in a leading role alongside Jack Black, and *August Rush* (Warner Brothers, 2007), where a young musical prodigy – the fictitious August Rush (see previous chapter) – who, when finding himself alone in New York City, makes his way in the world by playing an amplified acoustic guitar (before his teacher recommends him for the Julliard School of Music). Moreover, the popular culture of the guitar has spread widely across the domain of children's toys, the guitar being found in the form of everything from guitar-shaped clocks that make animal noises (when keys on the neck are pressed) to the miniature plastic guitars that accompany, for example, Bratz, Barbie and Hannah Montana dolls, not forgetting Woody, the cowboy figurine from the *Toy Story* computer-animated films of Pixar/Walt Disney Pictures (*Toy Story*, 1995, *Toy Story 2*,1999). Moreover, I recently (December 2008) bought a pair of jeans for my then four-year-old son from a supermarket chain with the styling '105437111' and 'Guitar Hero' on the label. Guitars pervade the form and iconography of children's toys and clothes, as much as they affect the lives of adults in various forms. Moreover, there are a variety of household items designed in the shape of a guitar, from toilet seats to coffee tables.[9] I was also reminded by Adrian Freed (of the Chordophone Research Group at the University of California at Berkeley) that guitar manufacturers such as Gibson and Fender also started out as furniture makers (Freed, personal communication).[10] An endorsement for the Fender Stratocaster Coffee Table reads: 'You don't need to be able to play the guitar to enjoy this, you don't even need to like coffee. All you need is an appreciation for one of the brands behind a great music genre and the overwhelming awesomeness of a cool piece of furniture' (www.fendercustomfurniture.com.).

But, clearly, spread out the across the domain or domains of material culture, *the guitar itself* becomes a problematic concept, as the physical object enters a virtual existence and also fades into thin air in air guitar (or, at least, becomes

---

[8]   www.youtube.com: 'Guitar Hero III: Herman Li "Interview"'.

[9]   See 'Toilet Seats Shaped like Guitars' at http://www.jamminjohns.com/home/. I am also reminded of David Kemp's 'Air Guitar' (2002), which is a 'found objects' artwork consisting of a toilet seat and a guitar neck.

[10]   See also cort.com (furniture and guitars); froggybottomguitars.com (furniture and guitars); ncguitars.com.co.uk (part of NC Design, including furniture, beds, sculpture, jewellery, guitars). Numerous further examples include anadalucia.com/craft/guitar.htm; finefurniturecaresecrets.com. The miniature guitars that seem to inhabit every curio/ ornament store are made as far away as Indonesia: visionbali.com.

embodied in the performance of the air guitarist). Yet to my mind, air guitars are very closely related to virtual guitars, which, in turn, may also be said to take on physical or 'real' form – for example, the small guitar-shaped controller for V-tune's mp3 accompanied 'virtual guitar' and the 'peripherals' that accompany the *Guitar Hero* and *Rock Band* games series. Moreover, those who win an air guitar competition invariably win a *real* guitar (which they may not be able to play)! The sounds and images of the guitar (even its physical shape and form) are continually and extensively reworked, transformed, re-contextualized and re-embedded, their characteristic signature shaping what may be viewed as an ever-changing reality – perhaps even part of developments in augmented reality – but certainly representative of a new way of looking at the instrument and a new way of looking at games controllers, among the many media with which the guitar is now intimately bound up.

Clearly, the potential of the guitar in cyberspace has been eagerly explored by manufacturers, including guitar manufacturers, in an engagement with the Internet that includes, but also goes well beyond, mere advertising. Evidence is readily available online, but a trip to Gibson's 'Second Life Island' seems to support the claim well: 'The first major manufacturer to establish an official island in Second Life, Gibson encourages consumers to participate in the new and exciting virtual world, complete with digital luthiers, instruments, and guest stars' (Gibson.com). The feature article on Gibson's 'Lifestyle' web pages goes on to say: 'In tribute to the legendary Les Paul himself, Gibson Island is in the shape of the famous guitar body that rises up from the ocean in Second Life. The "island" features full theatres, mini-theatres, humbucker mountains, and other areas resembling aspects of the Gibson guitar' (Gibson.com).

Guitar and 'Guitar'

> Right, let's get this out of the way: these Guitar Hero games aren't like playing a real guitar. However, they'll get your fretting fingers going, make you concentrate for a whole song, and they're a damn good laugh. ('Games' review, *Guitar and Bass* magazine (November 2008):15)

Place two Fender Stratocasters side by side. One of them will be less of a guitar to some people than the other one. Perhaps one of the guitars is set up differently (with too low a string action, for instance), has a different finish, or sounds different through the same amplifier. Perhaps the guitars just feel different, and one of them feels right whereas the other one does not feel right at all to the individual trying them out. There is developing here what seems to me like quite a reasonable argument along a line of questioning that focuses on what exactly makes the right guitar for the individual, but also what exactly it is in the new guitarscape that constitutes the guitar for the individual.

When one sees and hears a guitar in cyberspace, is the instrument that one observes any less of a guitar? Common sense would suggest that the once real, now virtual, guitar is a 'guitar' played by a 'guitarist' (note the use of inverted commas). It has become a virtual instrument. But what exactly does this mean? The series of pixelations or pixelated images and the pre-recorded sound (Second Life, further life) also reflect the guitar's existence (first life, former life, real life) in the world outside cyberspace, building upon but also re-contextualizing its well established effect and influence, its social agency, if you will. In cyberspace, the guitar no longer operates in 'real time', and so the affecting presence of the guitar in sound and image will be somewhat different through this fact alone. It also operates at a distance from the listener and viewer (but then again it is also split from source – at least from the listener's point of view – as a part of conventional audio recordings and DVDs). It can also be thoroughly manipulated in sound and image on the Internet.

As noted above, one person's Stratocaster is another person's 'Stratocaster'. However, it might also be said that a virtual Stratocaster is not merely a reflection of a real Stratocaster but just a different way of thinking about and interacting with *more or less* the same thing. But does the 'more or less' make a *real* difference? The main claim here is that the guitar offers a new way of thinking about cyberspace as much as cyberspace offers a new way of thinking about the guitar (including but also going well beyond cyberspace). In so far as the Internet is real, so are the sounds and images of the guitar in cyberspace. I am not suggesting that the virtual guitarist is real: the terms are distinct even if the justification for their application is not always clear. The guitar is still functioning as a sound-producing and iconic image of music, culture and society. It remains a hands-on phenomenon as much as it can be manipulated and controlled in cyberspace.

There is, of course, significant debate surrounding the fragmented presentation of the guitar (and everything else) on the Internet, the lack of information regarding the origins of the material one finds and the reliability of some sources. Nevertheless, regarding the problems that are surely inherent here, the evidence suggests that the guitar is firmly rooted in an array of musical, technological, social and cultural processes and interactions that transcend some limitations but impose others. The guitar on the Internet is but one admittedly complex example of a wide variety of processes and interactions with which the instrument is now bound up and which present a whole new set of questions, problems and challenges for those studying the wider significance of the guitar in the early twenty-first century.

Is the controller for the computer games series *Guitar Hero* a guitar or a 'guitar'? The controller is guitar-shaped, though it functions through the player pressing buttons rather than plucking strings. Hitting the right coloured keys in the right order (as played against a pre-recorded guitar part) gains the player several arithmetical scores (on different meters). There are, of course, many critics of the game who plead with gamers to pick up a 'real' guitar. Moreover, some manufacturers positively encourage gamers by providing them with more 'realistic' controllers from which players can control their video games. It is as if the leap into hyperspace now operates on a continuum: from real guitar to guitar controller to virtual guitar. One sees the stages of transformation taking shape before one's very eyes. The distance (or lack of it) between real and virtual guitars is explored ever further as manufacturers now seek to provide a guitar that is more guitar-like or real but can also function as a guitar controller for a video game. For instance, the Peavey Riffmaster is a $2,000 add-on for *Guitar Hero* that is said to take 'fake guitar playing very seriously', and moreover:

> For that money you get two controllers, which are authentic Peavey guitars gutted out and rewired for game-mode, a full P.A. system that houses a PS2, an amp head to control the unit, and a monitor so you can see the buttons you are pressing, just like the pros. But wait, there's more (cheesiness!): The guitar body is fully customizable, so if that Pantera logo doesn't do it for you, just send them a JPEG of Milli Vanilli and be the envy of all your friends. This unit is designed for bars, and will make you wish you never said anything bad about karaoke when it's replaced by 'Guitar Hero Night.' But seriously folks, it's nice to hold something heavier and more authentic in your hand than the standard controllers, and in a big group setting this could be a hit.[11]

However, some reviewers have also taken the opportunity to take a tongue-in-cheek look at guitar controller designs, taking their lead from how guitars are normally reviewed in guitar magazines. For example, the 'Guitar Hero Controller Roundup' on premierguitar.com begins, 'We see how five Guitar Hero/Rock Band controllers stack up' and continues:

> At Premier Guitar, we've made it a point not to cover *Guitar Hero* and *Rock Band* – they aren't real guitar, after all. But after talking to some friends, reading interviews with famous fans, and admitting to ourselves just how much we all actually enjoy playing the games, we decided it was time to look at the games through PG glasses. That's right, focusing on the gear.
> While the guitar decisions for rhythm games are generally made for you with a bundled controller, inevitably you'll find yourself in the market for another axe. So whether you're looking to upgrade from the original bundled controller, replace a broken one, or get into the games without buying a bundle, we have a guide to the most popular options out there. We spent time playing both Guitar Hero and Rock Band on Xbox 360 with all four of the major controllers from Guitar Hero II, III and World Tour, and from Rock Band. Then, we got our hands on one of Peavey's full-scale models. Which one's for you? Read on to find out …[12]

---

[11]   http://gizmodo.com/34240 2/real-peavey-riffmaster-guitar-takes-guitar-hero-rocking-to-the-extreme. See also http://peavey.com/products/custom.cfm.

[12]   Rebecca Dirks, Chris Burgess and Joe Coffey, 'Review: Guitar Hero Controller Roundup', http://www.premierguitar.com/Magazine/Issue/2009/Apr/Review_Guitar_Hero_Controller_Roundup.aspx.

The reviewers engage fully with a critical assessment of the pros and cons of each controller, as if they are reviewing a selection of real guitars. On inspecting the Gibson Explorer-shaped controller from *Guitar Hero II*, the review team notes:

> The strum bar and buttons all move with ease, and it's small and very light, which make it ideal for children. The guitar's size, however, is also one of its weaknesses for adults. Players with large hands might find the neck way too thin to be comfortable, and the small size certainly makes it feel like you're playing with a cheap toy. Also, the 'trem' bar is very loose, so you have to grab for it each time you want to use it. The biggest knock against the X-plorer is that it's wired; while that wasn't a big deal when the original game came out, with so many affordable wireless options, it seems more of a hindrance than it originally did. [13]

When posted on the Premier Guitar website the review of the Guitar Hero video games controllers sparked a good deal of debate and controversy about their value. Such a debate relates to fundamental issues about the real and the virtual, copyright, and the addictiveness of the game, with some players even dropping out of school to concentrate on their gaming.[14] The fact is that some players focus on video games guitar rather than learning to play real guitar, but some real guitar players comment on how much they enjoy playing the Guitar Hero series. Here are some comments taken from the Premier Guitar website in response to the review feature on video games guitar controllers as discussed above:

Comment 1

I'm not too cool to play *GH* [*Guitar Hero*] with my kids. I understand the game and am glad that my 8 year old son knows who Joe Perry [guitarist from Aerosmith] is because of it.

Comment 2

Whether or not this is a joke, *GH* is a serious business. Every generation has a way to reach its new audience with music and *GH* has done a phenomenal job of opening the youths' minds with music they never would have discovered without it. The fact that I hear from people all over the world every day about how the game has made them want to learn to play guitar is proof enough that it has a positive effect on kids. Sure, it's a game, and no, it's not going to make a

---

[13]   See n. 12 above.

[14]   See the following examples: http://www.rollingstone.com/rockdaily/index. php/2008/08/19/teen-drops-out-of-high-school-to-become-professional-guitar-hero/; http://www.premierguitar.com/Magazine/Issue/Daily/News/Riffs_14_Year_Old_One_ Man_Band_Guitar_Hero_Dropout_Guitar_Photocopier.aspx.

great player out of somebody who isn't serious about the instrument, but it does a lot of remarkable things besides make people fat and want instant gratification. I'm also biased because I've been involved with the game since *GH3*, but aside from that it still is clever and has merit.

Comment 3

The Peavey controller is great! And for all you nay sayers *GH & RockBand* have done more to get youth back into real music and out of the rap trap and pop slop pushed by most radio and video outlets. I love it and yes – my game controller is allowed in the same room as my real strings …

Comment 4

You're right. Sitting or standing in place for hours on end hitting buttons, not holding chords or working on scales is a great way to how to play guitar!

Comment 5

Mr. Guitar Hero, obviously you don't play *Guitar Hero* or you would know how much of a work out it actually is. I haven't seen one obese *Guitar Hero* player. The game is amazing and accurately mimics playing a real guitar so it was only a matter of time until the guitar community took notice.[15]

These comments clearly reflect differing views on the merits or problems of the *Guitar Hero* video games series. Debates rage as I write, including the furore that erupted on Yahoo's front news page over *Guitar Hero 5*.[16] It is clear that the games deserve significant attention: the sales figures show their phenomenal popularity and their global appeal for playing at home; they are now also replacing karaoke nights in some parts of the world as well as attracting large audiences at dedicated competitions. An article in *Classic Rock* magazine notes: 'Activision announced that the *Guitar Hero* series had broken industry records by grossing more than $1 billion dollars over 26 months in North America' (Yates, 2008b:50). The musicians featured in the games are clearly widely supportive of the genre and include Slash, Joe Perry of Aerosmith, Herman Li of Dragonforce and Metallica among a host of bands and artists who seem to be kindly disposed to the *Guitar Hero* phenomenon.

As Slash notes: 'Kids are being exposed to all this killer rock'n'roll that they would never otherwise hear' (Yates, 2008b:50). And as Joe Perry notes: 'The first

---

[15]   'Comments', http://www.premierguitar.com/Magazine/Issue/2009/Apr/Review_ Guitar_Hero_Controller_Roundup.aspx.

[16]   www.yahoo.com, front page news item: 'Legends Blast Guitar Hero', 25 June 2009.

time I played it, I thought, this is a really good opportunity to get our music out there' (Yates, 2008b:53). But it is not just the better-known bands that now find themselves in *Guitar Hero*: groups like Dragonforce have become widely known through the game, and some relatively unknown bands, such as The Answer, have become known through it. It is clear that the debate as to the merits or otherwise of the game continue to rage, as neatly summed up by Henry Yates: 'The future of rock'n'roll? A corrosive Trojan horse that will cut as many aspiring rockers as it creates? Or just a transitional teenage fad that will have burnt out by Christmas?' (Yates, 2008b:50).

I am intrigued by the fact that the monthly magazine *gamesTM* (76, 2008) features what appears to be the body of a Paul Reed Smith solid-body electric guitar on its cover. I think this seemingly odd juxtaposition is telling. Indeed, one of the reviews of *Guitar Hero* inside the same issue of *gamesTM* relates the success of the video games series to its peripherals, which 'give a more realistic experience' (*gamesTM*, 76, 2008). Indeed, Steve Waksman has picked up on what has been described as the 'aspirational element to *Guitar Hero* that's missing from games like *Dance Revolution*. Both satisfy the desire to interact physically with music, and both have a performance element'. Reporting further on his conversation with Steve Waksman, Rob Walker notes that the guitar-hero idea also implies an invitation to start your own band, and that the strength of the guitar tradition lies in its potential as a 'way of making music that's more physical'. Quoted in the same article, Rusty Welch, head of publishing for Activision (which owns the *Guitar Hero* franchise), notes that 30 per cent of *Guitar Hero* players are female, and that 20 per cent of all players are new to gaming.[17]

Rob Walker debates the fact that although some measurable skills are learnt, perhaps most gamers do not dream of musical virtuosity and stardom, but instead prefer to be 'a great pretender'.[18] So what is one to make of these comments? Is the *Guitar Hero* series aspirational or sheer fantasy, or a little bit of both? It is clear that *Guitar Hero* is not only played widely in homes across the world, but is also currently played at public events ranging from those taking place in small clubs to large-scale competitions. There is an interaction between the 'virtual' performance arena of the video game and the living rooms of gamers as well as those gamers who play outside the home in 'real' (or public) performance spaces (in competitions). Moreover, video postings of gamers playing *Guitar Hero* can be found on YouTube. Here the merits or otherwise of a gamer's performance skills receive comment, just like the real-life performances of the real-life guitar heroes featured in *Guitar Hero* – those who agreed to mime their performances in

---

17   Rob Walker, 'Consumed: The Pretenders', 25 November 2007, http://www. nytimes.com/2007/11/25/magazine/25wwln-consumed-t.html?_r=1&scp=1&sq=Consume d+The+Pretenders&st=nyt.

18   Rob Walker, 'Consumed: The Pretenders', 25 November 2007, http://www. nytimes.com/2007/11/25/magazine/25wwln-consumed-t.html?_r=1&scp=1&sq=Consume d+The+Pretenders&st=nyt.

movement sensor suits for the video games – whose 'real' work can be found on YouTube. Moreover, at the time of writing the music video game *Guitar Rising* had just been released. According to the manufacturer's web page: 'Guitar Rising is a music video game where the player plays a real guitar as cued by the game's visuals. Following rock music sequences and streaming notes, players play guitar melodies and rhythms. Beginner difficulty levels are designed for non-guitar players and hard difficulties will challenge experienced guitarists.'[19] Here, once again, one observes a complex ongoing negotiation of notions and combinations of the real and virtual as they bear upon the guitar, its performance, teaching and learning and its wider role in culture and society. Kiri Miller of Brown University, in her ongoing and extensive real and virtual fieldwork among players of the *Guitar Hero* series, will most likely get to the root of these and many other questions in her ongoing blog and a series of publications.[20]

The Guitar and the Internet

> 'Not surprising,' Clapton said to himself, 'that I am travelling so effortlessly through time and from one end of the planet to the other.' (Orsenna, 1999:21–2)

The Internet is said to offer a new era in guitar research (see Heck, 1998), enabling users to access to a wide range of sources based around the world (such as libraries and archives) that were once unavailable to researchers. Yet even one of the key means of such research can itself be transformed into guitar-like form or made guitar-researcher-friendly. The free offer of a mouse pointer in one such site was telling:

> I have bass and guitar cursors (mouse pointers). If you would like to use them, download and unzip to your c:/windows/cursor file, then click on your start button, then your control panel folder, then click your mouse icon, then click the pointer tab. Click Browse button and go through the cursor file till you

---

[19]   http://www.guitarrising.com/about.html.

[20]   See Kiri Miller at Brown University, USA: guitarheroresearch.blogspot.com/. See also the following articles and news items, which provide for a broad spread of issues related to the *Guitar Hero* phenomenon: 'The New Rock Revolution? Video Games', *Classic Rock*, 122 (August 2008):50–53; Michael Ross, 'The Real Heroes of *Guitar Hero III*', *Guitar Player* magazine, February 2008):58–63; respehttp://www.rollingstone.com/news/coverstory/24015954/page/49ct to beer pong, still the best party gameever;http://www.nydailynews.com/news/us_world/2009/02/03/2009-0203_guitar_hero_world_record_in_sights_of_te.html; http://www.premierguitar.com/Magazine/Issue/Daily/News/Gibson_Entwined_in_Guitar_Hero_Suits.aspx; http://www.premierguitar.com/Magazine/Issue/Daily/News/Gibson_v_Guitar_Hero_Dismissed.aspx;http://www.forbes.com/2008/03/13/guitar-hero-videogames-tech-personal-cx_er_0313guitar.html

see the guitar and click it. That will be your normal select 3d pointer (mouse pointer).[21]

I chose not to take advantage of this offer but it does show how one can customize one's desktop as much as one's guitar. There are, of course, significant and far-reaching questions about the reliability of information that one acquires on the Internet. It is the accessing of information at a distance that can lead to problems, not least in terms of checking the reliability of one's sources.

Debates rage, of course, as to the benefits or otherwise of the new musical environments created by broadband Internet and digital media (similar to those debates already discussed in relation to the *Guitar Hero* video games series). Issues at the heart of what is now a long-running debate include the nature of 'community' as created on the Internet and whether human relations are in fact fostered or destroyed; whether human creativity is enhanced or constrained; the effect on the art of performance; and how public (and thus private) space is configured. Several publications discuss these matters in some detail, including the ethnomusicological literature which I will focus on here (see Miller, 2007; Wood, 2008). A related but wider input to these debates is provided, for example, by Christine Hine in her *Virtual Ethnography*, where she notes the 'the ways in which the Internet is made meaningful in local contexts' (Hine, 2000:vii); Jamie Sexton's *Music, Sound and Multimedia: From the Live to the Virtual* (2007), a wide-ranging collection of papers that includes discussion and analysis of music videos, video games music, sound and music in website design and the Apple iPod; and Don Tapscott and Anthony D. Williams's *Wikinomics: How Mass Collaboration Changes Things*, which explores notions of consumer-controlled media such as YouTube and 'citizen journalism' (Tapscott and Williams, 2006:14). All of these areas of study are inextricably bound up with the new guitarscape. Moreover, even if many guitarists deny access to and feign knowledge of digital media, their audiences do not. It is common to see a video of a guitar player taken on a mobile phone or by a film crew on the Internet, and, moreover, specialist designers are employed to create and maintain the websites of the mainly professional guitarists who can afford them.

In this brief discussion of the guitar and the Internet, I want to pick up on the debate surrounding the construction or destruction of 'community'. René Lysloff's 'Musical Life in Softcity' is part of the ground-breaking collection of articles, mentioned already, with the title *Music and Technoculture* (Lysloff and Gay, 2003). Lysloff discusses the problems of fieldwork on the Internet – the overwhelming information, the amount of time spent online – and how it contrasts with his face-to-face encounters whilst carrying out field studies in Java. He states that his aim is 'to argue that at least some online communities like the mod scene, are as real as communities offline. Communities are, after all, based on social

---

    [21]   See Jan Norman, http://mysite.verizon.net/res8qqgs/hall.htm Orange County Register-June 13, 1994.

relationships, not necessarily physical proximity' (Lysloff, 2003:8). The Internet is, of course, but one important part of the new guitarscape. It is part of a larger network of social and cultural relations held in place by the guitar and by a variety of phenomena beyond the Internet. It might be said that in the new guitarscape, physical proximity also matters.

I asked Robert Urban, founder and moderator of the online site Gay Guitarists Worldwide, the question 'Has the Internet made a great difference to LGBT lives, freedom, and sense of community (or is this quite idealistic on my part)'? His reply is as follows:

> It is a fact that computers are more common among homosexuals than they are among straights. Laptop ownership, email use, and Internet use among gays and lesbians are all more than double that of the straight population. This is not surprising since studies reveal that gays and lesbians are more educated, more literate and more affluent than straights as a whole. So – you are not being idealistic. Advertisers know that the Internet is an important media source among LGBTs as a consumer group and is a major way in which brands communicate with them.
>
> Perhaps the most dramatic effect the Internet has had on LGBT sense of community is in how it has altered the geography of our social interactions with each other. During the years in which homosexuality was 'the love that dare not speak its name', gays and lesbians used gay and lesbian bars – often in clandestine fashion – for socializing. Now the internet has freed us from having to meet in bars. In fact, with advances in our human rights, we now can meet up, socialize and not feel threatened in a wide variety of places – even, say – a rock concert! (Robert Urban, personal communication)

To a significant degree, the Internet does enable contact to be made across the professional world of guitar playing and making, and not just from the point of view of marketing and sales (as discussed elsewhere). Sometimes connections are made between established professionals and those not so well established, at moments linking up the professional world of guitar playing with the world of the amateur and the aspiring semi-professional. Even with the canon of great guitarists still well in place, YouTube and MySpace, for example, provide a forum as never before for guitarists, guitar fans and other interested parties around the world with access to a computer (as discussed further in Chapter 8). Moreover, the names of the several hundred guitar sites that I have sampled, including infiniteguitar.com, alloutguitar.com and cyberfret.com, are all quite revealing about the aspirations of those who design and maintain them, and demonstrative of the embracing of cyberspace by those involved.

I believe some significance can be attached to the fact that one can virtually enter guitar worlds that were once exclusively the province of the widely travelled explorer and see what musicians are up to many thousands of miles away. I note a report on the Internet that reads: 'Budding Bedroom Guitar Virtuoso Finds Fame Online'. Here we are told that:

> Computers, backing tracks, recording software, digital video, and of course, the Internet, might even be seen to forge an international community of guitarists. 23-year-old Jeong-Hyun Lim provides us with a perfect example. Lim's YouTube. com video entitled 'guitar', in which he sits on his bed playing Pachelbel's 'Canon in D Major' with an ESP electric guitar, has received more than 7.5 million views, almost 17,000 comments and been the subject of a three-page (Internet) story in the *New York Times*.[22]

However, when I accessed the 'guitar' video on YouTube in early December 2008 it had been viewed 51.9 million times, and by 10 March 2009 it had been viewed 56.72 million times.

At the time of writing, there are now several videos on YouTube which relate to the 'Canon' phenomenon. According to CNN News, Jeong-Hyun Lim was tracked down by a *New York Times* reporter to his home city of Seoul, South Korea, where 'his story was plastered all over the South Korean media'. Interviewed in person by CNN in its video report, Jeong-Hyun Lim says: 'I was so embarrassed because, all of a sudden, I had too many phone calls and too many visitors.' In terms of his technique, the young self-taught guitarist, who had been playing for six years, gave himself 'fifty to sixty points out of one hundred'. Lim can be seen on YouTube Live (22 November 2008), going under the name of 'Funtwo' and playing with Joe Satriani and his band. The event was sponsored by *Guitar Hero World Tour*.

Such is the popularity of the guitar on the Internet, and its intimate relationship to this newer technology of globalization. Indeed, a search for 'guitar' on YouTube is described in 'millions' of 'hits' (sites logged), whereas for other musical instruments (accessed in early December 2008) the figures are more specific, for instance 561,000 for piano and 96,900 for violin.

On first embarking on an exploration of the virtual world of the guitar, I thought it best to try and acquire some idea of the scope of my project. That is, I wanted to gain some sense of the parameters of the new guitarscape as captured on the Internet, but also as constituted by it. I typed 'guitar' into a search engine. Yahoo came up with 638 million hits, and Google 280 million. Of course, I did not spend time checking through each and every site that my searches came up with, and it is clear from an advanced sampling that many of them mention the guitar only in passing. In cyberspace, of course, some sites close down while others remain open: that also happened during the period of my research. However, the vast majority of sites I sampled have been active for some time and mention the guitar in some detail. Some of the guitar sites are positively encyclopaedic in scope, leading in turn to may other sites through a multitude of links. I return again and

---

[22]   See www.nytimes.com/2006/08/27/27heff.html and www.modernguitars.com/archives/002282.html.

again to the content of some of these sites throughout this book. For the moment, it is necessary only to compare the quantity of hits gained for the guitar with those for other musical instruments, regardless of whether or not they are all made up of sites that actually focus on the musical instrument in question. These statistics are captured in Tables 5.1–5.5.

Table 5.1   Search results for names of musical instruments, 10 March 2009

Search term	Yahoo hits (millions)	Google hits (millions)
Guitar	821	211
Piano	720	187
Violin	117	35.9
Flute	95.5	23.6
Trumpet	84	18
Synthesizer	34.8	7.9

One must, of course, question any assumption based on this data. However, although I am not for one minute discounting the extent to which other musical instruments feature on the Internet, it is obvious that the guitar takes the lead in terms of the number of citations it receives. One might say that musical instruments *in toto* are in high profile on the Internet, boosted by references to the guitar. But how does my search for 'Guitar' compare with searches for other phenomena? The search results for 'Earth', 'God', 'The Universe' and 'existence' made for an interesting comparison:

Table 5.2   Search results for names of large phenomena

Search term	Yahoo hits (millions)
Earth	1.850
God	1.840
Guitar	823
The Universe	518
Existence	472

One can see that the guitar has a long way to go before it can compete with God and Earth in terms of gaining people's attention, that is, just as one might expect. But how do the number of hits for guitarists compare with hits for other significant people?

Table 5.3   Search results for names of important people

Search name	Yahoo hits (millions)
Jesus	906
Christ	491
The Pope	203
The Buddha	91.2
Jimi Hendrix	49
Eric Clapton	42.6

Hits for Jimi Hendrix and Eric Clapton fall short of hits for some of the holiest men in history. However, a search for 'Les Paul' revealed 219 million sites. But such a search is, of course, unreliable, given that 'Les' and 'Paul' might be counted as hits, and one cannot be sure (unless one undertakes the impossible task of visiting 219 millions websites), whether it is the Les Paul guitar or Les Paul the musician that is being targeted and counted as a hit. Figure 5.4 below represents an attempt to provide some insight into this dilemma.

Table 5.4   Search results for the name Les Paul

Search name	Yahoo hits (millions)
Les Paul	219
Les Paul (guitar)	24.2
Les Paul (musician)	10.2
Les Paul (guitarist)	4.73

Table 5.5   Search results for the names of types of guitar

Search term	Yahoo hits (millions)
Bass guitar	233.00
Acoustic guitar	129.00
Electric guitar	120.00
Touch guitars	99.50
Six-string guitar	13.00
Chapman Stick	5.00
Twelve-string guitar	3.58

At the time of writing, the guitar has what is described as 'portal' status in Wikipedia. The guitar portal information reads: 'Wikipedia: Guitar Portal (24,389 visitors, 442 members, founded No 6, 2004)'. At the Guitar Portal one reads that 'This is a WikiProject, a collaboration area and open group of editors dedicated to improving Wikipedia's coverage of a particular topic, or to organizing some internal Wikipedia process'. The viewing statistics for March 2009 show that the Guitar Portal was viewed 201,180 times up to that date and that the articles on the guitar ranked 976 in traffic on en.wikipedia.org. The other dedicated Wikipedia musical instrument site is that of the pipe organ. I asked Andrew Gray of Wikipedia the following question and received the reply shown below:

Q. What significance can be attached to the guitar's portal status?

A. There's no deliberately intended significance as such – only that it suggests there's enough of a group of editors interested in the topic to pull one together. The full list here illustrates that to some degree: http://en.wikipedia.org/wiki/Portal:List_of_portals – as you can see, the musical instruments we have portals on are the guitar (and a separate one on classical guitar) and pipe organ, which is certainly an idiosyncratic selection of three! The long-term goal is to have more comprehensive coverage, of course, but it's still a work in progress. What we have portals on so far is mainly a reflection of volunteer interest rather than any top-down selection – hopefully, as portals grow in use to our readers, we'll see a wider range created. I should probably clarify that what we've discussed – the inferences from the content – is reflective mostly of the interests of our 'writers', not our readers. It's a little tricky to gauge exactly what our readers are interested in, and how strongly, but we do have some limited viewing statistics that might be of interest. Compare, say: http://stats.grok.se/en/200903/Guitar (200k/ month), http://stats.grok.se/en/200903/Piano (150k/ month), http://stats.grok.se/en/200903/Violin (100k/ month) – and a more obscure instrument: http://stats.grok.se/en/200903/Piccolo (25k/ month).

The popularity of the guitar compared to other instruments is still noticeable in terms of what people read, it seems. (Andrew Gray, personal communication)

The questions raised in this chapter, including notions of real and virtual, material and immaterial, and subject and object, are being considered by a range of professionals and academics. One major question that has arisen is the degree of choice that musicians have in terms of their engagement with new technologies. Visionary Instruments note that their custom guitars and video guitars 'are for musicians who are serious about including the latest technology in their performance' and that their designs are only limited by 'imagination and the laws of physics'; they also describe their video guitars as 'the future of live music' (www.visionaryinstruments.com). The face of the video guitar includes a video screen that has various possible functions, including the potential to react (in its sequencing of images) to the music played upon the guitar (with its computer hard drive). Such developments may have wider implications and applications in guitar performance. However, drawing on previous discussion of the inter-relationships between technique and technologies in guitar performance, in the next chapter I focus on some of the ways in which the body and the senses are involved in learning and teaching, and in practice and performance. As much as musicians and manufacturers are exploring the outer limits of available technologies (and in the case of the video guitar, the visual aspect of performance), so performers are employing a wide range of manual techniques to produce sound on their instruments. The use of extended techniques often relies on new technologies to realize their full sonic potential in performance. Extended techniques also draw attention to vital issues surrounding the use of the body and the role of the senses in performance, involving matters of sight and sound, touch and feel, stasis and movement.

Chapter 6
The Sensual Culture of the Guitar

Best feel – Jeff Beck. (*Guitar Techniques* (December 2005):22)

'I can remember Bill said to Leo, "this guitar should fit you like a shirt" … the result was an aesthetic and ergonomic masterpiece.' (Minhinnett and Young, 1995:22)

I want to begin this chapter with reference to a film of black blues guitarist J. B. Lenoir performing 'I Feel So Good' in 1964. His vocal production, lyrics, facial expressions, body movements, guitar playing and zebra-striped tailcoat provide for a captivating performance. Yet Lenoir's demeanour is actually quite relaxed. He comes across as a smooth operator, a well-oiled musical machine. His excitement is contained, which is, perhaps, not surprising as he appears to be performing for the cameraman only. In the lyrics to 'I Feel So Good', Lenoir refers to his 'box', which is ostensibly his guitar with its 'natural top'. He states that he feels so good that he 'feels like playing my box' and 'blowing my natural top', that is, if he 'had one more shot'.[1] Yet, however else one might interpret the lyrics (and their possible sexual innuendo) or the restrained dynamics of his performance (not that he was known for being particularly restrained musically), one cannot deny that Lenoir sings about his most intimate feelings in the context of his guitar-based performance.

The guitar might be said to be readily available to accommodate those feelings, providing the musical context for an emotional exegesis, not only as the means for the realization of Lenoir's musical ideas, but also as the basis for an altogether more complex physical and psychological workout. As much as Lenoir can be seen to move with the guitar in his performance, so the ten musicians in Chapter 1 can be seen to be relatively still in performance. Of course the complexity of their co-ordinated body movements, as seen most clearly in their arm and hand movements around and upon the guitar, demonstrates a focused but, nevertheless, high level of physical activity (from two-handed tapping and percussive techniques to the leg and foot movements needed to push the buttons and depress the pedals of floor-based effects processor units, including now the ability to manually operate a laptop computer).[2]

---

[1]   J.B. Lenoir in Wim Wenders, *The Soul of a Man*, part of the seven-part series 'Martin Scorsese Presents The Blues', Snapper SMADVD031 (2003).

[2]   See Yung, 1984 for a seminal paper on the movements of the instrumentalist in performance.

Musicians like J.B. Lenoir often talk explicitly about the feelings they experience when taking up the guitar, expressing themselves with it and through it, when coming into contact with the instrument and its associated objects. The guitar is clearly an object that many people can relate to, engage with, and physically move with and upon. Perhaps its curves and contours, textures and finishes invite inspection and touch? At certain times, the instrument seems to take on the role of a person, its shape stereotypically linked to the figure of a woman (as noted in the next chapter). The early designs of the electric guitar (for instance, the 1950s Fender Stratocaster) were sculpted with the human body in mind, and were designed to be user-friendly and open to use by a wide variety of musicians, musical abilities and playing purposes.[3] Yet the guitar's shape has sometimes led to its interpretation as a phallic symbol, particularly in heavy metal, where the use of 'pointy' guitars is still quite common (and not just a relic of the 1980s). However many notions of gender and sexuality might be seen to be linked to a discussion of sensuality though, these subjects do not make up the crux of my argument as presented here. I take up the theme of gender and sexuality in the next chapter. As noted here, guitarists' comments also draw attention to the wider sensual experience that is playing the guitar, for men, women and children.

This chapter is largely about the ways in which musicians engage physically with the guitar and the means by which they organize their movements around it and upon it. The guitar is a site of musical performance that includes the exploration and agency of musical ideas as much as the activation of sounds and techniques. Cultural approaches and individual responses meet in performance, along with minds and bodies, wood and wire, and flesh and bone. As Simon Frith notes:

> The point here is that the body is also an instrument ... body movement is determined by other bodies ... and by the use of tools. The use of the body as an instrument involves, in fact, two components. On the one hand, the *material* we work on determines our movements (when writing, cuddling, driving, sewing) – in musical terms the instrument we play thus determines the instrument our body must be (standing up, sitting down, bowing or blowing, hitting or pulling). On the other hand, our body movements are also determined by our *purpose* (to write a letter, comfort a child, make a shirt, play a certain sort of note). (Frith, 1996:219)

With Frith's comments in mind, it is clear that learning to play and performing on a musical instrument involves a high degree of intentionality or goal-directed

---

[3] I note some of the more salient remarks here, but see also the extended discussion of the processes involved in guitar design featured in *The Story of the Fender Stratocaster: Curves, Contours and Body Horns: A Celebration of the World's Greatest Guitar* (Minhinnett and Young, 1995:22). For mention of the concept of 'optimal playing comfort' see, for example, the Plek technology advertisement in the Framus Guitar catalogue, 2008. See also: www.framus.de.

behaviour, whether to obtain some kind of ephemeral pleasure or a longer-lasting result. Guitarists do not play as automatons, however much of their technique might appear to be at times mechanical or even second nature. Although the ways in which guitarists use their body to move around on the guitar are noted, the focus here is on the ways in which the senses can be said to be engaged in the context of those movements in guitar performance. Working largely with reports from professional guitarists and published methods for guitar, I aim for a provisional fleshing-out of the sensual world of the guitar, providing an exploration of the ways in which we use our senses to engage with the instrument and how we are able to move around upon it.

Evidence suggests, as discussed, that there is indeed something amounting to a sensual culture of the guitar, connected as much to the lyrical interpretations of J.B. Lenoir as to the findings elsewhere of physical anthropologists and neuropsychologists. However many differences in the use of the body in performance might be put down to musically stylistic or cultural values and norms and codes of locally acceptable behaviour or their transgression, movements towards, away from, and around the guitar tend to happen within some broadly ascertainable parameters. These movements might be said to be visible in most cultural contexts, the subtleties of which are locally encoded and stylistically nuanced but, nevertheless, widely observable.

Guitar performance, like other instrumental performance, happens in certain places at certain times as dictated by consensus or convention. On the guitar, habituated playing positions and ways of standing, sitting and moving are readily adopted, involved, and relied upon at each and every performance or practice. Postures and deportments are also based on facets of an individual's character, physical make-up and social circumstance in relation to gender ideals, financial status and even political censorship. A complex orientation system is involved and is re-activated when needed, as cultivated by each and every guitar player, whether amateur, semi-professional or professional (even if it is constantly practised and ever finely tuned in the latter case). This orientation system is multi-sensory, re-establishing a sense of performance space, mapping out the immediate environment conducive to a meeting of the mind and body around and upon the guitar. Emplacement or 'body-mind-environment' (after Howes, 2005) is also experienced, felt, seen and heard, on, through and because of the guitar. It might also be claimed that the guitarscape is also a sensescape. I believe that a concept such as emplacement has the potential to model and probe fundamental questions about what kind of experience it is to the play the guitar, involving both the body and the mind in guitar performance. But it clearly has wider application in terms of how one might probe the wider sensual experience that is the guitar, involving all the senses and a variety of inter-media and inter-textual encounters.

Some Sensual Encounters with the Guitar

> 'The guitar is an instrument you cradle and caress,' she explains. 'You feel the vibration of the wood against your body. It's very sensual.' ('Sharon Isbin Unplugged'. in M.G. Lord, *Elle* (June 1996), from www.sharonisbin.com)

> So much happens in these few seconds of playing. My whole body is transported, altered by the feeling of the string landing between my nail and flesh, my left hand fingers pressing down on the strings with my thumb, balancing them in an opposing motion, the bass strings resonating against my chest, and the overall sound of these notes being played and felt by 'self-powered hands.' (Benjamin Verdery, in Gibson, 2008:70)

> My secret is one you have witnessed many times, and one that I can't leave to posterity, because it must with my body go to the grave, for it consists of the tactile senses in my finger pads, in my thumb and index finger that tell the intelligent maker if the top is or is not well made, and how it should be treated to obtain the best tone from the instrument. (Antonio de Torres Jurado, as quoted in Shaw, 2008:17)[4]

A few more examples might usefully help to introduce the broader range of ideas that I have in mind for this discussion on the sensual culture of the guitar. Surprisingly in the world of flamenco guitar, which is often presented as a world that is *muy macho*, tough, hard to get close to, one's attention is drawn to flamenco guitarists' wider sensual experience, which requires great sensitivity. Don Pohren uses vivid imagery to substantiate his claim that a flamenco guitarist 'only has to open *his* case and smell the sweet dry-wood odour of an old guitar to feel a certain enjoyment. As *he* strokes the deep strings of a quarter-of-a-century old guitar, the sonorous, age-mellowed sound will give a thrill, a *jondo* sensation, a desire to play and to play well' (Pohren 1962:73, my italics). The *jondo* or 'deep' sensation that Pohren describes (as the odour of the guitar diffuses throughout the room, and whilst the 'deep strings' of the old guitar set sound waves in motion) lends an element of romanticism (and perhaps even mystique) to his engendered description. But, more significantly in my view, Pohren also reminds us that playing the guitar is a sensual experience.

In this respect, I think Pohren points to something crucial. In uncovering some of ways in which the flamenco guitarist approaches and values the guitar, he provides a description of the lived experience of the guitar player as he or she engages with the instrument and its accessories. As the flamenco guitarist opens up their guitar case, so Pohren opens up for discussion the sensual experience that is guitar playing. Such reports are not just confined to the world of flamenco, which is, of course, a world that writers often wax lyrical about. From quite different musical and cultural perspectives, Johnny Marr reportedly commented:

---

4   See also Romanillos, 1987.

'I remember this red Stratocaster. I can recall the smell of the case and everything' (Carman, 2006:15). Moreover, Ben Verdery notes that 'Case opened, there lies the guitar ... not quite silent, as there's a slight resonance of the open strings from the opening of the case, as if preparing to be played' (Gibson, 2008:70).

Is one to assume that all the senses of the flamenco guitarist are as finely tuned to the guitar as their tendons and muscle reflexes? Clearly, their sense of touch must have been sensitized to the guitar in order to have conditioned their reflexes over time, the essential motor programming arising out of the learning or conditioning experience as observed by neurophysiologists. But their ears and eyes must have also been attuned to the sights and sounds of flamenco guitar culture.[5] In reading Pohren's description of the flamenco guitarist taking his guitar out of its case, it is clear that he conveys something of the multi-sensory experience involved, as if he had experienced this himself. Don Pohren is, of course, a highly accomplished guitarist able to write articulately about his findings within the context of seminal publications (see Pohren, 1962). He draws not only from personal experience in describing the world of the flamenco guitarist, but also from his immersion over many years in the flamenco guitar cultures of Spain and elsewhere.

In his report of nine-year-old Sharon Isbin's first introduction to the guitar, John von Rhien notes that 'The resonance of the guitar, the sensual contact of fingers against the strings – everything about the instrument appealed to her at once.'[6] This was a multi-sensory experience for the young guitarist. Steve Howe (Yes, GTR, Asia) reported though that during a concert 'The guitar gets hotted up and sweated up and you get hotted up playing it, and so it was a kind of, "Let's stay on this guitar because it feels good"' (Mead, 2004:126). These few examples give some indication of just how much talk about the guitar is shot through with references to 'feel'. To my mind, such phrases as 'strokes the deep strings', 'sensual contact of finger against the strings' and 'it feels good' point to an altogether more fundamental and complex experience, too easily and hastily cast off as anecdotal or even spurious. I claim that such references point to fundamental aspects of the guitar experience. Such descriptions of how guitarists interact with the guitar draw attention to certain underlying values, ways in which the guitar is valued as both a sound-producing device and a physical object making certain demands upon the body of the player.

A 'method' is what Fernando Sor refers to as 'a Treatise on the established principles on which rules are founded, which ought to guide the operations' (Sor, [1832] 1995:46). Principles provide the foundation for rules, which, in turn, should

---

[5]   If the guitarist is blind, other senses must compensate or, rather, make up a slightly different approach to sensing and playing the instrument. Notable guitarists who were blind include Blind Lemon Jefferson, Jeff Healy and José Feliciano. See also the video of a guitarist featured on www.youtube.com playing the instrument with his feet: 'amazing guitar player'.

[6]   John von Rhein, interview with Sharon Isbin, *Chicago Tribune* (30 May 2000), www.sharonisbin.com.

guide operations. In fact, his treatise touches on fundamental issues, concerning relations between mind, body and environment – that is, how the human being in the world interacts with his or her surroundings and the artifacts found there, in this case to create music. Sor explored the spatial and temporal dynamics of musical performance, and in his work on a method for the guitar he comes across as both physical anthropologist and aesthetician, searching for the 'right' sound and the means by which constantly to reproduce it, model it, establish rules and pass these on. Moreover, his and other methods provide a terminology, a means of explanation drawing on a teacher's experience (generally that of a performer too) reporting back from both the inner and outer world of the guitarist, introspective but also reflecting everyday concerns in terms of performance. Sor is clearly working with cognitive schema as he models the layout of the guitar, devises finger positions and carefully deploys chord voicings, concerned as much with ergonomics as aesthetics.

The diagrams in Sor's *Method for the Spanish Guitar* lead me to suggest that he also draws attention to links between culture and cognition in guitar playing. The diagrams represent and capture something of the degree of Sor's idealized involvement, of his physical and intellectual self with the instrument. Therefore a discussion of such elusive terms such as 'feel' and 'touch' must be linked to a wider discussion, particularly of the role of the body and senses in music making (and their cultural basis, dependent also on culturally based explanation or meaning). Here, I attempt to present what amounts to a preliminary modelling of guitar cultures as sensual cultures. I think Sor made significant inroads into such a study.

Victor Coelho notes Sor's experiments with techniques of moving the guitar *away* from the body: 'while standing and without the guitar actually touching ... this "sitting" method resulted in increased volume and projection' (Coelho, 1997:203). Clearly, models of touch (including suggestions of when to touch and when not to touch the instrument) have profound ramifications for sound production and the development of techniques linked to musical roles, as well as for the broader constitution of 'hearing cultures' (after Erlmann, 2004), all of which constitute the sensual culture or cultures of the guitar.

It seems most appropriate to me at this stage to draw primarily on ideas and perspectives offered by research into the anthropology of the senses, as taken up by music scholars, such as Veit Erlmann ('hearing cultures'), anthropologists of music and sound, such as Steven Feld ('senses of place'), and also historians writing on sound, for example Alain Corbain ('culture of the senses').[7] To do otherwise, I believe, would do little justice to the experiences informing not only the life of each and every guitarist but also to Sor's life as a musical being and culture bearer, and thus the distillation of that experience which is his method. As Brian Jeffery notes:

---

[7]   See Erlmann (2004), Feld and Basso (1996), Corbain (1998).

> Sor's method for the guitar is a quite exceptional book, transcending the subject of guitar technique to deal with harmony, mathematics, sonority, composition, and above all music as an art ... When the book was published in 1830, Sor was 52 years old. He had a varied life, many successes, many failures, a good deal of buffeting by fate, and a variety of amatory experience ... His method is a profound work, written by a man who had spent his life in music as a whole and not merely in the limited corner of it that is the guitar. The book is extremely detailed, always reflective and never dull. It shows a man who knew not only Haydn but also Molière, not only the guitar but also the piano and the voice. (Sor, 1995:iii–iv)

To my mind, Sor's personality is stamped on every page of the method. It is a treatise that distils a musical life well lived, and lived vigorously with and through the guitar. Clearly, Sor's technique of playing the guitar is not only a key to his personal musical aesthetic and physical awareness, but also a part of a more general response to the musical, social and cultural circumstances in which he found himself. His method demands a broader way of thinking about 'technique' and what it means to 'play' the guitar, providing goals, benchmarks and a broad range of questions applicable to both the pupil and the teacher (using his method). One might claim that in an effort to develop his playing upon the guitar, Sor was engaged in both a physical as well as a intellectual journey.[8] Sor reminds one of the cultural basis and embodied nature of the experience that is playing the guitar.

Bodies of Evidence

> At the beginning, the whole body or organism raises up a sculpture or statue of tense skin, vibrating amid voluminous sound, open–closed like a box (or drum), capturing that by which it is captured. We hear by means of the skin and the feet. We hear with the cranial box, the abdomen and the thorax. We hear by means of the muscles, nerves and tendons. Our body-box stretched, with strings, veils itself within a global tympanum (Serres, 1998:180).

Our bodies are particularly good sound catchers, but they are also relatively limited in the ways in which they can be used to produce sound themselves. We are even less able to control sound coming from our bodies once we have developed the means of producing it. Is the human body limited, then, in terms of its ability to produce and manipulate sound itself, of its own accord, beyond the highly practised but also gifted voice and the skilled percussionist that is the maker of 'body music'? Clearly, a musical instrument such as a guitar offers vast melodic, harmonic and rhythmic resources not directly available through the human body. Moreover, such a device offers a high degree of control over the

---

[8]   See also www.sorstudies.co.uk.

sounds produced. The potential that the body has to make but also *feel* music is surely tapped and stretched as it responds to the demands of learning to perform on a musical instrument. As noted earlier, some effort has been made by guitar manufacturers to consider the potential of exploiting links between the contours and surfaces of our body, and the contours and surfaces of technologies. This research involves the application of human factors and ergonomic principles in design theory (see Noyes, 2001). I note a report featuring a guitar called the Handle, made by Jim Reed Guitars. The report reads: 'the Handle was designed for comfort. Its concave form anatomically fits the body.'[9] However, this is a somewhat vague statement. Some scholars have a much broader notion of 'fit' and write of the ways in which we are said to 'inhabit' technology, a term which seems to have a particular relevance in a study of the guitar as it comes close to the body and as it grows in influence as an instrument of both global and contemporary performance. Nigel Thrift claims that 'object surfaces which interpose with our bodies are forming a new kind of carapace, a set of informational surfaces which, by dint of the combination of machine and theory, creates a new "inside" which is also simultaneously a new "outside"'(Thrift, 2005). Thrift does not seem to be suggesting a new kind of technological determinism. Instead he is surely arguing for a more intense study of the potential for creative interplay between the human body and new technologies.[10]

From studies undertaken of other lute cultures besides the guitar, we must also note that 'Factors such as the shape and size of the instrument, the material of the strings, the tension to which they are stretched, the height of the frets, and many other seemingly small details, are significant when we consider how the body interacts with them' (Baily, 1977:308). The guitar is designed to make music, but its shape, contours, ridges, materials and textures, as well as its weight, temperature to touch, the resistance to pressure of materials of construction, all contribute to the sensory experience that is playing it – that is, as the human body comes into contact with the instrument. Raymond Tallis usefully sums up the relationship between 'properties investigated' and 'exploratory procedure' as the hand comes into contact with an object: texture links to lateral motion, temperature to static contact, global shape and volume grasped by enclosure, hardness gauged by

---

9   See 'New Guitar Unveiled: The Handle', www.modernguitars.com/archives/001894. html.

10   In this respect, I note that Steve Vai appears as a guitar-playing cyborg (half human, half machine) on the cover of the CD *The Ultra Zone*, Sony Music/Epic 4947452 (1999). His guitar in this image is similarly exotic and futuristic, and straight out of science fiction. However fantastic this image may seem, it has some resonance with the direction of musical/ guitar technologies, which seem to rely on an increasingly symbiotic relationship between performer and musical instrument. I am reminded of various discussions of the subject of transhumanism, a term coined by biologist Julian Huxley in 1957. Transhumanism is 'the idea that we should use technology to transcend the limitations of our bodies and brains' (Hughes, 2006:70).

applied pressure, weight sensed by unsupported holding, and global shape and exact shape mapped by contour following (Tallis, 2003:143). In his discussion of tactile awareness Tallis notes that the 'hand is an organ of exploration and cognition in its own right', able to detect small changes in the environment as it feels its way around (Tallis, 2003:28). Tallis quotes John Napier, who describes the hand as the 'chief organ of the fifth sense', referring to the sense of touch. Napier notes that the hand is 'a motor and sensory organ in one' (Napier, 1971:176).[11]

But as if this were not enough of a significant connection to the body, guitar performance often demands much more of the performer. Simultaneously, parts of the body of the guitarist touch not just the guitar but the chair, stage floor, foot stool, foot pedal, and so on. The guitarist becomes spatially orientated, not only to the guitar, amplification and its accessories, but to the area of performance (and to other musicians who will generally be in a similar predicament). More than just approaching the guitar with musico-visual schema in mind (the positions of certain notes and chords on the fretboard, for example), the eye also registers the broader make-up of the instrument, looking down upon it, catching it out the corner of the eye, its indents, extrusions and extremities, in the way it catches the light and mirrors the environment around it. In the mind's eye of both performer and audience the guitar's iconicity is established in woodwork, metal casting and decoration, making it a recognizable and meaningful object of culture and society, an object with a history and with particular associations even in performance. Its design carries a great deal of information, as knowledge in the world that does not necessarily have to be carried in the mind of the player (cf. Norman, 2000:54–80) as it is already there on the guitar.

Touching the Guitar (and its Gear)

Musical instruments which are blown, such a nose flute or a saxophone, are held in place but also come into contact with certain parts of the nose or mouth which activate their sound. The guitar comes into direct contact with the nose or mouth only if one plays it like Jimi Hendrix or, indirectly, if one uses a talk box (a la Peter Frampton). Then again, if the odour of the guitar case reaches one's nose, as

---

[11]   Sociologist Chris Shilling draws on the work of Marx and Engels in his discussion of the 'productive capacities' of the hand, which, he says, 'emerge through its ability to invent and manipulate increasingly complex tools, while its gestural use is key to the cultivation of social relationships' (Shilling, 2005:29). Tool use itself must be seen as both an economic necessity and a symbolic gesture. Douglas Palmer notes that 'it is likely that the first tools were made of wood or other perishable materials that rarely get fossilised' (Palmer, 2005:147). His book provides a useful overview of current perspectives and debates in research on human evolution, including a chapter on 'Toolmakers and Artists' relevant to my discussion (pp.146–75), although it moves well beyond the scope of this chapter.

noted by Don Pohren, perhaps the smell of the guitar comes only indirectly into contact with the nose, and one can certainly taste the metallic strings as one tries to play them with one's teeth (Jimi Hendrix) or pluck them with one's tongue (Steve Vai). The methods and techniques of musical instrument performance (holding the instrument, posture and movement) can vary enormously and sometimes subtly, even when one focuses on such a discussion in relation to one instrument, such as the guitar. A more recent example of a call to attention concerning the use of the fingers on the guitar comes from Dave Hunter, who, when writing of electric guitar performance, says: 'That the sound chain begins at your fingers can sometimes be too easy to forget' (Hunter, 2005:8).

It seems highly appropriate here to mention yet again to Raymond Tallis's broad-ranging discussion of the hand, in which he notes its structural complexity, the incredible range of operations and manoeuvres possible through finger and grip combinations, how the fingers are capable of ever finer controlled movements (independently and co-operatively), the sensitivity of the fingertips (which are able to detect very small changes in surface textures, pressures and temperatures) and the protection offered by fingernails (Tallis, 2003). In this respect, it is interesting to note that guitar teachers have, from time to time, also been medical doctors, who may have advanced knowledge of both the physiology of the hand and its potential injuries: for example, Jorge Cardoso (Cardoso, 1973; Summerfield, 1996:70)[12], Mesut Özgen (www.mesutozgen.com) and Boris Perott (Summerfield, 1996:181).

As already noted, several guitar performer-teachers, such as Sor, have written extensively on what they consider to be the most appropriate methods for playing the Spanish classical guitar using knowledge and experience gained at a particular time and place (Sor lived in Spain, France, England and Russia). Despite Sor's concern for a whole-body approach to performance, his ultimate focus (and the crux of the matter in terms of how the body of the performer connects and interacts with the instrument) is the means of sound activation and production, that is, the plucking of the strings by the fingertips or nails (singly or in combination) and the resulting tone. This also depends, of course, on the type of strings used.[13]

In his book *The Dilemma of Timbre on the Guitar* (1960), Emilio Pujol compares the tonal quality of notes produced by the nails with those produced by the fleshy fingertips when plucking the strings of the guitar. In his seminal thesis Pujol says that 'Each style, however, embodies a distinct mentality: the one spectacular and tending to exteriorise one's personality, and the other intimate and sincere, deeply penetrated by the spirit of the art' (Pujol, 1960:58). Pujol also addresses this topic in his *Guitar School: A Theoretical-Practical Method for the*

---

[12]   See also Jorge Cardoso, *Técnica de la guitarra clásica* (;The Classic Guitar Technique'), DVD, RGB Arte Visual/Mel Bay Publications (2008). See acordesconcert. com/mamagementING.html. See also fretsonly.com.

[13]   See Rob MacKillop's extensive experiments with silk strings in the performance of Sor's repertoire: www.sorstudies.com.

Guitar ([1956], 1983:174–9). For Sor this is less of a dilemma, and he makes a choice (Sor, [1832] 1995:17). But guitarists plucking strings with their nails are not stuck with what nature has given them. They do not need to resort to the use of the plectrum as there is now a tried and tested alternative, should their nails break, in the form of false nails. Clearly, the use of fingertips or nails in plucking the strings can affect the sounds of musical performance. Mike Oldfield reports that he is continuously faced with both musical and technical choices, as seen in his comments on the difficulties of recording and eliciting the desired sounds from an acoustic bass guitar, for example: 'It took a lot of fiddling: it's not just a case of plugging in a microphone and recording it, you have to adjust this, change that, adjust the tone, even decide whether you play with your finger straight on or flick the strings with a little bit of your fingernail.' (Oldfield, 2007:175).

I note the extraordinary attention that some guitarists give to their nails. But what happens if they chip or break? What happens if the damage cannot be put right with the application of an emery board or a concert is too soon to allow nails to grow back? Although male guitarists might borrow women's nail care products, which include artificial nails and solutions designed to harden the nails, there is also a specialist industry devoted to nail care which is available for all guitarists, male or female.[14] As every fingerstyle player will know, the shape and smoothness of even the edges of one's fingernails matter greatly if one is to attain a clear tone. The care of fingernails is absolutely essential if one is not to continually break the means by which the guitar is played. This is important to professionals performing on a regular basis, of course.

Although strings are set vibrating (set in motion, activated) by the use of the left- or right-hand fingers, flesh or nail, guitarists may actually end up employing a wide variety of techniques to produce sounds (and notes): plucking, tapping, bending, sliding, scraping and slapping with fingernails, fingertips, the side of the fingers, the back of the nails, thumb, palm, full hand or various objects (such as a plectrum, bottleneck, violin bow, E-Bow, pre-selected objects) upon the strings. However, as part of the wide range of extended techniques now employed on the guitar, the instrument may also be used as a percussion instrument, its body and neck treated as if they are drumming boxes and percussion pads (popular at the time of writing with artists like Erik Mongrain, Tommy Emmanuel and Newton Faulkner). Then, of course, there is the 'twanging' or pulling, tapping and slapping, of the whammy bar, the body, leg and foot movements required to operate effects pedals and pedalboards, and (for some musicians) the movements to and from amplifiers or speakers to tweak controls or create feedback (or the hands-on approach required of Robert Fripp to operate his Lunar Module controls).

All such movements contribute to series of gestures, different within certain parameters, for each and every guitarist, providing for what appears to be in some cases a choreographed performance. Such is the integration of the use

---

[14] See, for example, www.guitarplayernails.com. The step-by-step process of attaching artificial nails is detailed here.

of technology and stage space in modern guitar performance, certainly among professional guitarists playing to fee-paying audiences. Movements with and around equipment may be performed openly as part of the unfolding compositional process (Fripp, Frith), or they may be quickly covered up and kept to the barest minimum, leaving the control of equipment to floor-based foot switches and pre-programmed processors (for example, Alex Lifeson). However, one of heavy metal's most dynamic performers, guitarist Zakk Wylde, has a comparatively straightforward rig: his stage equipment characteristically includes four effects pedals, four amplifier heads and two speaker cabinets.

How important is our sense of touch when we learn, teach and perform on the guitar? Touch requires movement and thus involves a web of sensation and co-ordinated actions. There are both cognitive and cultural factors at play, and one is surely caught up in 'the multiple ways in which culture mediates sensation (and sensation mediates culture)' (Howes, 2005:ix) when playing the guitar (see also Théberge, 1997). The player's fingertips and pads become accustomed to the touch of the various surfaces of a material culture, including a musical instrument (from strings to the body of the instrument). The guitar is a culturally defined sound-producing object made meaningful in certain social or personal contexts. As we grow up, we become accustomed to the 'sensuous materiality' (Howes, 2005:7) of a musical instrument: the feel of its surfaces and textures, the vibrations against our bodies, its dimensions and weight (both of which demand certain postures and movements to be adopted), all of which depend on the technologies and manufacturing processes available to various cultures and societies.

The way in which a guitarist learns or is taught has a profound effect upon his or her development as a musician (let alone his or her development as a social human being). Learning to play involves induction into a guitar culture where one is taught to sense the guitar with reference to values considered important within a given culture, and possibly according to the accepted wisdom of a school of guitar teaching (see, for example, Sor, 1832, Pujol, 1934 and 1956), that is, cognition situated in relation to cultural setting where 'Just as meanings are shared, so are sensory experiences' (Howes, 2005:4–5). In trying to bridge what are often regarded as separate worlds, Howes claims that 'This is why it is not enough to look at the senses as "energy transducers", "information gatherers", or "perceptual systems"; they must also be understood as cultural systems' (Howes, 2005:4–5). The anthropologist and musician Steven Feld also draws our attention to the fact that 'The sense of touch, the sense of feel, the sense of sound are so deeply and thoroughly integrated in our physical mechanism' (Keil and Feld 1994:167). Yet he goes on to say:

> Ironically, I'm a devoted reader of all the music psychology journals. I like reading research on musical memory, auditory illusions, perceptual universals, all those laboratory experiments. All of that is fascinating to me, but in a model of musical communication I don't want to privilege those perceptual things as

autonomous from the complexity of culture, experience, and interpretive moves. (Keil and Feld, 1994:165)

I try to keep my study of the guitar rooted in 'the complexity of culture, experience, and interpretive moves' (Keil and Feld, 1994:165), as discussed elsewhere in this book, though I draw attention to a limited range of work in music cognition in the next section.

Moving into Playing Position

It would be fruitless to try to show that musical performance is controlled exclusively by one sensory modality, such as vision, audition, or kinaesthesis, or within one kind of conceptual field. A range of possibilities are available which may be stressed to different degrees in different musical cultures, by different individuals in the same musical culture, and by a single individual at different moments in a single performance.

Nevertheless, despite this multiplicity of representations and the possibility of switching between them, it is quite clear that spatial relationships are very important at the cognitive level, being directly linked with the physical operations to be performed. Thus, one important conceptual model that the musician has at his disposal is actually a spatial model in which movements are planned and experienced in visual, kinaesthetic and tactile terms. (Baily, 1977: 309)

The guitar may be richly symbolic, but in principle its overall structure is simple. Basically it is a box or a plank, with a neck and four or more strings attached to it, running from its top to its bottom. The strings are tuneable. The hollow box, if there is one, usually has a soundhole. The plank does not. What exactly are we to make of these curious objects of culture and society? If we had not developed a love of the guitar, experienced the pleasure of holding it and playing it, might it seem just a little ridiculous that we reach out for it? Yet, like climbing into the cockpit of an aircraft or getting into the driving seat of a car, we move into playing position without question. The guitar demands a certain approach, it requires the player to have specialist knowledge which includes the skills to orientate quickly to the guitar's materiality (shape, weight, layout and sound). Of course, the aircraft, car and guitar also have a certain allure due to the physical and mental challenges they present, along with their rather glamorous and exotic associations. Often stereotyped as boys' toys, they are also objects of pleasure and leisure. If one is going to be able to fly, drive or play a musical instrument, a highly developed skills base involving the practised co-ordination of human faculties is required. It seems that speed and manoeuvrability are demanded not just of the aircraft, car or guitar, but also of the pilot, driver and player. Champions seem to be valued for the ways in which they court danger, push their machines and themselves to the limits, provide thrills for spectators, demonstrate mental and physical agility, athleticism and stamina, and the ways in which they might show off such qualities. The spectacle of the occasion is very important.

It is also clear that any study involving the body and the senses must include reference to work in music cognition, even by a non-specialist, as any moves upon an instrument of 'danger' must clearly be thought through carefully with a high level of preparation and concentration. In their article on 'situated cognition' in the journal *The World of Music* (1992), Davidson and Torff note that new perspectives have begun to challenge long-standing psychological concepts and methods: 'Instead of considering only the response of individuals within artificial settings, the researcher now has to consider three vantage points in order to develop a deep understanding of cognitive capacity' (Davidson and Torff, 1992:120). In their endeavours to provide a model of situated cognition in music, the authors list three vantage points, as follows: 'the development of the individual, the local support conditions leading to the mastery of the symbol system and materials of the domain, and the cultural setting which gives meaning and structure to the entire expression' (Davidson and Torff, 121). They explore this model with reference to 'two settings full of thought' (Davidson and Torff, 121): lessons on jazz piano and *yang chi'n* (Chinese zither).

Two questions frame their investigation: What is the scope of knowledge? How is knowledge used? Here the authors draw attention to the social and physical context in which cognitive activity takes place, the real world situation of music lessons in which cognitive skills are employed. They state that: 'Culture provides the means by which individuals make sense of the world, in a sense, a "tool kit" of concepts, categories, symbol systems, tools, conventions, values, aesthetics' (Davidson and Torff, 1992:127). Moreover, they propose clear links between culture and cognition: 'Cognitive functioning depends on the "tools" provided by culture, structures that enable individuals to make meaning out of situations and which generate direction and guide appropriate action. Cultural products, like language and music-theory systems, mediate thought and shape our representations of reality. We think *through* culture' (Davidson and Torff, 1992:127). Of course, there are elements of fundamental debate inherent in such statements, and it is clear from the inclusion of this literature where my own emphasis lies in this book (but for much broader perspectives see Clarke, 2005, as well as Green, 2001; Sloboda, 2004). It is necessary now to turn to examples of the ways in which, it has been proposed, musicians think *through* the guitar, which, like all instruments, is a product of culture and society but also sets a unique set of physical challenges to the individual who brings it to his or her body. What is it that we are mindful of as we approach the guitar? As we bring the instrument to our body what structures of thought guide our progress? Beyond hearing the tune in our head or engaging with a music score placed to the side, what further knowledge do we need to have in place to play the guitar?

In 'Spatio-Motor Thinking in Playing Folk Blues Guitar' (1992), Baily and Driver set out a model for the 'cognition of musical performance', a model that should instantly strike a chord with the guitar-playing reader. Here they examine the relationship between human movement and musical structure. They assert that creative spatial and motor grammars not only constrain musical performance but also account for the auditory structures of music itself. Seeking perspectives derived from a combination of anthropological and psychological approaches, the authors examine the playing style and technique of folk blues guitarist David Evans in an attempt to understand more of the creative role that spatio-motor thinking takes in structuring various improvisational musical forms. From their study of folk blues guitar (but also with reference to Baily's work on the lute cultures of Afghanistan) they note that:

> Musical styles vary widely with respect to the degree to which the characteristic motor patterns of their performance techniques embody the constraints imposed by the morphology of the instrument and use movements and sequences of movements that are intrinsically easy for the human sensorimotor system to organize. However, the constraints inherent in a particular layout may be transcended to varying degrees. (Baily and Driver, 1992: 58)

Research in situated cognition and spatio-motor thinking leads me to suggest that each and every performance on a musical instrument requires the establishment of a unique performance space. Performance spaces will, of course, vary enormously, being subtly or not so subtly redefined by the performer's personal response to a particular place, the particular social and cultural context of performance, the musical genre or style performed and the musical ideas and individual emotional state at the time. Cognition might thus be said to be situated by various social, cultural and individual factors. It is a process of contextualization and externalization as much as it is a process of internalization operating through the body (brain). Are not the many varied performances mentioned in this book evidence of this? As already noted for the guitar, habituated playing positions, ways of standing, sitting and moving, are readily adopted, involved and relied upon at each and every performance or practice. A complex orientation system is involved and is re-activated when needed. It also enables the performer to make sense of the performance space as a guitarist.

Emplacement or 'body-mind-environment' is thus felt, seen and heard through and around the guitar. There is a re-mobilization of a scheme of operations, appropriate moves, the tensing and relaxation of muscles and the application and relaxation of pressure from parts of the hands (and other parts of the body as they may be involved in holding and supporting the instrument). Performance is dependent on the player's ability to *move around* or *with* the guitar, as it were, whilst sitting quite still or traversing an allotted portion of a stage, studio or practice room. In turn, movement depends upon the co-ordination of the sense of touch. Touch provides the player with an orientating device, feedback, enabling the player to feel where he or she is on the instrument (feeling movement or acts from start to completion, departure point to arrival point). Touch not only affects the ability of the player to find or select the required notes but also affects tone production.

For instance, attack, decay and vibrato are felt and controlled through the fingers as much as they are heard. The result is either clarity or a fudging of the notes. Of course, all of this movement depends on the ability of the body of the player to generate the required energy, but also a sustainable amount in the muscles and tendons of the body, dependent on the rate at which oxygen is carried through the bloodstream and around the central nervous system. However, it is a fact that one can overplay or over-practise, sometimes leading to serious physical (if not psychological) injury. Repetitive strain injuries and back disorders (not to mention hearing problems) can plague the guitarist through life. Clearly, if only for the health of the guitarist, some form of guidance is necessary.

Taking a Position on Playing

The work of Fernando Sor can be seen as pioneering, and I see it as alluding to some of the ideas, principles and perspectives discussed above. However, there are more recent works that must also be mentioned in the context of this discussion. For example, *The Guitar Gymnasium* by Robin Hill (2001) is subtitled 'A Mental and Physical Workout, Designed to Develop Flawless Technique'. In his foreword, Hill notes that the book:

> not only deals with the technical aspects of guitar technique, but also with the many psychological factors inherent in the performance of music on the classical guitar. Most of *my* thinking on these matters has been precipitated by the 'front line' experiences of concertizing, recording, broadcasting and teaching. These practical experiences help to focus the mind ... wonderfully for serious thought on the matters in hand.(Hill, 2001:1)

I am reminded again and again (by contact with artists like Robin Hill, who currently teaches guitar at my university) that teaching materials are not meant to be set in stone, but provide the suggested means for getting the job done. Stressing the need for practice, the exercises and studies are those that are said to work for Hill, who is a guitarist at the 'front line' of the musical profession. One learns more about Hill's approach in a section entitled 'Performance and Practice: A Collection of Thoughts' (Hill, 2001:67–74), where his own comments are interspersed with quotes from other master musicians.

Besides the more practically orientated publications offered by teachers and working musicians like Robin Hill, guitar magazines offer monthly teaching columns (with both CD and DVD examples), there are legions of instructional DVDs on every conceivable guitar style, and publications such as the *EGTA Guitar Journal* (European Guitar Teachers' Association, published online at www.egtaguitarforum. org) which delve much more into the theory behind learning and teaching on the guitar. A selection of articles from this journal would include: 'Aspects of Technique' by Gordon Crosskey and 'Left-Hand Technique and the Limits of the

Possible' by Ricardo Iznaola. These more focused attempts at problem-solving are published alongside more general articles, for example, 'What Makes a Musician?' by John Sloboda and a piece critical of ideas about 'perfect technique' calling for increased awareness among guitarists about physical injury due to over-practice (by Dominique Royle, physiotherapist, and Nicola Culf, guitarist).

It is clear that there is a need for the provisioning of an adequate training not just for the performer, but also for the teacher. Such training as presented at the time of writing might also involve the student of the guitar in playing duos or playing in guitar ensembles. Richard Corr's *Guitar Academy* series of tutors is an excellent example of a broad and eclectic approach to guitar pedagogy, drawing on a wide range of guitar styles and techniques.[15] The iconography on the covers of Corr's books also speaks volumes about the serious attitude expected of students in a setting (the tutor with its accompanying CDs) which, in itself, has become something of an establishment (see Figure 6.1). The extent to which a school of guitar teaching can become something of an establishment is also particularly clear in the work of the Guitar Craft organization, founded by Robert Fripp and well documented in Eric Tamm's biography of Fripp (see Tamm, 1990). Guitar Craft is a series of guitar and personal development classes, founded and often presented by Robert Fripp, who is best known for his work with King Crimson. The 'Introduction to Guitar Craft' (2004) describes Guitar Craft as three things:

- A way to develop a relationship with the guitar;
- A way to develop a relationship with music;
- A way to develop a relationship with oneself.[16]

Clearly, the approach adopted in Guitar Craft might be seen to add rich musical, personal and philosophical dimensions to the often problematic and difficult tasks of learning and teaching on the guitar.

Methods for guitar contained in guitar tutors generally include maps of the guitar (note positions on the strings), diagrams of playing positions, scales and arpeggios, exercises and studies. These might be read respectively as: the installation and reading of cognitive maps, spatial orientation exercises, exercises in promoting proprioception, guidance on the most efficient ways of bringing the guitar to the body and how to keep it there, how to move the arms and hands ergonomically when in position, and where to find certain notes. This is the foundation of emplacement. Eventually one learns to feels one's way around the instrument whilst emplaced, one sees and hears the connection between note position and sound produced, one begins to touch the guitar in several distinct ways, locating timbral and textural effects, loud points and soft points, moving fingers, nails or plectra in certain directions. To my mind, with hindsight, Fernando

---

[15] See Richard Corr's website at: www.guitaracademy .co.uk. See also www. thewholeguitarist.com.

[16] www.guitarcraft.com/home.

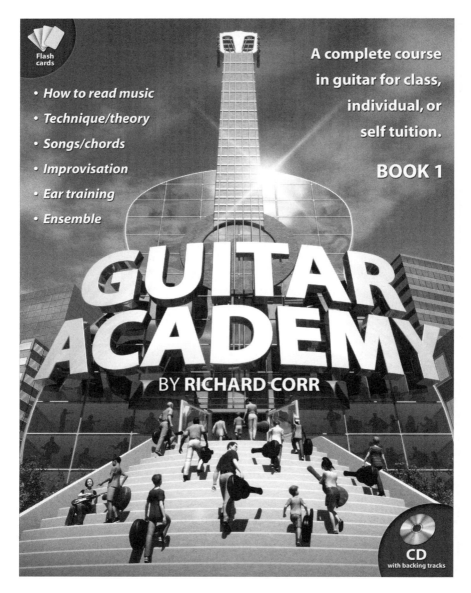

Figure 6.1   Cover of *Guitar Academy*, Book 1

Sor's *Method for the Spanish Guitar* (1832) as translated by Brian Jeffery (1995) might be seen as an early model of emplacement on the guitar (not that it is very likely that Sor had such a concept in mind).

   Yet Sor's method has sections on the following topics: the instrument, position of the instrument, right hand, left hand, the manner of setting the strings in

Figure 6.2   Guitar Craft: Orchestra of Crafty Guitarists, Barcelona, 27 February 2009[17]

vibration, quality of tone, knowledge of the fingerboard, fingering on the length of the string, use of the fingers of the right hand, fingering with both hands and the elbow, proceeding to problems of fingering for different intervals, harmonic effects and accompaniment. The obvious practical value of the layout of this method reflects a kind of cockpit model. What is striking about Sor's layout and analysis is the amount of detail surrounding his discussion of touch, pressure, movement, an awareness of the body, and the body's capabilities and limitations. He writes as both aesthetician and physical anthropologist. One can detect the cultural basis of this work, as questions of taste in relation to the values of his time surround Sor's recommendation of how to produce notes and tones, getting the 'best' sounds from his guitar. Unlike Sor's guitars (Lacote, Alonzo, Martinez), modern guitars now come in all shapes and sizes, generally have a wider range of sounds, are more responsive, project better, and are perhaps easier to play. But Sor's appreciation of both the sensuous materiality of the guitar, from how it should be held and touched to what kind of tone makes for 'good' music, is as clear as his tackling of the problem of orientating the body to the guitar or, rather, how one most efficiently might musically emplace oneself to the instrument(s) at hand. Slash's comments below not only bring me back to the subjects of feel, touch and emotional exegesis, but also point to some of the potential psychological benefits of the guitar experience. His personal reflections are telling:

> Practicing for hours wherever I found myself was liberating. Playing became a trance that soothed my soul: with my hands occupied and my mind engaged, I found peace. Once I got into a band, I found that the physical exertion of playing a show became my primary personal release; when I'm playing onstage I'm more at home in my own skin than at any other time in my life. There is a subconscious, emotional level that informs playing, and since I'm the kind of person who carries his baggage around internally, nothing has ever helped me tap into my feelings more. (Slash, 2007:38)

The company First Act sells portable acoustic and electric guitars (among other instruments) aimed at children. The blurb on the box of the instruments extols the 'powerful benefits of music' and states that 'music inspires learning'. To my mind, the way First Act develops the case for the benefits of learning a musical instrument is highly impressive, involving a quite detailed summary of what an instrument like a guitar can do for a child's 'intellectual development', emotional development', 'physical development' and 'social interaction' (www.FirstAct.com). These are grand claims not unconnected to Slash's testimonial above. I also note that both Slash and his wife are active on behalf of various equal rights causes.[18] The subject of equal rights is certainly one of the themes of my next chapter.

---

[17]   See http://www.dgmlive.com/diaries.htm?entry13749.

[18]   www.youtube.com: 'Slash & Perla on Pop 8'. See also, as a tangential reference, Schwartz, 1988.

Chapter 7
Gender and Sexuality in the New Guitarscape

I think of *La Guitara* as documenting a transition from woman guitarist as a unique and strange fruit to woman guitarist as an ever present contributor to the musical landscape of today. (Patty Larkin, personal communication)

I'm totally out now, and consider myself a guitarist/singer/songwriter who just so happens to be gay. (Carlyn Hutchins, interviewed in Gay Guitarists Worldwide at roberturban.com)

I am a transsexual and everyone usually figures that out sooner or later at the shows, I don't exactly hide it and am rather proud of who I am and how far I've come. (Tempest, bass player, harshreality.us/press.htm)

Women guitarists as ever-present contributors to the guitarscape, gay guitarists who are 'out' (or openly gay) and transsexuals respected for their bass playing? Is this but a minority of people expressing their right to be, or is it, in fact, a reflection of a wider, near-utopian reality now shaping up as reflected in the new guitarscape? Moreover, does this mean that the guitarscape is in some respects liberating? That would certainly add to the distinctiveness and newness of the guitarscape under study in this book. As noted later, the subject of 'girls with guitars' and question 'Can girls play guitar?' has garnered a great deal of debate, procrastination and, it has to said, puerile commentary for some time. Yet KT Tunstall and Avril Lavigne, as well as openly gay guitarists like Kaki King, are among many high-profile mainstream and alternative rock and pop women guitar players who have discussed their guitar playing in interviews in the popular press, revealing just how fundamental the instrument is to their differing approaches to song-writing, instrumental composition and performance (see, for example, Gannon, 2007; Pepper Rodgers, 2009).

The evidence suggests that talk about women and the guitar is not a localized, underground movement confined to a minority of artists (at the time of writing), such as Patty Larkin, Carlyn Evans or Tempest. But, of course, the Internet (despite its critics and detractors as noted in Chapter 5) now provides the means by which all of these artists can promote themselves to as broad a constituency as it will allow. It is also true to say that the subjects of women and gay people playing the guitar are under enquiry as, perhaps, never before. Not that women or gay guitarists have been totally left out of the world of the guitar or writing about it in the past (as noted below). But it is now clear and observable (particularly on the Internet) that both women and men are active in seeking out fellow guitarists regardless of their gender or sexual orientation (if known). For example, I observed a posting on acousticguitarclub.ring.com requesting information on female guitar players, that is, for the purpose of creating a long list of such individuals for general consideration. The section opens with the following call for contributions:

> Just wondering – who are your favorite female guitarists? Could be any genre or era ... famous or not so much ... It's fun for me to hear about my fellow ladies and to learn about new artists or ones I've never been exposed to – and they make great stories to inspire my students with.[1]

The many replies in response to this request included new names to add to the list each and every time. The list of women guitarists whose names are recorded on the web page began to grow exponentially. One of the responses to the call for contributions was from the Berklee College of Music guitar instructor Jane Miller, who commented:

> Great list going so far. On behalf of my colleagues at Berklee College of Music in Boston, I'd like to turn you on to the five female members of the Guitar Department Faculty (in alphabetical order): Abby Aronson, Sheryl Bailey, Jane Miller, Lauren Passarelli, and Robin Stone. We've got some great female students there these days, too. May the list grow ever longer.[2]

Of course, this is but one example where one can find mention of women guitarists on the Internet, and readers of this book would do well to conduct their own searches before reading on. But there was one name that continually appeared in the lists of women guitar players that I could find: Jennifer Batten. At a recent multimedia guitar concert and demonstration in York, England (15 March 2009, see also Chapter 4), I had the opportunity to watch and listen to Jennifer Batten perform. She is one of the foremost guitar virtuosi in the world and a former instructor at the Guitar Institute of Technology (Musicians Institute) in Los Angeles. Batten provided what seemed to me like a well-balanced show, playing several tracks from her latest album against the backdrop of especially collected video footage, as well as offering a detailed introduction to her guitar rig (Washburn J2100 guitar and Digitech RP1000 effects pedalboard, in particular) and playing techniques.[3]

---

[1]   Leanne Regalla, contributor to acousticguitarclub.ring.com/forum/topic, 'Ladies in Guitar', 20 February 2009.

[2]   Jane Miller, contributor to acousticguitarclub.ring.com/forum/topic, 'Ladies in Guitar', 20 February 2009.

[3]   Jennifer Batten, *Whatever*, CD and DVD, Lion Music LMC235 (2008).

Yet only a handful of the approximately seventy people who attended her concert made their way to the guitar shop across the road for a post-concert meet and greet. I must say that I was rather taken aback by this small turnout, given her high-profile work with such acclaimed musical luminaries as the late Michael Jackson and also Jeff Beck. However, it did give me and five or six teenage boys (aged roughly between sixteen and nineteen) the chance to meet this guitar heroine at close quarters, and to ask her some questions. The standard questions about Batten's career flowed, ones which she had obviously been asked several times before by professional journalists and star-struck onlookers: What is Michael Jackson like? Did you teach at the Guitar Institute in Los Angeles? Was Paul Gilbert one of your pupils?

But suddenly one of the youths made what was, to my mind, an extremely courageous comment: 'Why do you talk about Michael Jackson and Jeff Beck, Jennifer? We want to hear about *you*.' Batten proceeded to tell us of some of the difficulties for guitarists trying to hold a career together at a time of financial crisis whilst also, in her case, travelling alone and transporting all of her equipment herself. I mentioned to her that I had heard about the *La Guitara* CD project (as discussed below) on which she features, and her recent tour with Vicki Genfan. 'You guys seem to know more about my career than I do' was her reply. Moving on from my question about her work with Patty Larkin (*La Guitara*) and Vicki Genfan, I took the chance to ask her if she thought attitudes to girls playing the guitar had changed: Was this still a major problem? She did not get the chance to answer me. A tall Chinese man, who looked as though he might well be a student at the University of York, interjected: 'It wasn't a problem until you mentioned it!' 'Bravo!'" I said, 'In this instance, I think you are probably right', I thought. Perhaps I was the eager researcher almost too willing to put words into the mouth of my informant? However, just as this exchange in the music shop was not simple, so the subject of women guitarists is connected to a much wider world than that of the world of the guitar. The problems for women guitarists are really just not as simple as forgetting that they are women. In fact, as a guitarist – whether male or female – one is seldom allowed to forget that in the world of the guitar (among other worlds) gender and biology seem to matter greatly, as the following quote demonstrates: 'Armed with a wry sense of humor, an irrepressible spirit, and impeccable chops, Jennifer Batten is an oestrogen-powered supernova in the cluttered firmament of modern rock guitarists'.[4] I note too, the way in which Avril Lavigne is described as someone only just able to carry the weight of a guitar: 'She weighs less than seven stone and looks pushed to bear the weight of the guitar slung around her neck' (Gannon, 2007:13). Is this an astute observation, a sexist or condescending remark or a comment not to be taken too seriously? Given the comments noted above, one might question whether attitudes to women playing the guitar (stereotypical responses, sexist or condescending remarks) have changed at all, quite apart from

---

[4]   *The Monitor*, Peavey Electronics Corporation (1995–6):5, article on www.jenniferbatten.com.

gay and transgender or transsexual individuals taking up the instrument, despite claims to the contrary by some of those involved.

Theoretical Framework

Fortunately, keeping apace with changes in culture and society, if not intimately tied up with those changes, have been a growing number of wide-ranging academic studies, representative of multifaceted research into the subjects of gender and sexuality (or sexual orientation) in music. Quite a large collection of serious academic literature now engages with issues surrounding the politics of gender and the ways in which sexuality is expressed in music, around music or not in music in the lives of composers, performers and audiences. Several publications have been fundamental to my own understanding of gender and sexuality as expressed in the new guitarscape, and among a long list of publications I have found the following books particularly invaluable: *Queering the Pitch: The New Gay and Lesbian Musicology* (edited by Brett, Wood and Thomas, 1994), *Women and Popular Music: Sexuality, Identity and Subjectivity* (edited by Whiteley, 2000) and *Gender in the Music Industry: Rock Discourse and Girl Power* (Leonard, 2007).[5] In terms of my own research, these books, among others, have been crucial to my own appreciation of the predicament of women and gay musicians, and instructive in terms of guiding approaches that could usefully be adopted.

The key terms emerging from this relatively recent literature (surprisingly so, given the importance and fundamental nature of its subject matter) include 'identity', 'subjectivity' and 'power'. It is my intention here to focus on a critical evaluation of these terms, interrogating what they might mean in the context of a study of gender and sexuality in the new guitarscape, in the light of a range of evidence. It would be, of course, very difficult to do this without including an overview of the literature that, to my mind, usefully connects up issues of gender, sexuality and the guitar.

Because this chapter discusses gender and sexuality, it deals with fundamental issues relating to an individual's core identity, feelings and anxieties, constructs and concerns at the very heart of their lives as people first and as guitarists second. However, beyond the huge collection of writing on white male heterosexual guitarists, there has been limited serious attention given to the subject of women and the guitar. This seems an appropriate, if not ideal, place to start, then. Unfortunately, it is *not* exactly an ideal place to start, for the reason that most of the men, women, gay and transgender or transsexual guitarists I have corresponded with during the writing of this book desire to be known for their guitar playing or their musicianship, rather than for their gender, sex (male or female) or sexual orientation.

---

[5] For further fascinating material and important perspectives not discussed in detail here, see also MacAuslan and Aspen, 1997; Blau DuPlessis, 2006.

'Women and the Guitar'

The above-mentioned academic texts drew my attention to the fact that it was completely necessary to make my discussion in this chapter as broad as possible, by which I mean a discussion that proceeded without prioritizing men over women or women over men, or one gender over the other, but not forgetting to attend to the subject of sexuality or sexual orientation either. Moreover, 2009 was clearly not the time to still be writing a whole chapter on 'Women and the Guitar', at least not in a book on the new guitarscape, as not only had such chapters already been written (and written well), but such a chapter in the framework of this book might now be seen to ghettoize the work of one group of individuals unnecessarily. And, moreover, the subject of hegemony is never far away in a discussion of gender and sexuality in the new guitarscape. A model of hegemony demands a discussion of the perspectives and ideas of both dominant and not so dominant groups.

I have, however, tried to attend to Patty Larkin's view that 'Rather than marginalizing women guitar players or creating a circus oddity, our goal is to expose some of the most prodigious guitar talent that happens to also be female' (http://pattylarkin.com/laguitara/proect.html) – and, one might add for the purposes of this chapter, guitar talent that happens to be gay, bisexual, transgender or transsexual. Kaki King, a virtuoso multi-instrumentalist singer-songwriter, states, 'Ultimately, I'd rather be known as like, "Oh yeah, that sounds like Kaki King", rather than "Oh, she's pretty good for a girl".[6] Nowadays people are like, "Oh, she's a musician, and she plays guitar." There are less "guitar police" coming to my shows.'[7] Transsexual bass player Tempest also comments:

> I get to use music to bridge a gap ... If you can show them that this is your life and its not a put on, its not a gimmick and you command respect by being proficient on your instrument and your stage show then you can show them that life really can be different and yet [you] belong just like everyone else. (Tempest, harshreality.us/press.htm)

But I also keep in mind Alanis Morissette's comment: 'Even if the covers of a million magazines say "Women in Rock" or "New Women artists", at the end of the day I have to believe that most people are buying a record because they want to listen to it, and they forget about the gender as soon as they've put it in the CD player. I've always believed that it's "the best person for the job"' (White, quoted in Carson, Lewis and Shaw, 2004:44). The views expressed by Larkin, King, Tempest and Morissette resonate throughout most of this chapter, and are picked up and elaborated upon by a range of other guitarists.

---

[6]   'Kaki King's Dream World', Blast – The Online Magazine (2008): blastmagazine. com/2008/04/kaki-kings-dream-world/.

[7]   www.gibson.com/en-us/Lifestyle/Features/kaki-ki (page 3 of 3).

Moreover, two recent letters (written by male readers) to *Guitar Player* magazine show that readers as well as editors are not only engaging with the fact that there are now very many skilled women guitar players in the spotlight, but are also contesting the terms of reference by which women are represented in readers' polls (a high-profile phenomenon in the guitar world and one that guitarists pretend that they do not take seriously). The first letter contests the 'Best Female Guitarist' category, as follows: 'Sharon Isbin won an award without necessitating a separate category for women. Let's recognize the great women guitar players (of which there are many) based on merit' (Feedback, *Guitar Player* (July 2009):12).

There is also, obviously, a need for some care in the use of the terms 'female' and 'woman' when categorizing and judging an artist's work. The second letter takes the critique to a new level and points in the direction of some of the more fundamental issues surrounding the subject of gender and sexuality in the new guitarscape, as well as such profound concepts as self and society, nature and culture:

> Jennifer Batten gets the 'nod' for 'Best Female Guitarist'. 'Female' is an affirmative-action category, not a musical genre. Going down this road requires 'Best Asian/Pacific Islander Guitarist, 'Best White Guitarist', and 'Best African-American Guitarist'. Personally, I don't think about reproductive plumbing when I listen to music, and I suspect I'm not alone. If you're going to have a competition about an artistic endeavour, at least make it about art, not biology. Why do I have the feeling that Jennifer would agree with me? (Feedback, *Guitar Player* (July 2009):12)

Such comments open up a very wide debate and demand further intensive study. That readers of *Guitar Player* should actually write in to the magazine to take issue with its use of categories is one thing. The fact that *Guitar Player* magazine itself is willing to include these letters in its high-profile 'Feedback' section is something else altogether. It is also interesting to note that *The Guitar Player Book* (Molenda, 2007), in celebrating forty years of 'interviews, gear, lessons from the World's most celebrated guitar magazine'. included several contributions by women guitarists and journalists. Interviews with Jennifer Batten, Ani DiFranco, Kaki King, June Millington, Bonnie Raitt, Allison Robertson and Nancy Wilson are included among a total of ninety-six featured guitarists. Despite the small numbers, it has to be said that the women guitarists featured are in good company, the remaining forty-nine interview slots taken by men as varied in their guitar styles as Chet Atkins, Dimebag Darrell, Leo Kottke, Vernon Reid and David Torn.

I also note the fact that women are now being included on the cover of serious studies of the guitar, including Richard Chapman's widely accessible *Guitar: Music, History, Players* (2000). On the back cover of Chapman's book one finds a sequence of pictures: the Revd Gary Davis, Eric Clapton, Joni Mitchell and Jimi Hendrix (not only making reference to one woman and three male guitarists, but also acknowledging black and white guitarists). Among the many hundreds of pictures of men playing the guitar, photographs of the following women guitarists feature inside: Joan Baez, the Carter Family (including Maybelle and Sara), Sharon Isbin, Joni Mitchell, Mary Osborne, Ida Presti, Bonnie Raitt, Sister Rosetta Tharpe and Suzanne Vega. Chapman's book is refreshingly broad in scope, especially in its coverage of 'Latin and World', but is also honest in terms of its limitations. It is clear, from this and several other more recent publications (some mentioned below) that there are a number of women guitarists whose names have generally been accepted into the pantheon of guitar greats.

Ralph Gibson's book of photographs *State of the Axe: Guitar Masters in Photographs and Words* (2008) features eighty-one guitarists, including seven women, and contains representation of musicians (men and women) from a range of ethnic backgrounds. The women guitar players featured are Badi Assad, Sheryl Bailey, Amanda Monaco, Mary Halvorson, Michelle Webb, Ava Mendoza and Leni Stern. Clearly, even in Gibson's enlightened tome, women are in the minority. Not that I am suggesting that this is intentional on the part of Gibson or his publisher – yet again, at least women guitar players are included. But Chapman and Gibson among others, as well as their editors, have tried to cope with a major problem: if the women guitarists featured are not very well known (or do not provide role models for their mostly male readership), how can they possibly justify to a publishing executive committee that their book has selling potential? The 'great masters' of the rock guitar (mostly men) do have great selling power, and they tend to be repeatedly and dutifully rolled out and displayed. This represents less of a risk in terms of investment. Not that the iconic presence of the male rock guitar gods in the new guitarscape is any less important – it is crucial – than any other contribution. But this certainly represents a challenge that anyone writing a guitar-based book until very recently has had to face.

The challenge of including more material on women in a guitar-based book is very clearly taken up by André Millard in his edited collection *The Electric Guitar: A History of an American Icon* (2004). Millard includes many references to women electric guitar players in this book, and devotes a whole chapter to 'Women Guitarists: Gender Issues in Alternative Rock', written by John Strohm. The useful historical survey of women and the electric guitar (late 1970s–1990s) provided by Strohm recalls the often high-profile involvement of women electric guitarists in a range of genres (or subgenres) throughout what is a significant period in the history of popular music. That is, from punk to 1980s metal, indie and riot girl (riot grrrl), telling a story of rebellion and the hope of breaking down of barriers that has involved the musical talents of, among many others, Suzi Quatro, Joan Jett, Lita Ford, Jennifer Batten and Juliana Hatfield (see Strohm, 2004). Whilst Strohm's chapter on 'Women Guitarists' includes an overview of the work of women electric guitarists, it was preceeded, much earlier, by Charlotte Ackerley's article 'Women and Guitar' (1978) and then by Mavis Bayton's chapter 'Women and the Electric Guitar' (1997). Each of these, although dealing with a broadly similar range of musical genres, provides a different approach to issues noted (with nearly a twenty-year gap between Ackerley's and Bayton's publications).

Charles McGovern, in his chapter in Millard's collection *The Electric Guitar* discussed not only the multicultural nature of guitar playing in North America in the early part of the twentieth century, but also the highly significant role played by women as performers on the guitar, in factories making guitars and in the advertising and promotion of the guitar. McGovern notes: 'Women have been involved in the electric guitar's history from the first, although their roles have been overlooked' (McGovern, 2004:24). He mentions a long list of electric guitar luminaries in the discussion that follows, including Martha Carson, Mary Deloatch, Mary Ford, Memphis Minnie, Mary Osborne and Sister Rosetta Tharpe. Moreover, McGovern devotes one whole page of the book to a picture portrait of Cordell Jackson (the first such picture in the book among a small, but refreshing, selection) with the caption: 'Cordell Jackson was an early exponent of the electric guitar. She faced opposition from men because of her unrestrained playing' (McGovern, 2004:25). Arguably, some of these women have been more overlooked than others. However, McGovern's useful overview breaks new ground in a specialist guitar book designed for the general reader, whereas Bayton's highly academic analysis of girls playing guitars in largely guitar-based bands, based on interviews, begins to extend the academic terms of reference by which the guitar might be studied.

Guitarists, Gender and the Music Industry

> I think that women guitarists face some of the same challenges that many women in the world face at the workplace. It takes determination to go against the norm, and even once the desired skills are mastered, it takes focus and total belief in yourself to not let the naysayers detract you from achieving your goals. (Patty Larkin, personal communication)

Mavis Bayton's ethnographically based study of women guitar players revolves around themes also found central to her study of girl bands in *Frock Rock* (1998), wherein she presents evidence for a set of interrelated material constraints upon women making popular music. These constraints upon women can be summed up as follows: lack of money, equipment, transport, and private space; exclusion from public space; parental restrictions; constraints imposed by boyfriends and husbands; and exclusion by male musicians. Using similar interview techniques, Reddington (2007) also identifies a range of problems experienced by women punk musicians, but also how these were overcome, whereas Leonard (2007), who also draws on ethnographic techniques, is able to identify ways in which women may now be able to achieve their musical goals by adopting a DIY approach to online and offline promotion, among other avenues of career progression. I note also the comments made by the North American guitarist and singer-songwriter Patty Larkin on problems experienced by women musicians and on changing attitudes:

I think young girls in last half of the twentieth century in this country were shuffled towards the piano as an offshoot of Victorian parlour music. The odd thing is that there is a history of young women playing parlour guitar in the 1800s in America. Rock'n'roll changed the format, and along the way guitar was considered a sensual (read sexual) tool (sorry) that became an iconic symbol for young males. I always say that in order to play rock, your parents have to allow you to play LOUDLY and badly for long hours at a time. We're now seeing moms and dads who give their young daughters permission to do just that. It's not seen as unladylike, but as socially acceptable. (Patty Larkin, personal communication)

On her website devoted to both the promotion of her own solo work as well as that of her *La Guitara* CD of women guitarists, Patty Larkin notes, in a similar vein:

I have been asked repeatedly, 'Why are there no great female guitar players?' The answer is: there are. Demographics are changing as young girls and women take up the instrument with increasing dedication and commitment to technique and repertoire. It is my belief that women guitarists of the past played a part in the evolution of the instrument and that their story is largely untold. I also believe that there are women guitarists today who are actively changing our preconceptions about gender and guitar heroes. (Patty Larkin, http://www.myspace.com/laguitaramusic)

In relation to Patty Larkin's comment about guitar heroes, one of my questions to Robert Urban was: 'Who are the guitarists that LGBT admire, follow and aspire to be like'? His reply was as follows:

Talent and appreciation of talent is a universal. I think LGBT players worship the same guitar-gods that hetero players worship. I actually ask the same question in all my interviews of LGBT players – and I can testify that the great guitarists of classic rock are appreciated by all.

But as with any social sub-group, we have our special favorite guitarists who are gay – lesbian – transgender or bisexual. They speak to us in a special kindred way – perhaps because they are openly 'out' about themselves – which, if they are also singer/songwriters, is revealed in their song lyrics. They often headline at our huge LGBT PRIDE festivals – which are held annually in every major city around the world. (Robert Urban, personal communication)[8]

I consider it vital here to also make reference to an interview given by Kaki King in *Lesbian and Gay Times*. Here she draws on her own experiences of trying

---

[8]   See the following Robert Urban web links: http://www.roberturban.com/reviewsbyru.html; http://www.roberturban.com/gayguitaristsworldwide.html; http://www.roberturban.com/urbanprodliveconcertsindex.html.

to break into the music industry. King shows that as a young lesbian musician she was able to find her own unique route to a career in music:

> *Gay and Lesbian Times*: Your song 'Kewpie Station' was included on the various artists compilation *La Guitara: Gender Bending Strings* that Patty Larkin did. In addition to you and Larkin, there are other out female guitar players on the disc including Sharon Isbin and Mimi Fox. What do you think it is about guitars and lesbians?

> *Kaki King*: I think that anytime that women are breaking into a man's world, and guitar is certainly an instrument of machismo, it's typically lesbians that go first. If you're a guy, a young man, and you're a total geek and obsessed over car engines or computers, you're just normal. 'Oh, yeah, that's his thing. He holes up in his attic all day playing with his model trains,' or whatever it is, and that's fine. If a woman does that, it's perceived as being very odd. We're encouraged to be dilettantes, to be very social and have a normal group of friends and this or that. I think it's discouraged or frowned upon for women to ensconce themselves in something and ignore the rest of the world. If you're going to play music at a very high level, that's something that you're going to have to do. I think that maybe being different early on, if you're a lesbian or if you don't really fit in, it makes that an easier way to enable yourself to do that. It's a theory. There are obviously lots of very talented straight women out there, but I do find that that seems to be one of the reasons that women don't typically reach a more advanced level on their instruments than men, because it involves a lot of things that women aren't encouraged to do. (Shapiro, 2006)

Out of a range of literature that might have been included here, it is also necessary to mention the publication *Girls Rock! Fifty Years of Women Making Music* (Carson, Lewis and Shaw, 2004), which also draws heavily upon interview material, that is, interviews in the popular press and media, and those conducted by the authors. Chapter 1, 'Girls with Guitars', revisits many of the problems posed by Bayton in her 1998 study. Not focusing exclusively on women guitarists, the book expands on some of Bayton's themes by reference to work of a wide range of artists, including gay and lesbian musicians, some musicians well known and others who are, or were, less well known. A further important point can be gained from the work of all the girl band studies mentioned above: all of them mention musicians who are essentially amateur and semi-professional, as much as those who are budding professionals or professional already. The authors of *Girls Rock!*, Mina Carson, Tisa Lewis and Susan M. Shaw, include the work of women musicians from a wide range of genres, including riot girl (riot grrrl) and queercore artists. It is clear to see how notions and issues of gender and sexuality are negotiated and contested in the largely guitar-based music discussed, with examples ranging from Carole Kaye to the Indigo Girls, lead guitarists, bassists and singer-songwriters whose relationship to the guitar and to the music industry is explored in some detail.

However, as noted already, Charlotte Ackerley identified a range of problems for women guitarists back in 1978, at a time when there were even fewer well-known women guitar players besides such big names as Joni Mitchell and Bonnie Raitt. At that time, in response to the question 'Many female musicians express so much frustration regarding their difficulties in breaking into the music business. Have you run into this?' Bonnie Raitt replied:

> It's a terrible problem. You know it's hard for guys to break in too. There are just too many musicians around – especially guitarists. It could get easier if there were more women instrumentalists just sort of sprinkled around in more bands – and I don't mean the all-girl band situation, which is often exploited for it's own sake. I was lucky. I played the guitar, which seemed like a gimmick, and one of the reasons I got where I am is because I was cheap. When you hired me as an opening act, you didn't have to hire a whole band, you just hired me. I carried my own guitar, I did a little blues and some ballads, and I didn't threaten the male act on the bill.[9]

Clearly, since 1977 and Bonnie Raitt's comments as noted above, there has been much research into how the contest and negotiation of gender and sexuality (ranging from democratic debate to harassment and violence) actually affect the progress of musicians within the music industry, and some of the obstacles to progression are mentioned above. And by 'music industry', of course, I do not simply mean the recording industry but the wider commercial world involving the performance, marketing, promotion and dissemination of music, especially popular music (see Frith, 2001). Jennifer Batten's more recent comments demonstrate that, even with greater promotional resources and recording facilities available to musicians of all genders and sexual orientations, it would still seem prudent to not make too many assumptions about the greater presence of women playing the guitar, as if what are clearly signs of a slow revolution had suddenly toppled the status quo. Nor is it wise, I think, to assume that a well-established and secure role is now to be had for some of the better-known guitar heroines (or is that heroes?). Batten notes:

> The guitar god thing always reminds me of Saturday morning cartoons. It's nice to be recognized but I don't take it too seriously. I'm just trying to grow and keep myself inspired with new adventures in music. The industry is so male dominated. I'm not sure how far my acceptance has penetrated. Careers are always pretty fickle in music. I'm just glad to have made a living in it for a few decades. Having circumvented planet earth so many times, and seeing how

---

[9] 'Flashback', from interview with Patricia Brody, May 1977, *Guitar Player* (April 2009):160.

others live, you realize what a blessing it is to play for a living! (Jennifer Batten, www.6 stringheaven.com)

Even with several women players now widely known, including Jennifer Batten from the 1980s onwards to Kaki King in the 2000s, and the fairly high-profile work of blues musicians such as Joanne Shaw Taylor, Dani Wilde and Sue Foley, Michael Molenda (editor of *Guitar Player* magazine), in an interview for www.theworld, reportedly finds the situation of women guitarists still precarious:

> He says the players are there, it's just that they're not that well known. Molenda: 'It's that thing about breaking thru, kind of that cultural barrier where they sell tons of records and become like The Darkness or The Killers or whatever, that's been really hard, and we're absolutely looking for a time when it doesn't matter whether it's a female guitarist or a male guitarist, that the player is simply rated simply on how good they are, how they make you feel, and whether their tone or their notes just kind of send you all dizzy.' That's the scorching playing of Jennifer Batten – Michael Jackson's guitarist on his *Bad* tour, no less. (http://www.theworld.org/?q=node/151)

Yet in *Gender in the Music Industry* Marion Leonard shows how notions of gender and the potential for empowerment for all effect the workings of a rapidly changing music industry, a situation that the author has been able to monitor in a day-to-day study of the progress of female bands (Leonard, 2007). Leonard's work suggests that *anybody* going into the music profession is still likely to face enormous challenges, but all who do so may be able to make use of an enormous range of opportunities now available to both men *and* women (Leonard, 2007). She notes, among many other things in a broad-ranging discussion involving eighty-eight women musicians (many of whom are guitarists), the advent of online and offline DIY festival promotion (devoting a chapter to Ladyfest, also mentioned in *Girls Rock*), but also the rise and promotion of riot girl (riot grrrl) bands through the Internet and zines (printed and electronic).

The introductory quotes to this chapter show up something of that DIY ethic, as also discussed by Leonard in her book using different examples. For instance, Patty Larkin's *La Guitara* project (involving recordings of thirteen female guitarists), although signed to a record label, has also been promoted by her relentless schedule of interviews, touring and Internet promotion. Carolyn Hutchins and Tempest are now able to find some form of representation and further promotional opportunities online. Those playing the guitar, presumably as they always have done, include gay, lesbian, transgender and transsexual individuals. Some gay musicians are 'out', some are rumoured to be gay; other musicians are simply not 'out'. My Internet searches for 'girls and guitars' and 'gay guitarists' provided me with a huge range of links, from websites of guitars designed especially for girls

Figure 7.1   Banner of Gay Guitarists Worldwide

(see www.lunaguitars.com, www.daisyguitars.com)[10] to community sites for gay, transgender and transsexual guitarists (www.gayguitaristnetwork.com).

It became clear to me that any study of the guitar must include, but also go well beyond, discussion of the monolithic masculinity that has been said to attend the electric guitar, in particular, since the early inception of the instrument but especially because of its central role in rock music (as noted by Patty Larkin and Kaki King above). Not only is rock now present, to varying degrees, in many forms (for example, punk, riot girl, queercore, emo, indie, nu-metal, space rock, progressive metal, grindcore, symphonic rock, and so on), the meta genre of rock itself represents a specialist niche market (or several markets) and there are many other forms of music that do not depend on male posturing and pyrotechnics commonly (and in many cases, erroneously) associated with the electric guitar. It would appear that, at the very least, a monolithic masculinity approach to the new guitarscape is contested (and is being eroded) by a whole range of different perspectives, interpretations and positions. Moreover, a wealth of academic literature also reveals the highly nuanced and challenged state of notions of masculinity in a contemporary context, in North America and Europe (see, for example, Magrini, 2003; Bannister, 2006; Dawe, 2007) but also well beyond (see, for example; Gilmore, 1990, Magrini, 2003). Given the fact that most high-profile guitar players (especially electric guitarists) have tended to be predominantly male,

---

[10]   See Russell Hall, 'The Gibson Difference', 27 June 2007, http://www.gibson. com/enus/Lifestyle/ProductSpotlight/GearAndInstruments/The%20Gibson%20Differenc e/: 'Marlow cites the female-targeted Gibson Les Pauls, the Goddess and the Vixen, as examples of such "outside the box" thinking. In the tradition of Gibson's '50s space-age guitars – the Flying Vs, the Explorers, and the like – such designs evidence a willingness to take risks with regard to public acceptance.' See also http://www.gibson.com/en-us/ Lifestyle/Features/Electric-Ladyland/'Today's Top Female Guitarists Play Gibsons'.

white, and young – only now are the great rock guitarists of the 1960s–1990s, for example, showing grey hair and wrinkles – it is no surprise that the guitar as object has been read in performance as something amounting to an extension of the player's body, namely the phallus. As Robert Urban notes:

> True – the guitar – along with rocketships, skyscrapers, motorcycles, cigars, etc. – by its very shape and usage – is one of the most powerful phallic symbols of our age. Electric guitarists have tended to be placed on society's masculinity pedestal – I notice how audiences react to rock guitarists – it's quite empowering. It's a thrill be it gay or straight.
>
> Oh yeah … I always seem to notice that when straight guy musicians are asked, 'Why did you learn the guitar'? – the answer is usually 'to get girls!'. Well, in all honesty, my own answer is similar – only with a slight gender change – as a gay pre-teen, it was so hot being in a band with other guys! Even if they were all straight. (Robert Urban, personal communication)

Robert Walser's study of heavy metal (with a focus on the 1980s) showed that things musical are not as simply male dominated as they might first appear to be, or rather, as the rhetoric and hyperbole of performers, the popular press, and various commentators suggest. Even in the highly macho arena of supposedly testosterone-fuelled heavy metal music the boundaries of gender and sexual identity are contested and negotiated (Walser, 1993). Gender-bending, androgyny and the exscription of women are as bound up with playing with fire – part of the performance – as much as they are linked to the musical empowerment of both performers and audiences as commonly accepted (or stereotypical) gender norms are thrown into relief.

Walser interrogates the notion of virtuosity in both classical and heavy metal models where it can be seen as an empowering and engendering practice, and has also been linked to notions of male potency and power throughout history. Virtuosity can be considered to be a display of power where (often) men are in control (empowering for musicians centre-stage as well as audiences), and strut their stuff (rather like a cockerel, thus the term 'cock rock', although one might also assume innuendo). It can articulate a variety of fantasies and musical pleasures. But the prestige value attached to classical music makes the classical model of virtuosity extraordinarily powerful, not just in the classical music world but also when pulled in the world of heavy metal music. Through their virtuosic performance, heavy metal guitarists play not only with notions of gender *but also* with the boundaries that separate classical and popular musical worlds. There are, of course, various ways in which musicians can be seen to 'queer' the norm and, indeed, guitarists may queer the norm without being necessarily gay or bisexual. There are also rumours, for instance, of closeted metal guitarists, perhaps the most macho of all genres. But clearly, there are very serious ethical issues about 'outing' people who may be or may be not 'out'.

Susan Fast argues that it is not just men who are empowered by music made by men. In her book on Led Zeppelin she argues that 'it is empowering for female fans to gaze at male rock stars – that, in fact, they know they exercise control over the way in which rock stars dress and act in order for them to attract women, and also that their gaze on these men offers them an opportunity to explore and express something important about their sexuality' (Fast, 2006:366). The resulting 'highly complex and structured production of desire' as argued by Judith Butler (1990:123) is picked up by Steve Waksman in *Instruments of Desire* (1999). In his discussion of the guitar work of Jimi Hendrix, Waksman notes how the black guitarist remains a powerful and empowering musical figure, not least for reasons well beyond the sound of his guitar and voice (which in themselves are revelatory, path-finding, and remain the object of intense study). During his stage performances, Hendrix's movements with and around the electric guitar can often be seen to very sensual, sexual and literally playing with fire. He turns the guitar into an 'instrument of desire' as a racialized individual, his blackness but also his sexuality is seemingly extended by the guitar which, it has been suggested, takes on the form of a 'technophallus' in the socio-political climate of the late 1960s (Waksman, 1999:188). But the guitar was, seemingly, one minute a phallus, the next minute a woman, then a thing to be ritually doused with lighter fuel and set alight. Hendrix's stage performances show his ability to communicate using both the sound and shape of the guitar, as well as his own body and personality.

It would also be useful here to compare some of the findings noted above, which are based exclusively in North American and European popular music genres, with a less well-known guitar-based context. I turn next to my own research on the guitar in Spain where women take on the form of a guitar more than they take on the role of a guitarist.

The Guitar as Woman

In a Spanish context, fieldwork throughout the 1990s revealed to me just how much guitar making is an engendered occupation. My wife and I did not discover any women guitar makers on our travels, although in some of the workshops in Madrid women took care of enquiries and general matters front-of-shop. The subject of gender came up most forcefully in guitar makers' discussion of the form and temperament of their guitars. The luthier Francisco Manuel Díaz or 'Manolo' from Granada identified the guitar as 'totally feminine' given the shape of the body, with its shoulders, waist, soundhole and bottom, as well as its internal cavities. 'It is almost a woman', he said.[11]

---

[11]   See also a slightly different interpretation from Brazil: 'Anorexia is a disorder almost unheard-of here. Brazilian women have always had a little more flesh, distributed differently to emphasize the bottom over the top, more like the contours of a guitar rather than an hourglass. ... The ideal was what is known as "um corpo de violão," or "guitar-

This identification of the guitar with the body of a woman is a common notion expressed by guitar makers there. This metaphor was developed by José Ramírez III whilst describing his choice of woods for guitar construction: 'I will limit myself to expressing my innermost feelings on the basis of my experience with these two types of wood. I regard both the Picea-Falso Abeto (German Spruce) and the Thuja Plicata (Red Cedar) as two beautiful sisters – one blonde and the other brunette; one European and the other American, although I have to confess that I have a soft spot for the brunette, and by this I do not mean to scorn the blonde' (Ramírez III 1993:17).

After making considerable technical adjustments to his guitars, Gerundino Fernandez of Almeria was to note: 'It not only is still more feminine in looks than the traditional guitar, but has resulted in improved volume and tonal quality' (Gerundino, quoted in Pohren, 1990:208), whilst Manuel Reyes remarked, 'she was a crazy guitar. She used to get very cold, and colder more often than most guitars' (quoted in George 1969:47). Manolo regarded the guitar as 'a spirited woman', 'something alive', and the whole process of guitar making (in the sensual world of the workshop) as a process of giving life and giving birth – from selecting the wood to polishing the completed guitar. David George notes that Manuel Reyes used the term *dar a luz* (to give light, to give birth) to describe this process (George 1969:54). The guitar breathes, as it were, its wood sensitive to temperature and humidity.

In her extensive study of Hispanic folklore and literature Shirley L. Arora notes that 'Hispanic proverbs, riddles and folk verse offer numerous examples of metaphor in which a woman is compared – implicitly or explicitly – to a guitar or vice versa' (Arora 1995:1). Arora draws on a large number of examples to support her thesis. Juan Jara Ortega also makes reference to the guitar in his collection: 'A quien tiene escopeta, guitarra, reloj o mujer, nunca le falta un traste que componer' (He who has a shotgun, a guitar, a watch or a woman will never lack for something to fix), Jara Ortega 1953:105).[12]

Manolo, like other luthiers and *aficionados*, is a poet of the guitar. His poetic language intersects with a long tradition of writings about the guitar by poets such as Lorca, with the language of flamenco lyrics and the anecdotes of Don Pohren and with a range of social and engendered practices, such as the banter between the guitar maker and his friends. Indeed, no opportunities for a jibe or a joke are lost in this predominantly masculine world; a world in which the guitar is usually the only 'woman'.

In the male dominated world of flamenco guitar, it would seem that women have also had a role to play, and not just as singers or dancers. An Internet article

shaped body" ... thicker in the waist, hips and fanny and it was the rest of the world whose taste was questioned' (http://www.styleguru.org/entry/fashion-globalization-hits-brazil-hard/).

[12] See also *Receta para construir una guitarra* (Recipe for Constructing a Guitar) by Luis Lopez Anglada, 1984, in Leal Pinar, 1989:31–2.

which I accessed in 2005 on esflamenco.com reports that 'Guitar-playing is still a male-dominated field. Women are very slowly making some headway'.[13] However, Joaquina Labajo strongly supports the idea that men still dominate the flamenco guitar scene in Spain. She is less optimistic about the role of women as guitar players in the genre at the present time. In fact, she reports the strengthening of the flamenco guitar tradition as a masculine musical practice and views the guitar as a 'discrete witness of power relationships' (Labajo, 2003:76). But Loren Chuse provides a short chapter on 'Women and the Guitarra Flamenca' in her book *The Cantaoras: Music, Gender, and Identity in Flamenco Song* (2003). Historical evidence suggests that the tradition of female guitarists seems to have disappeared around the 1920s and 1930s, that is, with the growing importance of the flamenco guitar as a solo instrument of specialized accompaniment and virtuosity. However, Chuse includes in her discussion an interview with María Albarrán in 1996, whom she calls a 'pioneering gitana guitarist' (Chuse, 2003:212). It does appear to be the case though that women flamenco guitarists are still very much in the minority.[14]

Guitars and Glamour Girls

Women do not always feature in the new guitarscape as musicians, technicians or craftsmen, unlike most of their male counterparts. Take, for instance, a recent article on Gibson.com entitled 'Sexy Guitars'. Artist Jennifer Janesko uses the face of a guitar as a virtual canvas upon which to paint what has been described as her 'striking female images' (www.gibson.com).[15] Described as having been a 'renowned pin-up artist for over 15 years', Janesko works with New Jersey-based GZ Guitars to create one-off instruments with unique finishes, including several Gibson models which now feature 'her alluring airbrushed artwork' (www.gibson.com). The interviewer tries to understand Janesko's motivations more clearly:

> While some might argue that the genre objectifies women, Janesko is forthright about the medium's sexual allure. 'I embrace it,' she says proudly. 'To believe that sensuality exists is empowering.' So much so that Jennifer has occasionally modelled for other artists and photographers herself – including a cheesecake

---

[13] See http://esflamenco.com/scripts/news/ennews.asp?frmIdPagina=331.

[14] The reader might find the following web links useful: http://www.boston.com/news/globe/living/articles/2005/11/04/guitar_goddesses/; http://www.deflamenco.com/especiales/nimes07/index070128i.jsp;http://www.esflamenco.com/scripts/news/ennews.asp?frmIdPagina=331; http://www.boston.com/news/globe/living/articles/2005/11/04/guitar_goddesses/; http://www.deflamenco.com/especiales/nimes07/index070128i.jsp; http://www.esflamenco.com/scripts/news/ennews.asp?frmIdPagina=331.

[15] Jerry McCulley, 'Beautiful Bodies: Pin-Up Artist Jennifer Janesko's Sexy Guitars', 20 January 2009, http://www.gibson.com/en-us/Lifestyle/ProductSpotlight/GearAndInstruments/beautiful-bodies-pin-up/.

photo layout in *Maxim*. 'What's given me validation is that half of my collectors are women or couples,' Janesko explains. 'Women say (my paintings) are beautiful, sensual and passionate.' But guitar players and collectors will probably think her recent creations for GZ just plain *rock*.[16]

Clearly, sections of the guitar manufacturing industry appear to share Jennifer Janesko's views. For example, Gibson guitars and the lingerie chain Agent Provocateur recently premiered their new lines: 'Gibson Guitar, the world's premiere musical instrument maker and leader in music technology, announced its partnership with the luxurious lingerie boutique Agent Provocateur. This exciting partnership is to celebrate the new Gibson Les Paul Goddess an electric guitar designed specifically for women' (http://www.gibson.com/en-us/Lifestyle/Features/GodessRocks/).

Of course, such a partnership not only reflects the reality of the business world, but is a constant reminder of the presumed role of women as not just guitar gods, but as sex goddesses too. One finds women in advertisements in guitar magazines, sometimes as musical glamour models, posing as rock chicks, scantily clad or semi-nude with a range of guitar-related gear, as well as posing (apparently) nude behind guitars (also in 'girlie' guitar calendars). Guitar magazines now also feature mobile phone soft porn wallpapers and videos in their back pages (see, for example, *Total Guitar*, 184, January 2009:153). Leonard also notes that:

> Historically advertisements in these magazines have used images of scantily clad women to connote ideas of sexual attraction, social status and empowerment. This strategy of targeting male readers is still in operation. For example, the front cover of the magazine 2001 *Guitar Buyer's Guide*, published in June 2000, featured women wearing bikinis and high heels standing astride a guitar. (Leonard, 2007:39)

Leonard notes that this also reinforces the image of the guitar magazines as a male preserve, helping to include some individuals, but helping to exclude others. It must also be made clear that although guitar magazines do feature the images discussed, they may not do so each and every month (and may perhaps feature them much less than many other male-orientated or men's magazines). Moreover, guitar magazines also feature women columnists. I note, for instance, the regular teaching column by Rachel Woods in *Guitarist* magazine: see, for example, *Guitarist* (June 2009):167, 178–9). Also featured in this issue is an interview with Ritzy Bryan, female guitarist with The Joy Formidable (*Guitarist* (June 2009):35).

---

[16]   Jerry McCulley, 'Beautiful Bodies: Pin-Up Artist Jennifer Janesko's Sexy Guitars', 20 January 2009, http://www.gibson.com/en-us/Lifestyle/ProductSpotlight/GearAndInstruments/beautiful-bodies-pin-up/.

Critical Review and Evaluation

The reader will have already noted the fact that, in this chapter, I am as much concerned with what has already been written about gender and sexuality in guitar-based or guitar-related literature – and in the way such subjects have been presented – as I am interested in furthering such writing myself. To that end, I believe it would be useful here to try to point to some of the more problematic issues that have arisen, in an effort to evaluate critically the approaches taken and theoretical positions adopted. In providing an overview of a far greater literature on gender and sexuality in popular music than is covered here, Jason Toynbee creates a useful summary of positions on the subject, which helps to throw the above discussion into sharp relief. In relation to the discussion of gender and sexuality in popular music, Toynbee notes that:

> In the first place, there is an argument that popular music represents patriarchal society in microcosm. Guitar-toting men hold the desirable high ground of authentic rock'n'roll and women are either excluded or have to fight their way through against all odds. This critical feminist position can then be contrasted with what one might be described as a redemptive approach. Here the emphasis is on showing how women may, paradoxically, be empowered within existing structure of rock and pop. (Toynbee, in Bennett, Shank and Toynbee, 2006:343)

The reader will see from my discussion so far that I have tried to draw men, women, gay, transgender and transsexual guitarists into my discussion, from a range of genres and cultural contexts. I have been heavily influenced by readings in gender and sexuality that demonstrate the impact of the work of the 'new gay and lesbian musicology' (see Brett, Wood and Thomas, 1994), but also by a broad-ranging discussion of issues and debates relating to music, sexuality, identity and subjectivity contained in the work of Mavis Beyton, Marion Leonard and Sheila Whiteley (among others). I have found Whiteley's edited collection *Sexing the Groove: Popular Music and Gender* (1997) to be of significant help in judging the tenor and pitch of my discussion here as well as reaching a range of other writings through it. Clearly, we do not live in an ideal world, but in a world that is often idealized. It is difficult to remain objective when one is dealing with issues that one knows are close to another person's heart.

A case in point is the CD *La Guitara: Gender Bending Strings* (2005),[17] a collection of performances by women guitarists that epitomizes both the activism among women guitar players and the problems inherent in engaging with the very issues they seek to challenge, change and even eradicate. The album includes performances by Sharon Isbin, Patty Larkin, Memphis Minnie, Mimi Fox, Kaki

---

[17]   La Guitara: Gender Bending Strings: A Collection of Women Guitarists, Vanguard Records 79796-2 (2005).

King, Ellen McIlwaine, Badi Assad, Alex Houghton, Vicki Genfan, Muriel Anderson, Rory Block, Jennifer Batten and Elizabeth Cotton. All of the musicians are of the same gender, and musicians who are openly gay are included. Yet, apart from Badi Assad (Brazil) and Wu Man on *pipa* (China), all the guitarists on *La Guitara* are from North America. Are there any women playing the guitar in the wider world of the guitar? In my correspondence with Kamala Shankar in India, Shankar indicated that she had not experienced any problems in being a woman playing Indian slide guitar professionally as an exponent of Hindustani art music (Kamala Shankar, personal communication). Clearly, the observation of cultural differences enables one to hold up a mirror to one's own cultural predicament, and such a study is yet to be completed in terms of the guitar.

Figure 7.2   Back cover of *La Guitara* CD

Moreover, one imagines the aspiring women flamenco *guitaristas* in parts of Spain positively rejoicing in the *La Guitara* CD, whilst it would perhaps elicit quite a different reaction among some male flamenco guitarists. But, clearly, more in-depth cross-cultural surveys of both men and women guitarists are needed (as well as surveys of lesbian, gay, transgender and transsexual musicians). Such a survey is to some extent going to be provided by Sue Foley's 'Guitar Woman' project, which includes interviews with women guitarists from countries as far apart as

Brazil and Iran.[18] But, clearly, given the great many musical instruments around the world, and the extraordinary range of ideas about musical instruments and about the ways in which they are engendered, one wonders if and where such ideas have found their way into a local interpretation of the meaning of the guitar.[19]

Beyond their obvious collective virtuosity, the women on the *La Guitara* CD represent very different approaches to performance, playing techniques and uses of technology. Steve Waksman reminds me that, even on *La Guitara*, it is the acoustic guitar that predominates (Steve Waksman, personal communication).[20] Out of thirteen women guitarists playing on the album, only three are playing electric guitar (although some of them have mastery over both, as demonstrated elsewhere). The point is that women have always played the acoustic guitar in all its forms, but the electric guitar has presented them with a range of challenges (most of which have been noted above).

However, does *La Guitara* represent a turning point, a record of the current state of the axe, an act of rebellion or a sign of recalcitrance? I have already mentioned the fact that *La Guitara* is a largely North American effort: it represents the social and cultural predicament of eleven women guitarists based in North America and Brazil, not Iran or India or Spain. Yet still the musical-stylistic-ideological basis of the women guitar players' work differs enormously from that of men guitarists, despite what might be interpreted as an *en masse* call for acceptance and emancipation.[21] As noted, a great many concerns are raised in and through the work of the guitarists featured, including feminist and gay issues, but also issues of race and historical accuracy, and electricity and acousticity. Clearly, these concerns contrast with but do not necessarily contradict those held by some of the other women mentioned in this chapter, for example, Jennifer Janesco and her guitars painted with naked women and also Gibson's partnership with the lingerie firm Agent Provocateur, which are essentially business-driven developments. Moreover, *La Guitara* itself walks the fine line between promoting women guitarists on the one hand and selling them (or risking misrepresentation as trying to sell them) as some kind of 'circus oddity' on the other (the very thing

---

[18] http://guitarwoman.com/; http://www.suefoley.com/; http://www.suefoley.com/index.php?option=com_content&task=view&id=13&Itemid=28.

[19] A broad survey of such matters is beyond the scope of this book. But see Veronica Doubleday's extremely useful cross-cultural survey of relationship between musical instruments and gender (Doubleday, 2008).

[20] Women may have been associated with acouctic guitars, but there have also been high-profile women bass guitar players, from Suzi Quatro and Tina Weymouth to Charlotte Cooper and Grog (see McIver, 2008; see also the interview with Grog in *Bass Guitar Magazine*, 37 (July/August 2008): 20–22).

[21] See also the following two links: http://www.guitarplayer.com/article/shredmistress-rynata/Jul-06/21606; http://www.rockrgrl.com/conference/; http://www.girlswithguitars.co.uk/.

the producers want to avoid). But despite the challenges that *La Guitara* represents to both its creators and it audiences, Patty Larkin remains optimistic:

> I think that for all intents and purposes, the guitar revolution has indeed already happened, but I think that the far reaching effects will be a long time coming for many who hold to the belief that only boys/men can really play guitar with any technical proficiency. Ask any thirteen year old boy to name two women guitarists he admires. I think that women like Sharon Isbin, crossed into the male dominated sport of guitar decades ago, and she is considered by aficionados to be a world class musician. It comes down to technique and repertoire. If the girl can play, there's nothing more to say. Does she get the gig? It depends. That is still dependent upon social norms. (Patty Larkin, personal communication)

When I asked Robert Urban if he thought there really was a new guitarscape for LGBT musicians, he threw the question into relief with reference to what one might call the 'bigger picture', to broad changes in attitude, social norms, politics and governance:

> There are more openly-out recording and performing LGBT guitarists and bassists, succeeding, than ever before. My own LGBT guitarists Internet networking group has nearly five hundred LGBT players worldwide. In this 'age of Obama' – it's actually an entirely new 'Landscape' period! It's a very exciting time for LGBT people everywhere – as barriers against our being able to marry, against our being able to serve in the military, against our being able to hold public office, against our being able to be open in the film and television industries, against our being able to be ourselves in all aspects of society – and yes, against our being able to be openly gay AND be in a rock band – finally seem to be falling away.

It seems appropriate to end this chapter on an optimistic note, as directed by my interviewees. The next chapter shows further how notions of power and agency might not only be theorized and tested guitaristically, but also how the influence of many very different individuals has been felt through the guitar. Moreover, although matters of gender and sexuality are fundamental to the new guitarscape, the guitar phenomenon can be seen to be inextricably linked to, caught up in and shaped by a great many causes, concerns and contests, as well as ambitions, aspirations and atrocities.

Chapter 8
The Power and Agency of the Guitar

We were late, and it was all the guitar's fault. (Wendy Harrison, *The Guardian* (10 February 2009):6)[1]

He said, 'Listen, there's something you should know. For our readers, the day *Guitar Player* arrives in their mailbox is a big day in their lives'. (Wheeler, 2007:x)

Then, thankfully, his mind and his glance wandered back to me, La Guitarra, and a warm smile brushed his face, 'And because of her, I was fortunate enough to meet Jorge, Enrique and Maria'. (Cezar, 2005:519)

The ways in which social agency can be invested in things, are exceedingly diverse. (Gell, 1998:18)

When Woody Guthrie wrote and stuck the words THIS MACHINE KILLS FASCISTS onto the front of his guitar he was surely aware of the iconic power of his instrument in performance, which was able to carry messages far and wide, beyond the confines of his native North America to the world at large. Combined with Guthrie's own genius as a singer-songwriter, the guitar and its message became highly significant at a particular time and place. In sound and vision it was a part of a political rallying call for Dust Bowl migrants in North America during the 1930s and 1940s. But it might be said that if the medium is the message, the guitar has delivered many a political address. In this respect, I do not believe that its role has been merely incidental.

Furthermore, the notion that the guitar can be used as a kind of symbolic weapon to help thwart and even overcome oppression is clearly manifest in the concept of the 'guitar as gun' which can be found in the form of a slogan in several cultural contexts, as far apart as South America and sub-Saharan Africa.[2] Victor Jara,

---

[1] In this article Harrison reports on the predicament faced by a mother when taking her children to school, only to find that her ten-year-old son had forgotten his guitar. She and her children went back to collect the guitar, arriving at the school two minutes after nine. But they were spotted by what the mother called the council's 'Late Man'. The normally punctual young boy was horrified as his mother had to give her name to the Late Man. 'But on the upside', says the mother, 'I bet he never forgets his guitar again.'

[2] For more information on the 'guitar as gun' see: http://www.theglobalist.com/DBWeb/printStoryId.aspx?StoryId=3870; http://www.akpress.org/2007/items/guitararmy. See also *The Guitar as Gun: Highlife Music from Ghana*, Stern's Music/Earthworks STEW50CD

for example, who has been described as the brightest light of the *nueva canción* movement in Chile in the 1960s, has been quoted as having said: 'The authentic revolutionary should be behind the guitar, so that the guitar becomes an instrument of struggle, so that it can also shoot like a gun' (Fairley, 1994:572). Jara's hands and wrists were broken during the torture that preceded his death. He was to finally die in a hail of machine-gun bullets that silenced forever the distinctive voice and guitar style of a widely inspirational individual (see Schechter, 1996:436; Jara, 1983:243). Of course, Jara left a powerful legacy to the Chilean people in the form of his songs and his recorded output: his influence lives on.

At certain times, those singer-songwriters and other musicians who have taken up the guitar have believed that it might contribute to a wider social agenda and even to social protest and political activism,[3] particularly, as noted also in the previous chapter, through the work of a range of gay, lesbian, bisexual, transgender and transsexual singer-songwriter guitarists, from Ani DiFranco to the Indigo Girls. The 'Buck Owens American' red, white and blue guitar also springs to mind at this point as an object carrying a political message. It was a guitar which Owens as a patriot had made during the Vietnam War.[4]

Guitars continue to be seen as fitting musical vehicles for the expression of political affiliations and allegiances. Although it is not just the instrument alone that is responsible for the impact of the music of a Guthrie, Jara or Owens, it continues to play a prominent role in what one might call the ensemble power of music. The messages left by Woody Guthrie and Victor Jarà, in particular, live on, the guitar acquiring from them, but also from many other thousands of high-

---

(2003). The album was recorded, produced and compiled by John Collins. The cover features a Ghanaian soldier sitting to play an electric guitar with a rifle on his back. See Turino, 2000 for a discussion of guitar traditions in Zimbabwe and political resistance in *chimurenga*. See also Eyre, 2003. See the picture of the US Marine carrying his guitar and gun at Khe Sanh, Vietnam, in 1968 in Kingsbury and Nash, 2006:262, and similarly the Sandanistas pictured in *World Music: The Rough Guide*, vol. 2:368 (Broughton et al., 2000). As quoted in Wong (2003:135), the Vietnamese musician Pham Duy recalls: 'a gun in one hand and a guitar in the other, I went to war with songs as my weapon'. Examples of gun-shaped guitars include the Johnson Machine Gun Guitar and the Hondo Tommy M16. Pictures of these guitars are to be found in *Guitar and Bass Magazine*, 19/ 2 (February 2008):98 (as well as the Internet, of course). In his chapter on the MC5, Steve Waksman includes a picture of the guitarist Wayne Kramer 'in revolutionary pose, facing the American flag with guitar and rifle on his back' (Waksman, 1999:218). Waksman's discussion fully situates the MC5's musical guerrilla tactics in a complex political milieu, which can be seen to have had a radical effect on its approach to performance, song-writing, guitar playing and use of technology.

   [3]   In terms of social activism, see 'Jail Guitar Doors: Rehabilitating Prisoners through Music', www.jailguitardoors.org.uk; donated guitars for the New Orleans Musician Relief Fund, http://blog.nola.com/chrisrose/2008/07/jammin_generosity_of_two_famil.html; 'No Strings Attached Donates Guitars to "Needy Kinds"', http://news.bostonherald.com/news/regional/genral/view.bg?articleid=1072322%srv.

   [4]   There is a clear picture of this guitar in Kingsbury and Nash, 2006:264.

profile figures, an empowering legacy with historical, social, cultural, political and economic dimensions.

The guitar now delivers its messages well beyond the confines of the concert stage or the CD player, even if such outlets remain prime locations for its musical performance. More than just a sound-box yet sonically crucial to the contemporary musical landscape, the guitar continues as an affecting presence in the lives of those people who possess or do not possess knowledge of it. In the previous chapters I have already noted the wide variety of contexts in which one can find writing about the guitar. Here I feature the six news items which I believe illustrate further the points above. The first example is from the *Gulf Times*:

'Tsunami guitar' sold to Doha-based donor

Canadian rock star Bryan Adams said he was extremely pleased to associate with the 'Reach out to Asia' humanitarian initiative launched by Qatar to help the underprivileged and disadvantaged across Asia. 'H.E. Sheikha Mayassa invited me to Qatar and I consider it a great privilege to take part in the charity drive,' said Adams who began the 'tsunami guitar' project shortly after tragedy struck several Asian countries in December 2004. Speaking to reporters here yesterday soon after his arrival from London, Adams said he would display at the charity dinner the guitar signed by legends from the world of music. They include Mick Jagger, Keith Richards, Eric Clapton, Brian May, Jimmy Page, David Gilmour, Jeff Beck, Pete Townshend, Mark Knopfler, Ray Davis, Liam Gallagher, Ronnie Wood, Tony Iommi, Angus and Malcolm Young from AC/DC, Paul McCartney, Sting, Ritchie Blackmore and Def Leppard. The guitar has already been sold to a Doha-based philanthropist, he revealed. Proceeds from the sale of the guitar would be used to build a new school in Thailand, one of the countries affected by the tsunami last December.[5]

For Blair at 50, Salutations (Sweet and Sour)

[Mr Blair] was too old to keep posing for pictures with his guitar. Newspapers all week have run old photographs of him at Oxford ... In one picture, he sat

---

[5]   17 November 2005, 08.58 am Doha Time, http://www.gulf-times.com/site/topics/article.asp?cu_no=2&item_no=61198&version=1&template_id=36&parent_id=16.   See also 'Stars Sign Gibson Flying V at 2009 Brit Awards Jeremy Singer' (2 February 2009), http://www.gibson.com/en-us/Lifestyle/ArtistsAndEvents/Stories/stars-sign-flying-v-220/. 'At the 2009 Brit Awards which was held at London's Earls Court Arena a Gibson Flying V guitar was signed exclusively by the likes of Kyile Minogue, Brit Award winner Duffy, The Killers lead singer Brandon Flowers, The Pet Shop Boys, Sir Tom Jones, The Ting Tings, Take That, The All Saints, Lady Ga Ga, Actor Simon Pegg and World Champion Boxer Joe Calzaghe to name a few. This specially signed guitar will now be auctioned off to raise money for The Brit Trust Charity later on in the year.'

strumming the offending guitar. Striking his regular-bloke pose for the newspaper editors.[6]

TOKYO, April 25

Prime Minister Shinzo Abe will have a hard act to follow when he arrives in Washington on Thursday for his first trip to the United States as Japan's leader. President Bush took his predecessor, Junichiro Koizumi, on a high profile visit to Graceland in Memphis, where Mr. Koizumi put on Elvis's shades and played air guitar while mugging for the camera.[7]

An Exhibit On Campus Celebrates Grisly Deed

... of the young Palestinian ... who carried into the restaurant some twenty pounds of explosive reportedly hidden in a guitar.[8]

Chirac unhurt as man shoots at him in Paris

[The President] passed by in a jeep, standing and waving to spectators. Mr. Brunerie then took a .22-caliber hunting rifle from a brown guitar case and was able to fire at least one shot in the direction of the president.[9]

Kibbutz Maabarot, Israel, July 26

The Arazis finally had enough when a Hezbollah rocket crashed within a few yards of their home last week. The family of five loaded the car with a cooler full of food, a duffel bag stuffed with clothes and sheets, a guitar and their eleven year-old Dalmatian, Dali, and headed south to find safety.[10]

---

[6]   7 May 2003, by Warren Hoge (*New York Times*), World News, http://www.nytimes.com/2003/05/07/world/for-blair-at-50-salutations-sweet-and-sour.html?scp=54&sq=Guitar&st=nyt.

[7]   26 April 2007, http://www.nytimes.com/2007/04/26/world/asia/26abe.html?scp=5&sq=Guitar&st=nyt.

[8]   26 September 2001, by Ian Fisher (*New York Times*), World News, http://www.nytimes.com/2001/09/26/world/an-exhibit-on-campus-celebrates-grisly-deed.html?scp=1&sq=An+Exhibit+on+Campus+Celebrates+Grisly+Deed&st=nyt.

[9]   15 July 2002, by Alan Riding (*New York Times*), World News, http://www.nytimes.com/2002/07/15/world/chirac-unhurt-as-man-shoots-at-him-in-paris.html?scp=1&sq=Chirac%20unhurt%20as%20man%20shoots%20at%20him%20in%20Paris&st=cse.

[10]   31 July 2006, http://www.nytimes.com/2006/07/31/world/middleeast/31displaced.html?scp=9&sq=Guitar&st=nyt.

What is one to make of the significance of the guitar in these reports? The first report is the easiest of the six examples to interpret. The guitar gains both symbolic and economic cachet when autographed by celebrity musicians. It is seemingly used to represent the willingness of musicians from the West to help those less fortunate in the world, and becomes the basis for apparently generous economic exchange between nations. The guitar is signed by wealthy musicians as if it is some kind of cheque – perhaps it is. Moreover, the signatures of famous musicians add to its value, appearance and influence. The instrument itself becomes a site of cultural brokerage, if not a kind of cultural broker not only between those rallying to the cause, but between nations in whose name a significant amount of money would be exchanged on the basis of the signatures on the guitar.

In the second and third reports, world leaders appear to use the guitar to appeal to a wider constituency, perhaps condescendingly for the lumpen proletariat as 'regular' blokes, or to the widest age range. They may appeal to our fondness for the guitar by posing with it or playing air guitar, in this case arousing a cynical response in the reporter. One Japanese prime minister is said to be 'a hard act to follow' in his willingness to play air guitar, perhaps in imitation of Elvis Presley. Apparently, even the guitar cannot function as the basis of what seems like harmless fun to the uninitiated in global politics. In the fourth and fifth reports, harmless fun does not feature at all as the apparent harmlessness of the guitar is exploited and undermined in subterfuge. This may have led to the taking of human life in one case and the near assassination of the French president in the other. Is the fact that appearances can be deceptive exploited here?

A guitar and a guitar case, which are surely normally perceived as innocuousness objects, are turned into the vehicles for malicious intent. These commonly taken-for-granted, everyday items (generally symbolic of youthful vigour for many people) are used for the stowing-away of lethal explosives and the hiding of a firearm. In cinematic films featuring gangsters or representatives of 'The Mob' from the 1920s and 1930s, it is the violin case that tends to have a weapon concealed within it. But the guitar's unimportance as a relatively non-threatening object was reportedly devastating in the first instance, its ubiquity a camouflage in both cases. In the sixth example, a family flees the threat of missile attacks. Here a guitar comes before the family dog in the reported pecking order of essential and cherished possessions to be taken to safety.

I argue here that, in these six newspaper reports, the guitar (and a guitar case) can be seen to be surprisingly agential in the lives of a diverse range of people, the instrument also being implicated in tragic or near-tragic events. I claim that these examples show up the potential of the instrument to act as an agent of individual and collective will, as the basis for social action but also anti-social behaviour, with sometimes quite unexpected, serious and far-reaching consequences. For those of us inclined to treat the guitar as an innocuous object more in line with a pleasure pursuit, as the basis for music making, courtship and growing old disgracefully, such revelations might be shocking. One is aware of the guitar's most obvious symbolic use in gender politicking (as noted in the last chapter), but the reports suggest a much broader role for it. Yet how seriously should we take these reports? Are they perhaps representative of one-off instances on the periphery of the new guitarscape? What further literature might provide some insight into what is happening here, as we stand back and survey the guitarscape as the basis for social interaction and cultural exchange?

In *Art and Agency* (1998), Alfred Gell considers art objects to be akin to social beings; that is, as extensions of the agency of certain individuals within a particular culture, with the power to influence the thoughts and actions of others, they come to embody complex intentionality and mediate social agency. The actual making, but also the dissemination, of things such as masks, ritual objects or musical instruments (and their decoration and symbolism) might be considered a means of ultimately influencing others, their very existence becoming an extension of this intention, presumably arising from a conscious decision and, therefore, premeditated. Eventually, Gell proposes, these objects become a form of instrumental action.

To draw on Gell's theory, a guitar – Gell uses the example of a car – might be seen by its owner as a body part or prosthesis. However, Gell also takes the step of introducing the concept of things as a locus of a form of autonomous agency in certain social situations. It is relevant to the newspaper reports above that where it is used in two instances of lethal and potentially lethal social action, the guitar, like the explosives or the rifle, is not the agent of destruction, and is perhaps not even the tool of destruction. It seems to function more like an accessory to the crime. I use the examples in the following sections to try and substantiate my claim that the guitar has become powerfully and even unexpectedly agential in the lives of all those who make and play it. Or, at least, it is a powerful channel of their influence. But I have a further claim to make. It is also active in the lives of those people who may or may not recognize the extent of its affecting presence, nor its potential for social action.

Jimi Hendrix and his Fender Stratocaster (if not his Gibson Firebird) are entangled and almost inseparable parts of Hendrix's iconic status in the history of popular culture. Certain makes and models of guitar naturally retain strong links to and associations with the performers who use or once used them (and in some cases even designed them), for instance, Les Paul's Gibson guitar, Chet Atkin's Gretsch, B.B. King's Gibson 'Lucille', Eddie Van Halen's customized and signature guitars and Steve Vai's Ibanez Jem guitars, particularly those named 'Evo' and 'Flo'. It is also common for guitarists to put their names on their guitars, for example, Jimmie Rogers, Lefty Frizzell, Joe Memphis, Elvis Presley (who wrote 'Elvis' on his guitar), Stevie Ray Vaughan ('SRV'), and Elvis Costello, to name but a very few. Signature guitars made in for and in consultation with well-known and popular guitarists carry their names on the headstock of the instrument. Then again, Willie Nelson's Martin N-20 classical guitar has been 'autographed by many of his heroes and friends' (Kingsbury and Nash, 2006:278), including Johnny Cash. The list below contains several more examples of the names by which guitars are identified, in this case examples of signature models, although it is by no means exhaustive.

> Gibson Alvin Lee Signature ES-335
> Gibson Barney Kessel Custom
> Gibson Jimmy Page Les Paul
> Guild Duane Eddy DE-500 Blonde
> Harmony Roy Rogers H600
> Ibanez GB-10 George Benson
> Jackson Randy Rhodes
> Martin 00-18 Steve Howe
> Martin 00-45 Jimmie Rodgers
> Music Man Steve Lukather 'Luke'
> Music Man Van Halen Signature
> Ramirez 1A Segovia model

Guitarists also talk of the very special bond that they develop with their instrument. Eric Clapton notes: 'it has become a friend, and we have had a deep relationship that has lasted over forty years. These days, I never like to be without a guitar somewhere near me; it has enhanced my life, and healed me in ways that are beyond words' (Chapman, 2000:6). Joe Nick Patoski and Bill Crawford might also be seen to note the importance of the guitar as crucial to an individual's musical and social power in their account of the life of Stevie Ray Vaughan. They recall what Ray Hennig, owner of a guitar store in Austin, Texas, said of Vaughan's battered old Fender Stratocaster:

> He lived for that guitar ... It just became part of him. He told me it was the only guitar he ever had that said what he wanted it to say. Isn't that weird? It was like it was alive. That's what he thought. That guitar actually helped him play. That's how much confidence he had in it' (Patoski and Crawford, 1994:76).

If this is but guitar myth and legend taking on a life of its own in popular music journalism, the point about the power of the guitar is still made.

As if to celebrate the symbiosis of guitar and guitarist, guitars are brought to life and given character through their distinctive design features, model type and purpose, which are interwoven in the descriptive terms used by guitar designers and manufacturers to identify particular guitars. More specific terms are used to describe the type of build of the instrument, the guitar types, and finish. Models may also be given a number.

Type	Model Role	Model/name	Finish/colour
acoustic	handmade	Hummingbird	natural
electric	custom	Heavy Stud	satin
classical	boutique	Assassin	high gloss
flamenco	vintage	Baby	gloss natural
jumbo	replica	Cyclops	mid-gloss
dreadnought	re-issue	Black knight	thin gloss
parlour	prestige	Tennessean	fireglow
tenor	special	Jazzmaster	flamed
baritone	standard	Firebird	fireburst
bass	deluxe	Jaguar	super -flamey
solid-body	prorotype	Mustang	Bengal burst
acoustic-electric	family reserve	Zephyr	two-tone burst
electric-acoustic	limited edition	Skyhawk	three-tone burst
hybrid	relic	Defender	tobacco sunburst
thinline	historic	Frontier	transparent
hollow body	memorial	Pacer	aircraft grey
arch-top	anniversary	Mystic	jet black
flat-top	double-anniversary	Casino	blonde
f-hole	classic	Explorer	antique blonde
doubleneck	heritage	Stingray	trans black
double six	studio	Dark Fire	whale blue
fretless	presentation	Country Gentleman	tortoiseshell
touch	premier	Goddess	nitro-cellulose lacquer
slide	concert	Olympic	Lake Placid blue
resophonic	project	Breadwinner	goldtop
experimental	tribute	Thunderbird	aged goldtop
lap steel	special edition	Lightning	shiny nickel
travel	centenary	White Falcon	synthetic varnish

In her seminal book *On Concepts and Classification of Musical Instruments*, Margaret Kartomi (1990) shows that the meaning and significance of musical instruments as cultural phenomena for 'insiders' in a particular culture or cultural context can be very different from the meaning and significance they have for 'outsiders'. Kartomi's study of a great variety of indigenous classification schemes shows how musical instruments are connected to fields of meaning that at one end of the scale pervade entire cultures and even nations, whilst at the other end are tied to quite specific contexts and localities. These semantic fields also intersect with and form the basis for indigenous theories of music and musical performance practice.

The Power and Agency of Genre

> Over the last twenty-five years, Cline has dabbled in jazz, punk, rock and country, frequently trampling all over the boundaries between these genres. (Nels Cline, *Guitar Buyer*, 86 (October 2008):130)

> The first P of PPA stands for *pinche*, a Mexican term meaning fucking asshole. So pinche personal assistant is dedicated to all those people in 'certain' areas of the music industry, that we have had to put up with, who believe they know and understand what's going on, but who actually don't have a fucking clue. ... Note: A lot of people, when discussing our sound, say we play flamenco. We don't. We blend a lot of styles into our playing, but this area of music is not one of them. (Liner notes to *Rodrigo y Gabriela*, Rubyworks Ltd RWXCD37L, 2006)

Simon Frith argues that musicians, especially in the field of popular music, are entangled in the genre rules and regulations that shape audience and music industry expectations of them, however much they may try to pull against them. Whilst Alfred Gell writes of the power of the artist in non-industrial societies, Frith draws attention to the power of the music industry to shape audience expectations and thus, to some extent, musicians' actions, not just in highly industrialized societies, but also in societies across the planet whose music is now coming within the reach of a widely spread but centrally based music industry (in North America, the UK and Japan). He argues:

> The particular way in which a guitarist gets a guitar note, for example (whether George Benson or Jimi Hendrix, Mark Knopfler or Johnny Marr, Derek Bailey or Bert Jansch), is at once a musical decision and a gestural one: it is the integration of sound and behaviour in performance that gives the note its 'meaning'. And if nothing else this makes it impossible to root explanations of popular music in consumption. It is not enough to assert that commodities only become culturally valuable when they are made 'meaningful' by consumers: they can only be consumed because they are *already* meaningful, because musicians, producers and consumers are already ensnared in a web of genre expectation. (Frith, 1996:94)

If one subscribes to Frith's view, it is clear that the 'web of genre expectation' can be seen to have a profound effect on what musicians can and cannot do in the workplace, also influencing public perceptions of musicians' work down to the level of a single note. Musicians, producers and consumers are all apparently implicated, although it is not clear how one ascribes meaning in terms of genre expectation in the case of Derek Bailey's free jazz improvisations, for example, which were hardly the same from performance to performance, let alone from record to record or track to track). Yet Jason Toynbee develops a persuasive argument for the inevitability of genre using Bailey's claim to 'free' improvisation as one of his case studies. Referring to an interview given by Bailey, Toynbee states that 'acknowledgement of the generic aspect of free music can be found throughout Bailey's discussion' (Toynbee, 2000:109).

Genre expectations as mapped out by the music industry or recording industry would indeed seem to provide an inevitable source of inspiration for much of the classification of guitarists into musical categories in the online encyclopedia Wikipedia (which, one assumes, is not controlled by the music industry). The ten guitarists featured in Chapter 1 are all included on various pages within Wikipedia. However, their genre classification also merits discussion here.[11] Steve Vai comes under 'Instrumental Rock', 'Hard Rock' and 'Progressive Metal'. But he also comes under 'Experimental' on the 'List of Guitarists by Genre' page, and features in two other lists: one of heavy metal guitarists, one of rock and pop guitarists. Vai features above George Van Eps in a list of 'Artists who Use Seven-String Guitars'. Both Fred Frith and Robert Fripp feature in the 'List of Guitarists by Genre' under 'Experimental'. Sharon Isbin features in Wikipedia in the 'List of classical guitarists' under 'Contemporary'. Dominic Frasca and Erik Mongrain have developed unique styles of playing that seem to confound any simple genre classification. They are not featured, though they are as well known as many other guitarists who are featured. One could apply a 'minimalist' label to Frasca's work (but that might not mean much to a general audience and it instantly pigeonholes him). 'Lap tap' is more a style than a genre and might be subsumed into something like 'Experimental Acoustic' or 'Percussive Guitar'. Perhaps these styles could come under 'Extended Techniques', but then how 'extended' does a playing technique have to become before it can feature in such a category? Kamala Shankar and Hasan Cihat Örter play the pieces and musical forms of the art music repertories of their respective home countries. Both improvise on what one might loosely define as modes which contribute to the structural basis of their musical compositions and improvisations. Shankar is clearly based in Hindustani classical music, whereas Örter is a musical polyglot, playing across a wide range of genres and styles. Although neither musician is afraid to experiment, genre boundaries are also clearly respected.

The popular press is renowned for its yearly readers' polls of guitar players, but it has also tried its hand at providing a further scheme that would seem to try and establish some sense of order in the changing soundscape produced by successive generations of guitarists. *Rolling Stone* magazine's 'New School of Guitar Gods', which, as the magazine says on its web pages, 'come with cute descriptors. Jack's is the best', exemplifies a desire on behalf of the magazine to find ways of placing guitarists into categories that one might say are 'of the moment', but draw on previous stylistic, genres and other musical references in order to put into words the distinct qualities of the guitarists singled out for inclusion. *Rolling Stone*'s

---

[11]   I refer to the following web pages in the discussion below: en.wikipedia.org/wiki/ Steve_Vai;   en.wikipedia.org/wiki/List_of_guitarists_by_genre;   en.wikipedia.org/wiki/ Category:Artists_who_use_seven-string_guitars;en.wikipedia.org/wiki/List_of_guitarists_ by_genre; en.wikipedia.org/wiki/List_of_classical_guitarists.

descriptors are made up of a series of criteria, actually a mixture of proposed genre, band and album influences (as seen in Figure 8.1. below).[12] 'Jack's' apparently successful descriptor is 'The Crawling King Snake'. Such descriptors clearly point to the complex and difficult task of trying to put into words a short summary of a guitarist's sound, positioning him or her in relation to current influences and past reference points, creating an image which most readers would be able to associate with and use to qualify the descriptors in the scheme.

Such schemes are helpful here not only in highlighting individual differences between musicians' work, but also in providing landmarks in a musical 'map' of the contemporary world of the guitar. Schemes like this can also be quite sensationalized! Of course, such schemes are but one interpretation of what actually is going on musically, with little reference to broader social and cultural considerations. In this case, the scheme makes reference to a largely North America-based cohort of musicians, and to musicians who are members of bands (apart from Kaki King, who has her own band and is the only female musician mentioned). The 'newness' of this school is, presumably, also linked not only to the sonic dimensions of the musicians' work and their visibility or popularity at the time of writing, but also to the youthfulness of several of the guitarists listed (see Table 8.1).

Table 8.1   *Rolling Stone* magazine's list 'New School of Guitar Gods'

Descriptor (Genre/band/album influences)	Guitarist (band)
The Avant Romantic	Nels Cline (Wilco)
Blues-Rock Warrior	Warren Haynes (The Allman Brothers Band and Gov't Mule)
Skynyrd Art-Theorists	Jim James & Carl Broemel (My Morning Jacket)
Prog-Metal King	Adam Jones (Tool)
Van Halen Meets Bootsy	Kaki King
Four-Armed Monster	Mike McCready and Stone Gossard (Pearl Jam)
Iron Man Of Hip-Hop Guitar	Tom Morello (Rage Against the Machine)
Space Guitar Heroes	Chuck Garvey and Al Schnier (moe.)[13]
The Extremist	Omar Rodriguez-Lopez (Mars Volta)
Dark Side Of The Moon Explorers	Ed O'Brien and Jonny Greenwood (Radiohead)
Stoner Metal Ruler	Matt Pike (Sleep and High On Fire)
The Crawling King Snake	Jack White (The White Stripes and The Raconteurs)

Clearly, *Rolling Stone* assumes a developed knowledge of popular music history, and past and present genres and artists, among its readership. I note again, then, that such knowledge as is ѡssumed here displays a sophisticated musical understanding and common terms of reference not only between journalist and

---

[12] See http://stereogum.com/archhives/rolling-stones-new-school-of-guitar-gods.
[13] See http://www.moe.org/.

reader, but also between journalist and musician and, perhaps, between musician (who obviously wear some of their influences on their sleeve) and audience. Moreover, such terminology must seen to be run through with romantic and mythical aspirations for the musicians concerned, as if they were involved in some science fiction fantasy epic, as real musicians soon to become uploaded as virtual players in a new guitar computer game. Whatever meaning such a classification scheme has, it would seem to create legends of musicians in their own lifetime and offer new genre schematics.

A second example of a classification scheme that I have found particularly revealing in terms of linking musical and other descriptors (such as genres) to the sounds of particular guitarists is that contained in *The Illustrated Encyclopedia of Guitar Heroes* (2008). The mapping-out of the new guitarscape from current but also historical perspectives proceeds in the following manner. The notion of 'virtuoso' strays across genres, though as generally applied here it is used for the meta-genre of rock (from alternative rock to progressive metal). However, there is a clear suggestion of a relationship, overlap and continuum between particular genre and subgenre (stylistic?) markers, with headings such as 'blues to rock', 'hard rock to metal' and soft rock and pop' revealing a clear, simple and logical ordering of musical, social and cultural continua and emphases. In fact, the publisher states: 'Our 181 guitar heroes have been grouped into seven chapters based on the genre of music they are most closely associated with', and goes on to say: 'Whilst we have resisted the temptation to rank our guitar heroes according to their talents, we have hinted at our personal favourites by kicking things off with a special Virtuosos chapter, covering a range of genres' (*Guitar Heroes*, 2008: Publisher's Note).

Further study and analysis of the book *Guitar Heroes* revealed that 181 guitarists were featured in the main text and that the additional appendix of 'Other Great Guitarists' featured 492 musicians. It is surely telling that only two women are mentioned in the main text – Bonnie Raitt and Maybelle Carter – although some are mentioned in 'Other Great Guitarists' (Jennifer Batten, P.J. Harvey, Sharon Isbin, Joan Jett, Joni Mitchell, Ida Presti, Sister Rosetta Tharpe and Suzanne Vega). Ali Farka Touré (Mali) and Peter Tosh (Jamaica) are the only two non-European and non-North American musicians among a total of 181 guitarists. In 'Other Great Guitarists', guitarists from African, South America, India and Japan receive some mention, including such contemporary guitar luminaries as King Sunny Ade, Alirio Díaz, Vishwa Mohan Bhatt and Kazuhito Yamashita. In this section musicians are not placed in genres but feature alphabetically, each entry stating whether they were or are solo or with a band, and the decades they have been or had been active.

Table 8.2   Examples taken from the classification of guitarists by genre in the book *Guitar Heroes* (2008) (ordered as in the contents list)

Descriptor	Guitarist
virtuosos sample = 7 of 19	Frank Zappa, Jimi Hendrix, Steve Howe, Eric Johnson, Steve Vai, John Petrucci (Dream Theater), Jonny Greenwood (Radiohead)
blues pioneers 5 of 14	Charley Patton, Muddy Waters, BB King Johnny 'Guitar' Watson, Stevie Ray Vaughan
from blues to rock 11 of 33	Chuck Berry, Bully Holly, Hank Marvin, Jerry Garcia, Alvin Lee, Ry Cooder, Carlos Santana, Rory Gallagher, Bonnie Raitt, Sonny Landreth, Gary Moore
hard rock and metal 8 of 25	Leslie West, Ted Nugent, Alex Lifeson, Angus Young, Kirk Hammett, Mary Friedman, Zakk Wylde, John 5
soft rock and pop 6 of 18	James Burton, George Harrison, Stephen Stills, Todd Rundgren, Steve Lukather, The Edge
alternative and indie 7 of 22	Tom Verlaine, Peter Buck, Paul Weller, Johnny Marr, Jeff Buckley, Dave Navarro, Jack White
beyond rock 21 of 50	Andrés Segovia, Django Reinhardt, Les Paul, Chet Atkins, Joe Pass, Ali Farka Touré, John Williams, John McLaughlin, Bert Jansch, Peter Tosh, Robert Fripp, Allan Holdsworth, Paco de Lucía, Adrian Legg, Richard Thompson, Bill Frisell, Mike Oldfield, Al Di Meola, Pat Metheny, Vince Gill, Stanley Jordan

The guitarists mentioned in *Rolling Stone*'s 'New School of Guitar Gods' as well as the many featured in the book *Guitar Heroes* have been or are (at the time of writing) widely influential. Their sounds certainly carry across the planet on recordings, on tours and via the Internet. Yet, as the reader will be aware, there exists across the world a very large number of equally contested musical genres and styles to which the guitar belongs (and often makes a defining contribution). Some of the exponents of these musical traditions are noted in *Guitar Heroes*.

But a genre list designed to reflect the current state of the new guitarscape might include Calcutta slide and bottleneck blues, gumboot and grunge, metal and *marrabenta*, stringband and surf, slack key (Hawaii) and *ranchera*, *karoo* blues (South Africa) and guitar song (Sardinia), Brazilian *carioca* and Rioplatense guitar in Argentina and Uruguay, Mande guitar, the guitar in *maskanda* and *soukous* and so on. In these rich musical contexts the guitar features solely or predominantly, and remains recognizable even in customized form.

The Power and Agency of the Guitar in a Specific Cultural Context

In this section, I present a case study to draw attention to the ways in which meaning is constructed around and through the guitar in a particular social and cultural context. I will also discuss some of the ways in which the guitar is made meaningful within a range of cultural and artistic domains normally seen to lie outside of musical performance. Of course, one expects some interchange of ideas between music, literature, poetry and art, but here I emphasize the further reconstruction of the guitar in the media, advertising and promotional culture. One might call this the guitar's inter-textual expression, a feature of the new guitarscape which adds to its symbolic and economic cachet. In Spain, the guitar's influence has spread widely and is apparent, for example, in the works of great poets and artists like Federico García Lorca (1898–1936)[14] and Pablo Picasso (1881–1973 see, for example, his *Guitar*)[15] as much as it is present in the politics and poetics of world of the guitar making.

The guitar is influential across the entire realm of expressive culture in Spain, as a multimedia phenomenon. Examples of this include the interdependency and dynamic interplay of the guitar, voice, dance and percussion within a flamenco performance or Lorca's ability to capture the guitar in words with 'poetry at once musical and painterly in its effects' (Ward, 1978:232). Lorca, poet, playwright, artist and musician, belonged to a long line of polymaths whose work was often centred on or greatly influenced by the culture of the guitar and who, in turn, made a significant contribution to the construction of guitar culture. Similarly, Vincente Espinel (1550–1624) was a poet, novelist, composer, guitarist, soldier and priest. He was either responsible for adding a fifth string to the guitar or, at least, for the popularization of this idea. This freed the guitar from the restrictions of a limited strummed repertoire, encouraging greater physical dexterity and

---

[14]   See, for example, *La guitarra* (1922) and 'La guitarra' from *Cante Jondo* in Leal Pinar (1989: 29).

[15]   27 April 1927, Paris. Oil and charcoal on canvas, 81 × 81 cm. Picasso used the form of the guitar in many of his works and in different media (including paintings, collage and sculpture). I recommend the following books as starting points as they provide a broad range of examples of the ways in which the guitar features in Picasso's work: Robson, 1991; Harrison, Frascina and Perry, 1993.

notably the refinement of plucking techniques (see Chase, 1959:61–2, Ramírez III, 1993:11–13).

The names of many Spanish art music composers are synonymous with guitar music. These composers have all written pieces especially for the guitar or have had their work arranged for it. This group of Spanish composers, whose work now forms a large part of the classical guitar repertoire, includes Fernando Sor (1780–1839), Francisco Tarrega (1852–1909), Isaac Albeñíz (1860–1909), Enrique Granados (1867–1916), Manuel de Falla (1876–1946), Joaquín Turina (1882–1949) and Joaquín Rodrigo (1901–1998). The second movement (Adagio) of Rodrigo's Guitar Concerto, the *Concierto de Aranjuez*, is one of the most popular art music compositions to come out of the twentieth century. One of the greatest 'foreign' interpreters of Spanish music, Julian Bream, says that the concerto 'is a lasting tribute to Spain, yet it is also an inspired incantation for the instrument that has personified and illuminated so beautifully her musical heritage' (Bream, 1985). However, the idea that the guitar is *the* national instrument of Spain is a subject of intense debate, as is the role and work of a great many of its champions (for example, Andrés Segovia and Paco de Lucía).

The cultural politics of flamenco has been written about elsewhere (Manuel, 1989, Pohren, 1962, 1992, Washabaugh, 1994, 1995, 1996, 1998). These studies have shown how flamenco is tied up with the identity politics of 'the nation' and what it is to be 'Andalusian' and 'gypsy' in relation to what it is to be 'Spanish'.[16] Peter Manuel also notes how notions of class are reconfigured in the 'contemporary flamenco complex' in relation to Andalusian and gypsy identity (Manuel, 1989). The politics of authenticity are played out in the flamenco club or *peña* circuit, where guitarists, as well as dancers and singers, are seen as 'true to the tradition' or 'purer' than others if they are of gypsy origin (see deWaal Malefyt, 1998).

The ubiquity of the Spanish guitar in Spain cannot be explained by the flamenco phenomenon alone, nor does flamenco have the monopoly on debates about authenticity. The Spanish classical guitar has a significant and increasing role in regional musics, including the *laudes españoles* ensemble.[17] The Spanish guitar features little in the regional musical traditions of northern Spain, particularly Galicia, where *gaita* or 'bagpipe' ensembles form the major musical instrumentation. Nevertheless, flamenco and flamenco guitar are found throughout Spain, even if they are seen as something *quintessentially* Andalusian. Similarly, for some ethnic communities in Spain, particularly the Basques, the guitar is not symbolic of Basque national identity. The guitar has a problematic role in the construction of centre–periphery relations in Spain, adding to the tensions that arise in the construction of 'the nation' from a set of autonomous regions.

---

[16]   John Hooper's *The Spaniards* provides an account of the development of 'New Spain' after Franco's death (see Hooper, 1986).

[17]   This is the 'Spanish lute' ensemble consisting of a *bandurria*, guitar and *laude*. See the excellent book on this subject by Juan José Rey and Antonio Navarro (1993).

Figures ideally 'central' to a construction of Spanish musical identity, such as 'national composers', sometimes do not quite fit in with the master plans of the spin doctors and image makers. For example, both Francisco Tarrega and Joaquín Rodrigo were born in peripheral and coastal Valencia, and factory-made guitars from Valencia pose something of a threat to the established *centres* of guitar making in Andalusia and 'central' Madrid. Many flamenco guitarists in Andalusia play, for example, Conde Hermanos guitars that are made in Madrid rather than Andalusia (and played by non-Spanish guitarists like Al Di Meola), so there are also tensions between these *centres*. However, all 'top' guitars are generally 'handmade' *wherever* they are made. Fernando Sor, perhaps the greatest exponent of the classical guitar during the late eighteenth and early nineteenth centuries, was from Catalonia and a native of Barcelona. Ripples such as these merge to create waves in the stream of national consciousness.

Cities, towns and villages actively encourage and incorporate guitar events as part of their national and cultural heritage agendas. They organize *festivals* which seek to reaffirm the position of the guitar, firstly as a part of that city's cultural and artistic heritage and secondly in Spain's national heritage. Marcos notes that 'the 1991 Guitar Festival of Córdoba has gone a long way to ensuring that the city achieves its goal of becoming the guitar capital of the world' (Marcos 1991:13). The Córdoba International Guitar Festival (begun by Paco Peña in 1981) is an attempt to bring together professional performers, teachers, composers, students and constructors of the guitar from around the world.[18] The festival is good news for guitar buffs and students, as well as providing yet another opportunity for administrators, politicians and sponsors to make a statement about the role and position of their 'guitar city' in regional, national and international settings. In 1998 the International Guitar Festival in Córdoba included the internationally acclaimed performer Pepe Romero and the Cuban, Córdoba-based composer-guitarist Leo Brouwer. Whilst at the 1998 festival, my wife and I met the artist and museum curator Eugenio Chicano from Málaga. Chicano's Picasso-inspired guitar pictures constituted a major exhibition at the festival and attracted the attention of the Romero brothers (Pepe and Celi) and Manolo Sanlucár, among many others.

The modern forms of both the classical and the flamenco guitar evolved from the mid-nineteenth century in the Spanish workshop of Antonio Torres Jurado (c.1817–1892). Don Pohren notes that 'Torres was not only the creator of the modern Spanish guitar, but was also the first constructor to begin successfully differentiating between *flamenco* and classical guitar construction techniques' (Pohren, 1990:201; see also Romanillos, 1987). These forms have their origins in a long and dynamic interplay between Spanish musical culture and a confluence of Mediterranean cultures from the medieval period to the mid-1500s. This interplay later shifted to a solely European context where, for example in Italy, France and England, guitar making also became established (see Chase, 1959; Grunfeld,

---

[18]   See MacFarlane, 1989, and Marcos, 1991, for reports on the Córdoba festival in 1989 and 1991 respectively.

1969; Turnbull, 1991). However, from around the 1500s 'the Spanish' are said to have 'never wavered in their fidelity to the guitar, which they revered as the king of instruments' (Chase, 1959:53).

From my own fieldwork among guitar makers in Spain, I discovered a fascinating poetics of place informing a modus operandi for construction.[19] In trying to convey the rich tapestry of sounds that one can extract from a guitar, Francisco Manuel Díaz or 'Manolo' used powerful imagery drawn from his local surroundings (the city of Granada). Like the soothing fountains of the Alhambra Palace and its gardens, the guitar's sonorities were related to a rainbow-like continuum of colours and scents. Aesthetics and wood ecology were combined in an elaborate poetics of the guitar in relation to the environment in which it is found. This poetics, despite its almost mystical inflections, underlined the very real dependence of a guitar's tuning systems, timbre and sonorities upon weather, temperature, humidity and the quality of the timber from which it is made. Manolo believed that guitars made in Granada lend themselves to personal interpretation and reflection; they are 'perfectly' constructed, like the gardens of the Generalife. In fact, the guitars of Granada and the gardens of the palace were said to incorporate similar aesthetic and physical qualities. The Alhambra dominates the geographical landscape of the city and the surrounding area, and is a landmark of historical, political and economic importance. Similarly, the guitar dominates the local musical landscape, in performance, the media and the iconography of advertising and display.

Clearly, musical instruments are empowered in a variety of ways, not only by the distinctiveness and effects of their sound but also by the ways in which they are written about, talked about, painted and photographed. Moreover the gestures and movements that accompany their performance, choreography and iconography extend and reinforce their presence and impact. In Spain, this model of expressive culture could be applied, for example, to flamenco shows as much as to the workshops of guitar makers. In these contexts, meaning is, so to speak, embodied, ingrained and absorbed into the woodwork of the guitar and in turn reflected and played out from it. Moreover, like the tarantula, guitar players, makers and enthusiasts are sensitive to the slightest tremors in the intricate material, social and cultural webs that they weave and within which they are entangled. Strings are pulled and monitored for slack, and websites (including Internet sites) are maintained.

---

[19]   In Granada, my wife and I interviewed the following guitar makers: Casa Ferrer, Antonio Morales, José Lopez Bellido and Francisco Manuel Díaz. In 1998 twenty-four guitar makers were listed on the official Granada website, but I found evidence for up to thirty-one makers. We also spent some time in Madrid interviewing guitar makers, including the families of Ramírez, Contreras, Rozas and Conde Hermanos. See also Clinton (1989), 'Escuela Granadina de Luthiers' (Granada School of Guitar Making), *Guitar International* (series of articles from July 1989).

Guitars in the Cyclical Process of Social Reproduction

The guitar is a thing, but not just a thing. It is a commodity (bought and sold), but it is not *just* a commodity, a thing with use or economic value. The terms with which we describe the guitar (and many other phenomena of material culture) such as 'object' and 'artifact' need careful application, as Ian Woodward notes in his *Understanding Material Culture* (Woodward, 2007:15–16). As part of a process that includes phases of production, exchange and consumption it is, like other cultural objects, caught up in 'the cyclical process of social reproduction' (Gell, 1986:113) or, as Arjun Appadurai notes below, the meaning that people attribute to things necessarily derives from human transactions and motivations, and particularly from how those things are used and circulated (see Appadurai, 1990).

> Even if our own approach to things is conditioned necessarily by the view that things have no meaning apart from those that human transactions, attributions and motivations endow them with, the anthropological problem is that this formal truth does not illuminate the concrete, historical circulation of things. For that we have to follow the things themselves, for their meanings are inscribed in their forms, their uses, their trajectories. It is only through the analysis of these trajectories that we can interpret the human transactions and calculations that enliven things. Thus, even though from a *theoretical* point of view human actors encode things with significance, from a *methodological* point of view it is the things-in-motion that illuminate their human and social context. (Appadurai, 1990:5)

Caught up in 'the cyclical process of social reproduction', even in its place of manufacture and in pieces on a workbench the guitar is a site of meaning construction. Handmade, signature and vintage guitars have greater economic and symbolic value than other guitars. But the fact that a guitar is handmade does not necessarily mean that it was built by a single maker, or without manufacturing processes involving advanced machine work. Could something be 'hand built by robots' (after Newton Faulkner)? When a guitar is sold, its sound, look and associations (as endorsed by certain professional players), along with a range of other considerations, are tried out, tested and imagined by potential buyers. Such things as playability, type of pick-ups and weight, but also sound projection and colour, for instance, will also be scrutinized. Taste and subjectivity play a hand in making, buying and playing practices.

More often than not, the main motivating and deciding factors for purchase include the fact of whether the guitar has associations with a famous guitar player (and given the guitar's long history at least in acoustic form, most makes usually do, even if a guitar hero has not owned the particular guitar in question). This is important for the buyers who wish to sound like, but also try to take on or emulate, the sound and image of their guitar hero. The guitar remains US- or Korean-made, vintage, handmade and signature, descriptors which carry specific meanings and help shape how guitars are received and understood, given an identity, a status, a place to belong and a role to play in a musician's life.

The fact that a musical instrument does not just make sound – other consumables, such as a motor car, make sound – but have the potential to make music makes it a very particular kind of commodity and well beyond a commodity. The potential for music making on musical instruments is, of course, not of the same order as the potential one has to make music on a radio. That potential is usually and largely beyond our control. The guitar, turned out not exclusively in high numbers by a large-scale manufacturing industry, is, like the radio, commodified but with added value: it has the potential for making the music of its owner-to-be a reality; in addition, as it is often claimed, every guitar is different (perhaps like the radio and the car?). One does not have to learn very much at all to become an accomplished player of the radio (unless, that is, one goes on to become a radio ham). Motor cars, radios and guitars have particular effects on the lives of their owners. Perhaps that is why a recent reciprocal advertising deal between PRS (Paul Reed Smith) guitars, General Motors and Corvette Racing was put in place. Such a business deal, also shows how proactive guitar manufacturers are in promoting their instruments, as well as the faith placed in the guitar by Paul Reed Smith's co-investors.[20] Moreover, the Guitar Broker store in Weston, Florida, chooses to advertise its guitars for sale alongside such classic cars as the Vector M12 and the Lamborghini Murcielago.[21]

Once the guitar is sold it undergoes subtle transformation. No longer *just* a commodity, it is Robert's guitar, Sharon's guitar and so on. It takes on new meaning in the hands of its owner. For its owner, particularly one filled with youthful aspirations, it may present the means of social transformation, of turning the self into some other person (at least for a moment) and of personal growth. One might call this the beginning of its career (and possibly the beginning of the owner's career). It may move on to another owner. Its original identity, the concept and design that shape its appearance and effect, is carried with it as it is distributed among the community over time. Its influence spreads, or rather, the influence of those who made it or once played it spreads if not grows, for they have bought into but also re-energized and passed on the guitar as an object (and as a concept) that retains its symbolic and economic value. But its career might also be seen to have begun in the workshop.

The guitar can be the basis of significant individual or group investment – that is, financially, especially in terms of vintage guitars and those owned by famous guitar players, but also in terms of creative investment. Most people on an average

---

[20] 'Report: Paul Reed Smith Guitars Signs Racing Deal with Chevrolet' (3 June 2007), www.wbaltv.com/money/4103689/detail.html. See also www.prsguitars.com/corvette/index.html.

[21] See the advertisement by the Guitar Broker company in *Vintage Guitar* (September 2008):77.

income would have to think twice about buying a good guitar. One feels the loss of a first guitar as one climbs up the guitar ladder, but however cheap and nasty they are, first guitars will never be forgotten. This sense of loss quickly fades as one's first Fender or Gibson guitar arrives, at least for a while. A guitar gains interest and provides collateral, in both symbolic and economic terms.

Appadurai makes another crucial point. In a discussion that ranges from oriental carpets to human relics, the distinction between contemporary economies and simpler, distant ones is less obvious. Beneath the seeming infinitude of human wants and the apparent multiplicity of material forms, there in fact lie complex, but specific, social and political mechanisms that regulate, or at least influence, taste, trade and desire.

Guitars and 'the Extended Mind'

Guitarmorphosis:

Greg Wintergreen woke from uneasy dreams one morning to find himself changed into an electric guitar. He was lying on his back, which was of a lacquered hardness, and when he lifted his headstock a little he became aware of his belly with scratch plate and tremolo arm. His strings, of a pitifully light gauge, vibrated ineffectually. (Nicholson, 1998:155)

Through the study of these artefacts we are able to grasp 'mind' as an external (and eternal) disposition of public acts of objectification, and simultaneously as the evolving consciousness of a collectivity, transcending the individual *cogito* and the co-ordinates of any particular here and now. (Gell, 1998:258)

In the many contested cultural arenas mentioned in this chapter, the guitar is certainly able to *stand for something else*. But the guitar also *stands for itself*. Like that of a totem pole, its power does not just emerge from its transformation into metaphor in the mind of the carver or the eye of the beholder. Its power also comes from its materiality, as a three-dimensional object that presides over a society – it also claims space, place and can be touched. (Presumably an object's history provides it with a potential fourth dimension, if time really does exist.) At large, out in the world, the object is now not just of the mind but part of the sensescape. That makes it and what it stands for all the more *real*. It becomes a focal point but also a *durable* means of providing and sustaining a sense of place and communal identity. Images project from the totem pole, as much as images and sounds come out of the guitar.

Like those of the totem pole, the symbols and metaphors of the guitar are a ready-made source of meaning in local society, in the case of the totem pole reflecting a very local cosmology (a cosmology in which certain values and beliefs brought the object into being in the first place). One can see how the physical form of both the totem pole and the guitar are crucial to the role that they perform as social and cultural phenomena. Not that the totem pole or the guitar have roots in the same culture, but they both, like many other objects, exude influence. Of course, the totem pole (or at least the template for its design) can actually move, but it may not move anywhere, even if its influence projects and moves afar with its adherents. The guitar tends to move around, and there are many guitars and as many people moved by the guitar.

I refer again to Alfred Gell's notion of 'distributed objects', and use the Spanish context to provide one example of how the influence of the guitar, from the maker out, has spread far and wide. In turn, the guitar maker is embedded in a local milieu, highly informed by the tradition of guitar making that is a part of the social and cultural context in which he lives. His quest for the 'perfect' guitar is as much an ideological stance as it is an engagement with the physical and acoustic properties of wood. So too the guitar is an engendered object holding power and authority bestowed upon it by a long tradition of male luthiers and performers (who have also carved out a niche in society worth defending). More than this, musical instruments in the past and present have been embedded in cults of the dead, of ancestors, spirits or deities. Is the guitar a cult object? Certain guitar-based bands, but also guitarists, clearly have a cult following. In some cultures, instruments are so sacred that they cannot be played (see Fischer, 1986). This is not the case with the guitar, unless it is rare and priceless, has special connotations or is placed in a museum. But Dale Olsen's study of musical instruments in ancient South American music cultures reminds one of just how firmly embedded musical instruments (as sound-producing objects and symbolic artefacts) can be in rituals of transcendence and transfiguration, and in matters pertaining to life and death (Olsen, 2002). In his important book *The Soul of Mbira*, Paul Berliner documents the complex and wide-ranging role of the *mbira* (a hand piano, thumb piano or lamellaphone) as an instrument of spirit possession among the Shona people of Zimbabwe (Berliner, 1978). Beverly Diamond demonstrates the ritual and metaphorical significance of musical instruments in her seminal study of First Nations music, culture and society in North America (Diamond et al., 1994). It is clear that we should expect musical instruments to have different social lives, but no less complex ones, whether they be a Shona *mbira*, an Ojibwe drum or a guitar taking on local meanings around the world but also lending itself to one might call a global synthetic folklore (with strands of narrative or common meaning interpretable by the Shona, Ojibwe and guitarists everywhere else).

Appadurai's thesis about things having careers and mutating roles is applicable to musical instruments as much as any other objects of culture and society. However, beyond commodification, power and influence, which also have economic and symbolic value, are not just represented by objects but given life through them. I dare to suggest that guitars appear as agents of 'the extended mind' which Alfred Gell discusses in relation to carved objects from the South Pacific area (Gell, 1998). Importantly, Gell shows how the influence of objects can grow when they take on three-dimensional form (like a carving or a sculpture) and how when they are moved around they may accumulate influence and thus power out of all proportion to their size. One might also question how a technology of globalization, such as the Internet, will also affect the power and agency of the guitar.

Like other musical instruments around the world, the guitar has its own mythologies. One of the better-known myths is the one about Robert Johnson selling his soul to the Devil in exchange for technical wizardry on the guitar. Then again, there are those guitarists (as noted above) who believe that their guitar has a life of its own, as if it contained a spirit, rather like a fetish. Certainly there are those guitarists who have tried to animate the guitar, bring it alive, with a voice of its own that echoes or is in conversation with the human voice. I recall Merle Travis's 'Muskrat', where Travis imitates the phrases of the vocal melody on his guitar, the introduction to 'Yankee Rose', which features a conversation on guitar and voice respectively by Steve Vai and David Lee Roth, and also George Benson's improvisations on 'This Masquerade' with his voice and guitar playing unison lead lines.[22] But by no means are these examples isolated phenomena, and Jeff Beck's song 'Pork-u-Pine' amply sums up the phenomenon with the line: 'If the voice didn't say it, the guitar will play it'.[23] At the time of writing, guitarists such as Robert Fripp and Trey Gunn use samples of human speech triggered by the guitar with words and syllables pitched by the guitarist.

The *Oxford English Dictionary* (tenth edition, 1999) gives the following definitions of 'fetish': 1, an inanimate object worshipped for its supposed magical powers or inhabited by a spirit; 2, a form of sexual desire in which gratification is linked to an abnormal degree to a particular object; 3, a course of action to which one has an excessive and irrational commitment. Typically, the anthropological perspectives on objects provided by Gell show up a range of effects that can be achieved through material culture, technological artifacts seemingly unrelated to the guitar, which take on and accrue meaning in cultures and societies at different times and in different places around the world. I argue that the cult of the guitar involves a similar fetishization of musical material culture and that Gell's ideas on the 'extended mind' are just as applicable to the guitar as any other forms of what he calls 'enchanted technology' (Gell, 1998:163).

---

[22]   The three tracks mentioned can be found on the following albums: *Merle Travis: The Definitive Collection*, Delta Leisure Group 38286 (2 CDs) (2008) (originally on the album *Folk Songs of the Hills*, Capitol Records T-891, 1947); David Lee Roth, *Eat 'Em and Smile*, Warner Brothers, 25470 (1986); George Benson, *Breezin'*, Warner Brothers B000J5LN3Y (1976). See also 'Getting Better: Wah's Going On? How to Use your Wah, Plus the Most Classic Tone of All', *Guitarist*, 316 (June 2009):19. This short article includes a discussion of how the wah or crybaby pedal can be used to mimic human vowel sounds (as featured on the CD accompanying that issue).

[23]   'Pork-u-Pine', from the album *Jeff* by Jeff Beck, Sony Music Entertainment, Epic EPC 5108202 (2003).

Musical Instruments on the Move

The networks that carry musical instruments around the world are complex and multifaceted. They extend the power and agency of musical instruments. But as musical instruments leave their point of origin they are also received into the hands of culturally distant musicians at journey's end. As such they are also subject to appropriation. I have already discussed the fact that musical instruments are empowered and empowering in many different ways. At the same time as they are subject to a process of continuous induction into the world of museum culture (the Enlightenment project carries on unabated), they are increasingly drawn into transnational industries that import and export material culture and 'ethnic' goods through means that set up networks akin to the 'travelling cultures' described by James Clifford (1992). For example, complete gamelans (percussion orchestras) are shipped from Indonesia to university music departments, among other venues, around the world to provide the basis of ensemble work experience for a range of students, professionals, therapists and patients. The *mbira* from Zimbabwe is an instrument which was once at the heart of widespread spirit possession ceremonies (see Berliner, 1978), but is now played around the world. The Australian didjeridu, as manufactured and played by Aboriginal people – they call themselves *Yolngu*, and in north-east Arnhem Land the instrument is called *yidaki* (see Neuenfeldt, 1997b: vii) – is very much a part of a unique cultural heritage and features as a symbol of Australian aboriginality, solidarity and protest which has now been taken into New Age productions and sensibilities. Karl Neuenfeldt notes that although the didjeridu is 'an ethnically and racially identified musical instrument, its ubiquity as a commodity allows networks of cultural production to encompass people from diverse cultural heritages' (Neuenfeldt, 1997a:117). He goes on to discuss the experiences of both Aborigines and non-Aborigines involved in the retailing and performance of the didjeridu in the local economy of Alice Springs, and the ways in which the instrument and its culture are carried by global information flows and advertising.

Musical instruments, like other material culture, may even become 'art'. James Clifford refers to the ways in which 'ethnic' material culture is transformed into 'art' in the museums and galleries of the world via the 'art-culture system' (Clifford, 1988). In turning to the way objects such as musical instruments are transformed into such things as 'art' on their 'travels', it is appropriate to introduce the term 'bricolage'. I use the term here as defined in a seminal work edited by Hall and Jefferson, although it appears earlier in the work of Claude Lévi-Strauss (1966). 'Bricolage' refers to 'the re-ordering and re-contextualisation of objects to create fresh meanings, within a total system of significances, which already includes prior and sedimented meanings attached to objects used' (Hall and Jefferson, 2006:177). What has become abundantly clear is that

> some instruments in the late twentieth century operate as indispensable ingredients of artistic expression simultaneously at the levels of culture,

> commerce and creativity. They are now part of a global cultural economy and circulate in transnational networks of practice, commodities and aesthetics. Instruments migrate along with musicians or are bought, sold and bartered in a multi-million dollar-a-year musical marketplace. (Neuenfeldt, 1998:5)

Musical instruments are a part of this profound 're-ordering and re-contextualisation' of objects in what Pierre Bourdieu has called 'the field of cultural production' (Bourdieu, 1993). Bourdieu describes fields of 'restricted' and 'large-scale' production which affect the creation, dissemination and circulation of material goods. These fields are tied to systems of hegemony and cultural dominance and to the contestation, negotiation and working-out of power relations in social and cultural exchanges on a worldwide scale.

Increasingly, anthropologists are interested in not only how culture travels but also in how, as a consequence, it (along with culture bearers) should be approached in any study that aims to understand the 'predicament of culture' (after Clifford, 1988). In his more recent seminal publication *Routes: Travel and Translation in the Late Twentieth Century* (1997) James Clifford asks the reader to reflect on a series of fundamentally important questions: 'Why not focus on any given culture's farthest range of travel whilst *also* looking at its centres, its villages, its intensive fields? How do groups negotiate themselves in external relationships, and how is a culture a site for travel for others?' (Clifford, 1997:25). Clifford even presents a case study of the Moe family, an all-singing, guitar playing and dancing troupe that toured the world for fifty-six years. The home movies of the celebrated guitarist Tau Moe provide for what Clifford calls a 'travelling Hawaiian view of the world' (Clifford, 1997:26). Such a study reminds one that the study of the guitar is also a study of cross-cultural encounters, interactions and exchanges. The guitar travels, as much as it is a site for travel. But how does it fare as a site for translation, as well as positive and productive dialogue? I discuss such matters in the context of the next chapter.

Chapter 9
Guitars, Travel and Translation

It is a world of motion, of complex interconnections. Here capital traverses frontiers almost effortlessly, drawing more and more places into dense networks of financial interconnections; people readily (although certainly not freely and without difficulty) cut across national boundaries, turning countless territories into spaces where various cultures converge, clash, and struggle with each other; commodities drift briskly from one locality to another, becoming primary mediators in the encounter between culturally distant others; images flicker quickly from screen to screen, providing people with resources from which to fashion new ways of being in the world; and ideologies circulate rapidly through ever-expanding circuits, furnishing fodder for struggles couched in terms of cultural authenticity versus foreign influence. (Inda and Rosaldo, 2006:3–4)

I do not accept that anyone is permanently fixed by his or her 'identity', but neither do I accept that anyone can shed specific structures of race and culture, class and caste, gender and sexuality, environment and history. I understand these, and other cross-cutting determinations, not as homelands chosen or forced, but as sites of worldly travel: difficult encounters and occasions for dialogue. It follows that there is no cure for the troubles of cultural politics in some new vision of consensus or universal values. There is only more translation. (Clifford, 1997:12–13)

The guitar can function as a portable culture translator. (Bob Brozman, in Smith, 2003:232)

In the new guitarscape, evidence suggests that the exploration of the cultures of the guitar by guitarists and others around the world has never been so intense. But how far does this interest in the guitar cultures of the world go beyond mere musical tourism? Rock guitar heroes, for example, Joe Satriani and Steve Vai, despite all their achievements, also readily cultivate a mystique around their playing with their use of 'exotic' scales, 'Eastern' sounds and references to, if not collaborations with, musicians from Turkey, India and Japan. It seems likely that chord accompaniments on electric sitar-guitar are used purposely to create a fantasy of some Eastern or Oriental musical Otherness, that is, scene setting with mystical, exotic and erotic dimensions and overtones. Satriani's electric sitar chords in 'Lords of Karma' and the Hindustani vocal samples in Vai's 'The Blood and the Tears' are but two well-known references to 'the East' (among many others) in their work. What is one to make of such well-established and recurring sonic tropes in the work of two of the new guitarscape's best-known performers? To my mind, such tracks are a mixed blessing. There is little doubt that the textures and timbres created enrich the aforementioned guitar instrumentals, as well as broadening the sonic palette of the guitarists concerned. Moreover, evidence suggests that Satriani and Vai are well known and lauded among guitarists throughout the continent of Asia, rather than chastised for their 'Oriental' appropriations.

But what of the wide range of essentializing, romanticizing and exoticizing tropes that regularly attend the appropriation of now familiar sounds (from sitar-like imitations to samples of Pygmy vocal polyphony) borrowed from a diverse range of music cultures? These are borrowings from musical contexts that often have very little to do (outside of a musical fantasy) with the rock and pop music mixes into which they are drawn. For instance, Steven Feld provides an in-depth critique of such tropes in relation to the use of samples of African people's music (especially ethnographic recordings of Pygmy polyphony) on the album *Deep Forest* by Deep Forest (Feld, 1996:26).

Steve Waksman has discussed in some detail what might be described as the exotic elements found in the music of Led Zeppelin, including the group's fascination with the apparent mystique of so-called Celtic, Indian and Arab musics. He also discusses in some detail how this fascination with these musics began to take shape sonically and lyrically in Led Zeppelin's recordings, especially in the guitar work of Jimmy Page (Waksman, 1999:267–74; see also Fast, 2001). Waksman provides an in-depth critique of Led Zeppelin's approach to the appropriation of sounds from distant lands, involving issues of copyright and ownership and a serious lack of understanding (at that time) of the cultural value of the sounds borrowed. He puts forward the view that this was a part of a further attempt by Led Zeppelin to negotiate 'between economic and artistic imperatives', fostering 'a sense of expansive artistic possibilities even as they participated in the standardization of rock music as a cultural product' (Waksman, 1999:267).

Such problems do not, of course, rest solely on the shoulders of musicians from North America or Europe. On a slightly different note, what of guitarists in Iran or China, for example, who play rock music which is often regarded as subversive? Appropriating music by Led Zeppelin, Satriani or Vai in these contexts could be potentially problematic, 'furnishing fodder for struggles couched in terms of cultural authenticity versus foreign influence' (Inda and Rosaldo, 2006:4), with sometimes dire consequences for those involved.

In this chapter I now move out again to the broad picture, to the point where the guitar can be seen as an instrument of global performance and, therefore, subject to a similar array of problems that attend any other travelling culture or technology of globalization. As noted elsewhere, by the use of the term 'global' I do not assume that the guitar is the predominant instrument in every musical culture the world over. This is very clearly not the case. Moreover, I do not see the new guitarscape as some trouble-free zone, as if it were free of cultural politicking, economic imbalance and inequity. But it is also true that the more globally mobile styles and techniques of the guitar are played alongside a great many culturally specific musical traditions not involving the guitar. In several cases, as noted throughout this book, the guitar has been assimilated into local music cultures (in parts of sub-Saharan Africa and India, for example). Local music has been *translated* onto the guitar. As if viewing the new guitarscape as but one facet of a planetary musical system, the ten vignettes in Chapter 1 provide, I hope, some vivid examples of the guitar's rootedness in various musical contexts whilst also drawing attention to its travelling state.

But just as there are a multitude of reasons why guitars travel, there are many interpretations possible of the musical results. The argument here is that in a 'world of motion' with all its 'complex interactions' there are also 'difficult encounters' in need of the establishment of clear 'dialogue', explanation, analysis, interpretation and, ultimately, translation. The aim here is to provide a critical assessment of some the ways in which the guitar forms the basis of cross-cultural musical encounters. The claim is that these encounters are difficult, not in any sense because a lack of camaraderie, nor necessarily in terms of the musical results, but certainly in terms of their cultural, political and economic underpinnings. The focus here is, of course, on the role of guitars and guitarists in these 'difficult encounters'.

As an instrument of global performance, to what extent is the guitar's rootedness and, therefore, particular role, meaning and value in various musical cultures understood? Guitarists across the world, just like other musicians, have borrowed techniques, phrases, styles and instruments from cultures of which they have limited experience. But it must also be noted that this is not always the case, and some musicians have moved ever closer to the musical traditions that interest them. Marty Friedman (ex-Megadeath) now lives in Japan and has recorded with a wide range of Japanese musicians (see www.martyfriedman.com). Banning Eyre, guitarist and journalist, has written a book based on fieldwork in Mali (as discussed elsewhere). Bob Brozman trained as an ethnomusicologist before recording albums with musicians from countries as far apart as La Réunion, India, Papua New Guinea, Japan and Hawaii. What is one to make of this wide and varied engagement with the world of music as guitarists continue to play across cultures? Are Friedman, Eyre and Brozman in the minority in terms of the depth of their engagement? Surely this leads quickly to the question: Is the guitar in some instances the mediator of rich cultural exchanges? If so, in general is it the facilitator of less rewarding cultural exchanges?

Moreover, guitarists such as Ry Cooder, Banning Eyre and Bob Brozman are often seen as quasi-ethnographers, curators, cultural brokers, mediators and translators in terms of their engagement with guitar-based music (among other forms) found largely in the Third World, or on the periphery of the so-called First World. The evidence suggests to me that the new guitarscape is part of a world in which 'there is no cure for the troubles of cultural politics in some new vision of consensus or universal values' (Clifford, 1997:13), despite what some world travelling guitarists might otherwise claim (as noted below), and with some even eschewing responsibility for their actions altogether.

The New Guitarscape goes Around the World

Hasan Cihat Örter plays a wide range of music, with origins both inside and outside Turkey. He knows the modes, microtones, melodies, phrasing, rhythms and so on of his homeland extremely well. Örter also has a virtuosic command of rock, jazz and classical guitar. I Wayan Balawan's music demonstrates a local sensibility but also acknowledges globally mobile genres, most obviously rock and jazz. He has assimilated ideas from Balinese gamelan traditions into his playing as well as metal and be-bop, studying the gamelan from childhood as well as studying popular music at college in Australia. Kamala Shankar has drawn the guitar (especially its Hawaiian variant), in customized form, further into the Hindustani classical music tradition. She is a virtuoso in a long-established art music tradition, the bearer of musical knowledge and practices that make extraordinary demands upon performers and teachers. It is clear that in any book that comments on the guitar's global reach, one cannot simply talk about musicians from North America or Europe discovering musicians playing guitars elsewhere. Just as Lionel Loueke tries to bridge both his African roots and his knowledge and flair for jazz (as a part of the New York scene), so the three musicians mentioned above also negotiate and articulate notions of cultural identity in relation to the guitar in very local contexts but, nevertheless, are open to assimilating musical ideas and musical instruments from elsewhere as well as discovering the work of guitar players in distant lands or even travelling to them.

With respect to what has been said so far in the book, there are two main points to make. Firstly, in claiming that the guitar is an instrument of global performance, I have tried to provide a range of examples demonstrating its existence in the hands of musicians in quite different cultural contexts, where it takes on a particular role and identity. Secondly, I have tried to make reference to a body of reliable research publications that are enabling of a critical evaluation of my observations. It is very difficult, if not perverse, to talk about the global reach of the guitar without reference to writings on musical globalization. Musical globalization is, of course, a topic that has been subject of much comment and theorization among academics (as noted in Chapter 3). However, there are few studies available at the time of writing that make detailed reference to the cultural predicament of particular musical instrument traditions (but see, for example, Polak, 2000; Neuenfeldt, 1997b; Bennett and Dawe, 2001; Coelho, 2003).

It is also clear that the meta-genre of World Music created by the music industry has been able to provide guitarists (among many other musicians) from around the world with not only greater exposure, but also some gainful employment. As yet there is no genre with the label 'World Guitar', but one detects the potential as, after all, several high-profile guitarists have been involved in guitar-based collaborations, with the guitar becoming a primary mediator 'in the encounter between culturally distant others' (Inda and Rosaldo, 2006:4). Related to these encounters is a well-developed and forceful critique of the processes, practices, poetics and politics of World Music (see, for example, Meintjes, 1990; Erlmann, 1993; Garofalo, 1993; Feld, 1994a, 1994b, 1996; Taylor, 1997; Guilbault, 2001).

In developing a scholarly critique of World Music, researchers have tended to focus on the more problematic aspects of the phenomenon, such as processes of commodification and appropriation as they configure and impact upon the work, representation and reception of local musicians in an international musical arena. Typically, Third World musicians do not have the resources to compete with North America- or Europe-based musicians, producers and promoters. For one thing, they are not on a level footing economically. Moreover, the control over production and consumption, ownership and royalties often rests in the hands of someone from elsewhere, usually a North American or European pop star or star producer. These individuals may literally fly into a local studio, make a recording with locals and disappear again. It is clear that musicians, wherever they are based, are open to exploitation and misrepresentation (and that includes North American or European pop stars and star producers). But such problems are particularly acute for musicians coming from extremely difficult socio-economic circumstances, including those who may have very little understanding of how the global music industry operates (even if they have experience of working in local music industries). Generally, but not always, they have little power to challenge the results of their recordings and collaborations or, indeed, to question the fees.

Moreover, various tropes of the other, namely exoticism, orientalism and primitivism given musical form, not just in World Music, but particularly in Western art and popular music, have now been widely identified and interrogated (see Born and Hesmondhalgh, 2000; Taylor, 2007). Such a study has begun to reveal much about the musical ideologies behind the work of composers and performers, producers, record companies, promoters and advertisers in approaching the music of cultures that exist outside North America and Europe. Not that the problems and issues arising out of trying to bridge aesthetic considerations and commerce can be confined to the West (see Taylor, 1997; Stokes, 2004, 2007; Bernstein, Sekine and Weissman, 2007).

It is in the aforementioned academic writing that one also has the chance on occasions to glimpse how guitarists and guitar-based music feature in an international setting, as the guitar becomes a locus for musical and cultural interactions within and across cultures. As the basis for interaction – I hesitate to use the word 'exchange' – between 'culturally distant others' one might assume that guitar-based recordings, especially those consigned to World Music, would also throw into relief some of the concerns as noted above. After all, it is likely that numerous problems of translation (language, ideas, beliefs, values, intentions) will arise in this context in so-called exchanges between various musicians. The main problem arising is the extent to which collaborations between Western popular music stars and Third World musicians represent a form of musical and economic exchange or a form of commercial exploitation.

Two particularly well-known popular music productions are regularly cited by scholars and others in their attempts to address such concerns: firstly, Paul Simon's

Graceland, album which features the work of several South African artists, including guitarist Ray Phiri and bass guitarist Bakithi Kumalo (see, in particular, Meintjes, 1990, 2003; Feld, 1994a); and secondly, Ry Cooder's recordings with the Buena Vista Social Club and collaborations with Vishwa Mohan Bhatt and Ali Fraka Toure, as well as Chicano and Hawaiian musicians (see some comments in Fairley, 2001; Stokes, 2004 and 2007; and more recent interviews by Shaar Murray, 2008; Simmons, 2009). *Graceland* has received extensive academic analysis and critique in terms of the extent to which it represents 'collaboration' over exploitation, because of the political context of its recording and performance. The contexts of Ry Cooder's collaborations have also received critical analysis. For example, according to Charles Shaar Murray, 'In the 1990s, Cooder went global…but his crowning achievement as an explorer of non-Anglophone musical cultures came with Buena Vista Social Club … which recaptured the lost glories of Cuban music and landed him in hot water with the US government …' (Shaar Murray, 2008:53).

As already noted, guitar-based collaborations across cultures take place well beyond the boundaries of the marketing category of World Music. Moreover, there is a rich legacy of guitarists working across cultures. Some of the better-known collaborations are to be found in the recordings and concerts of guitarist John McLaughlin, who has worked with musicians from India and Spain since the early 1970s (see Farrell, 1997; Stump, 2000). The connections made by musicians often reveal an underlying complexity in terms of the power relations involved, as musicians from North America or Europe reach out to musicians from economically poorer and politically weak parts of the world. Clearly, what often motivates Western musicians is the search for new sounds and musical experiences. For musicians in Third World countries there are these are motivations among a host of others, but the prime motivations are obviously money and greater exposure (not that the musicians involved always have limited financial resources). No wonder that such exchanges are often viewed cynically and seen as ultimately exploitative (perhaps on both sides). In other words: Who tops the bill, and who is further down? Who provides the foregrounds, and who provides the backgrounds? What proportion of the revenue made from the production goes back into the local economy (see Guilbault, 1993)?

To my mind, John McLaughlin's engagement with Indian music has been a long-standing and serious one.[1] McLaughlin took courses in Indian classical music performance, for instance, and brought musicians over from India to live, work and perform with him for several years in New York (see Farrell, 1997). The evidence suggests that there was a deep reciprocal immersion in the cultures that came together in the Shakti project, a group in which both musical ideas and cultural norms seemed to be shared and valued, producing a meeting of

---

[1]   See the following web links:www.cs.ut.ee/~andres_d/mclaughlin/; www.angelfire.com/oh/scotters2/jmc.html; www.innerviews.org/inner/mclaughlin.html; www.johnmclaughlin.com/.

cultures and approaches as much as spirits which in the-mid 1970s proved to be refreshingly new. Shakti stands out among what might be regarded as World Music experiments, not just because of the intensity of the musicians' engagement with the actual musical processes, but also because of the ways in which the project took anything but a superficial approach. It did not rely on providing audiences with an exotic trip to the East through musical pastiche. There was a diligent engagement with the musical structures of the both North and South Indian musical systems (Hindustani, Karnatic), as well as with the problem of including instruments not normally found together in an ensemble setting (guitar, violin, tabla and gatam).

In his book *Indian Music and the West*, Gerry Farrell explains with great acuity some of the more problematic issues surrounding 'the West's cultural encounter with India' (Farrell, 1997:220). He argues persuasively that during, but also in the wake of, the British Empire in India 'Indian music was the incidental music to the colonial re-creation of India. This was a mysterious, unpredictable, unknowable place, composed of opposites which were defined by foreign rulers; not a geographical location, but a place in the Western imagination' (Farrell, 1997:220). Shakti's recordings may be seen to be difficult to locate culturally, clearly emphasizing Indian music systems, modality and phrasings, but also incorporating the musical inflections of a jazz-based eclectic guitarist. Moreover, the combination of instruments used contributed to the highly distinctive melodic and rhythmic characteristics of the Shakti sound. But the evidence suggests that Shakti's highly imaginative music was intended to transcend cultural boundaries rather than reinforce them.

Ethnicity, Identity and the Guitar

The reader will note the changing emphasis throughout the chapters in this book in terms of the coverage of North American and European guitarists and those musicians based elsewhere. This lack of consistency is due to the dearth of written evidence on how the guitar is used outside North American and European contexts at the time of writing. As also noted previously, guitar makers and manufacturers are keen to locate their guitars in particular places, rooting them in local cultural and geographical contexts to distinguish them further from competitors' guitars, but also investing them with further aesthetic appeal as they become emblematic of particular places (for example, Maingard guitars from South Africa). This also applies to genres, for instance, Malagasy guitar or karoo blues from South Africa (see also Bennett and Dawe, 2001). As established in previous chapters (and strange as such a claim might sound), the guitar is not just a vehicle for the realization of musical ideas. Not only are musical ideas consistently tied up with a wider social and cultural narrative, commentary or agenda in the first instance, but guitars are also sites of meaning construction where individuals try to make further sense of various markers of identity, including notions of race, history, ethnicity, gender, sexuality, class and status. I have already made reference (in the previous two chapters) to my own studies of these subjects in a Spanish context, and these studies show up a very clear cultural response to the guitar, guiding the ways in which the instrument is valued by successive generations.

The most fully documented evidence for the life of the guitar outside North America and Europe exists for its use in sub-Saharan Africa (as noted below). In the previous chapter, I also provided a wide-ranging example of the power and agency of the guitar in a Spanish context. The instrument's role as a national symbol is, as I have discussed, contested despite its status in various parts of the Spain as an instrument of flamenco, the archetypal Spanish instrument and a pillar of the social and cultural establishment. In Chapter 1, the three guitarists from Asia also show three varying local responses to the use and role of the guitar in Turkey, India and Bali.

The ten performances described in Chapter 1 differ in their ability to locate musicians in a specific musical and cultural context, although this aspect of their work is clearer in the case of Kamala Shankar, Hasan Cihat Örter and I Wayan Balawan. However, the subtleties of the musical contexts in which they live and work, and how these affect their approach to the guitar, will not be immediately obvious to readers if they have not spent a good deal of time immersed in the guitarists' cultures of provenance. However, the differences between the world views and cultural understandings held by outsiders and insiders, the emic and etic perspectives as posited by ethnographers, have not been questioned by researchers; it is more accurate to say that the subtleties and complexities of each cultural predicament – outsider, insider, – have been demonstrated.

In Chapter 1, I also present performances by Robert Fripp in Tokyo and Fred Frith in Mexico, but also by Steve Vai and Erik Mongrain playing to what one might regard as national 'home crowds' in Denver, Colorado, and on French-Canadian television respectively. From Benin, Lionel Loueke plays African music and jazz in New York. One of the most significant influences on Balinese guitarist I Wayan Balawan was Swedish guitarist Yngwie Malmsteen, who is based in North America. But according to his website, www.balawan.com, the guitarist now plays what he has called 'ethnic-jazz fusion', a mix of local gamelan sounds with jazz and rock. Some of these musicians travel further or more often than others, but they all now travel in cyberspace as well as the real world. In the context of various 'intensive fields' one finds a demonstration of how those musicians mentioned above, among others, 'negotiate themselves in external relationships' and how, as emblematic or expressive of musical ideas, cultures, times and places, a guitarist's work 'becomes a site of travel for others' (Clifford, 1997:25), whether the guitarist is Lionel Loueke or Yngwie Malmsteen.

As the reader will note, the model developed in this book draws heavily on perspectives offered by more recent research and publication in anthropology. Anthropological models of human cultures and societies provide a useful reminder of the often very different cultural contexts in which the guitar and its players produce music and the various ways in which their work is consumed, perceived and received. There are, of course, very many different types of music played upon the guitar, for often very different reasons: debates about what is 'authentic' or 'true to tradition' are vexed. But just as the anthropologist studies particular patterns of social behaviour and organization in depth within often quite specific cultural contexts, so he or she also defines the field of anthropology through a comparative study of human groups with the same kind of intensity. As an ethnomusicologist adopting anthropological perspectives in a study of the guitar, I am as much aware of musical, social, cultural, ideological, technical and technological links across guitar traditions as I am of the ways in which the guitar has featured in studies of local musical contexts-become-fieldwork sites around the world. Such is the predicament of the travel guitar and the travelling guitarist (and those of us studying them) as they operate within a world of globally mobile or travelling musical genres, styles and audiences.

Guitarists may operate with reference to a single point of origin or more than one, as defined by a sense of their own cultural identity and ethnicity but also by their musical influences (which in the case of guitar players tends to be very broad indeed). Where do we *place* Lionel Loueke? Of West African origin (Benin), he is fast becoming an integral part of the New York jazz scene. Clearly, the subjects of space and place were among the critical concepts and terms of analysis that needed to be interrogated in the context of a guitar study.

The guitar travels and is subject to translation, assimilation and customization in many different ways. Yet in a special edition of the journal *The World of Music*, 'The Guitar in Africa: The 1950s–1990s' (1994), Cynthia Schmidt makes an important observation. There is no doubt that the guitar has been a decisive influence upon pre- and post-independence music making in several African countries. Yet she notes that in an African context, 'Fundamentally, guitar music is not defined by ethnicity and lacks the association with long-standing traditions, yet it has been integrated to varying degrees into musical traditions' (Schmidt, 1994:5). Schmidt and her contributors show how the guitar has a well-established role in Mande musical traditions, even accompanying the oral tradition of the Sunjiata epic by Mande speakers in West Africa; how in South Africa, Zulu performers translate and re-create aspects of the musical bow performance on the guitar in the *maskanda* tradition, as well as acknowledging connections between the *mbira* (hand or thumb piano) and guitar traditions of Zimbabwe; and how, in the urban music of Zaire (now the Democratic Republic of Congo), bandleaders such as Luambo Makiadi or 'Franco' employed up to three lead guitar players, patterning the guitars after local rhythm instruments. 'Most striking', according to Schmidt, is 'the role of the guitar as a symbol of national identity in various African countries' (Schmidt, 1994:5).

The emergence of the electric guitar on local African music scenes brought with it 'increased institutionalization of music. Guitars became a vehicle for explicit use by the nationalist leadership in disseminating their ideas and shaping national identity' (Schmidt, 1994:7). Professionalism, musical economy, creativity and virtuosity in guitar performance all map onto older ways of being a musician in some African contexts, especially among the *jeli* musicians of West Africa, as exemplified in the work of Djelimady Tounjara from Mali. Banning Eyre notes: 'Portable, rugged, versatile, and relatively easy to construct, the guitar has thrived in African settings to the point where today it is among the most pervasive instruments continent-wide, second only to the drum' (Eyre, 2003:44). More recently, Djelimady Tounkara features in the book *In Griot Time: An American Guitarist in Mali* (2000), in which the author, Banning Eyre, provides readers with a rich insight into the lives and music of some of Mali's master guitarists. Eyre even includes field recordings of some of his guitar lessons with Djelimady on the accompanying CD to *In Griot Time*.[2] The book represents one of the first attempts to capture the everyday life of an African guitarist in an effort to understand the music played on the guitar, the playing techniques employed and the musical ideas and people behind them.

Banning Eyre manages to capture the musicians' predicament well. In his book, he notes:

> Djelimady Tounkara has powerful hands. His muscled fingers and palms seem almost brutish to the eye, but when he grasps the neck of a guitar and brushes the nail of his right index finger across the strings, the sound lifts effortlessly, like dust in a wind. In Bamako, Mali, where musicians struggle, Djelimady is a big man, and all of his family's good fortunes flow from those hands. (Eyre, 2000:1)

The future of the Tounkara family rests in the hands of Djelimady. He earns his living through playing the guitar, an instrument that has changed his life and the life of his family.

Banning Eyre, a columnist with the widely respected and distributed magazine *Guitar Player* for many years, also embarked on a guitar-based journey to foreign lands. He went to Mali to learn to play the local guitar styles of Mande musicians, specifically Djelimady Tounkara. Eyre provides a rich and detailed account of his time in Mali. The cover blub to the book states:

> In 1995, Banning Eyre went to Bamako, the capital of Mali to study guitar playing with Djelimady Tounkara, a former start of the Super Rail Band. In Griot Time is the extraordinary account of his trip – a unique insider-view into African music. Banning Eyre quite literally goes behind the curtain to reveal the triumphs and failures of the African music scene as it becomes an important player of the world music industry. (Eyre, 2000, cover notes)

How much of an 'insider-view' is presented by Eyre boils down to the quality of his fieldwork. It is quite optimistic to assume that he presents an 'insider-view'.

---

[2]   *In Griot Time: String Music from Mali*, Stern's Africa STCD1089 (2000). The CD that accompanies Eric Charry's book *Mande Music* (2000) includes guitar music among a variety of local sounds.

Yet in her review of the recording, Bonnie Raitt notes: 'I can't remember when a Westerner has been able to dive so deeply into another culture with such soulful results'.

Gerhard Kubik's work on the guitar in Africa is also represented in a significant selection of audio-visual field recordings made between 1966 and 1993. He presents a highly detailed documentation of the life and work of African guitarists over a long period of time, drawing on decades of fieldwork in sub-Saharan Africa and elsewhere. Entitled *African Guitar: Solo Fingerstyle Guitar Music from Uganda, Congo/Zaïre, Central African Republic, Malawi, Namibia and Zambia*, the films capture the work of some of the guitarists whom Kubik came across in his travels through the continent, including Mwenda Jean Bosco (Zaïre), who featured in academic studies of the African guitar in the 1950s (see Rycroft, 1961–2). Kubik makes these important comments about the purpose of the project and their value:

> It offers an intimate, off-stage look at African solo guitar performances and for the first time presents to a wider audience some important guitarists who are largely unknown outside of Africa. Often, I was the only outside eyewitness to this music as it was actually happening. I've lived through its background and it's meanings; I've shared the hope and frequently the intimate thoughts of some of these musicians, many of whom I've stayed or travelled with for long periods. This intimate experience has sharpened my sense of responsibility to make a historical record of what I've witnessed. (Kubik, 2003, accompanying booklet)

Further key writings on the guitar in Africa include Andrew Kaye's wide-ranging overview of sub-Saharan guitar traditions (1998), Banning Eyre's overview of selected styles with musical examples (2003), Eric Charry's highly detailed analysis of the Mande guitar style (2000), Christopher Waterman's analysis of the role of the guitar in *jùjú* bands in Nigeria (1990), Louise Meintjes's discussion of the work of *mabaqanga* guitarists in South Africa (2003) and Graeme Ewans's account of the life of the Congolese guitarist Franco (Ewans, 1994). This body of literature not only provides a rich and reliable source of information on the guitar in Africa, but also reaches deep into the cultural contexts in which the guitar is found, eliciting details about its role, value and meaning and thus providing the basis for translation across cultures.[3]

---

[3]   See, among many excellent CD recordings, *Gumboot Guitar: Zulu Street Guitar Music from South Africa*, recordings by Janet Topp-Fargion and Alfred Nene, text by Janet Topp-Fragion, Topic Records Limited TSCD923 (2003).

Guitars that Rule the World

The compilation album *The Guitars that Rule the World* features work by guitarists born in North America and Europe, including such well-known names as Zakk Wylde, Richie Sambora, Paul Gilbert and Yngwie Malmsteen.[4] There is probably an unintended note of triumphalism in a production whose vision of the guitar world is quite narrow. Of course, musicians in Indonesia and Brazil, for example, have also been playing rock and metal styles for decades, and include among their ranks guitarists whose virtuosity extends to rock and metal as much as more locally based musical styles. However, there is little doubt that guitarists such as Wylde, Sambora, Gilbert and Malmsteen are well known to guitar-playing audiences throughout the world, not everywhere at all times but certainly among a large and widely based fraternity in countries as far apart as Indonesia and Brazil.

The new guitarscape is a place where knowledge of the canon of the great guitarists and their masterworks still fire the imaginations of musicians across the planet. In the early twenty-first century, musicians, record producers and media executives from the most powerful nations still call the tune in the world of guitar playing, in contradistinction to those small companies and musicians existing on a ledge. The fact remains that a small group of famous guitarists can be seen to be empowered across the planet, especially in rock and jazz guitar but also, to some extent, in classical and other acoustic guitar styles (even if Asia is producing some of the finest classical guitarists who are in high profile).

The well-established names of the guitar world – mostly white, middle-class males – seem to retain a tenacious hold upon the new guitarscape. Even on YouTube and MySpace, I have observed musicians young and old, from very different cultures, consistently inspired by the latest work of several well-known North American guitarists. For example, although posted comments on the work of such guitar heroes as Steve Vai are both admiring and sometimes highly critical, his videos have hits in the hundreds of thousands. One also finds the work of North American guitarist Joe Satriani, celebrated locally, for example on his *Live in India* DVD. In the accompanying documentary film footage, Satriani's Indian fans can be seen to wax lyrical about their guitar hero whilst learning his music from a highly skilled Indian guitarist.[5]

In turn, though, in the new guitarscape, one can also purchase the latest CD release by Paris-born guitarist (of Vietnamese parents) Nguyên Lê in which he plays in a fusion style that combines contemporary jazz-based grooves with phrasing inspired by traditional Vietnamese music, on a fretless electric guitar.[6] Moreover, as mentioned elsewhere, guitarist Erkan Oğur from Turkey is a multi-instrumentalist who has achieved national recognition and given concerts outside Turkey, but only

---

[4]   *The Guitars that Rule the World*, various artists, Metal Blade B000007T6Z (2002).

[5]   *Satriani Live! Joe Satriani.* Joe Satriani, DVD (2 disks), Epic/Sony BMG Music Entertainment 88697025019 (2006).

[6]   Nguyên Lê, *Tales from Viêt-nam*, CD, ACT/WDR, ACT92252 (1996).

now, through the Internet, is he able to reach a wider international audience to begin to solidify his position as a serious musical innovator within the world of the guitar.[7]

In Chapter 1, I featured the work of ten guitarists, including musicians from Africa and Asia, but also mentioned examples of guitar music from South America. The claim is that in any discussion of the world of the early twenty-first-century guitar, one *must* now include musicians whose provenance lies outside of North America and Europe. A significant amount of writing on the guitar draws attention to the instrument's apparent cosmopolitanism (a problematic term: see Stokes, 2007), as well as the world-travelling outlook of many of its performers and devotees. I have already mentioned the thick and heavy tome *Guitar Heroes* (2008), with its inclusion of guitarists from outside North America and Europe. However, in the main text, only two non-European, non-North American musicians are featured among a total of 181 guitarists. In the appendix entitled 'Other Great Guitarists', guitarists from Africa, South America, India and Japan receive some mention, including such contemporary guitar luminaries as King Sunny Ade, Alirio Díaz, Vishwa Mohan Bhatt and Kazuhito Yamashita, though their countries of origin are not mentioned in the book:

> King Sunny Ade (Nigeria)
> Oscar Alemán (Argentina)
> Laurindo Almeida (Brazil)
> Carlos Barbarosa-Lima (Brazil)
> Vishwa Mohan Bhatt (India)
> Debashish Bhattacharya (India)
> Luiz Bonfa (Brazil)
> Alirio Diaz (Venezuela)
> Juango Dominguez (Argentina)
> Sol Hoopii (Hawaii)
> Enver Izmailov (Ukraine/Crimea)
> Ledward Kaapana (Hawaii)
> Agustin Barrios Mangore (Paraguay)
> Yuri Naumov (Russia)
> Koo Nimo (Ghana)
> Paulinho Logueira (Brazil)
> Baden Powell (Brazil)
> Bola Sete (Brazil)
> Akira Takasaki (Japan)
> Peter Tosh (Jamaica)
> Ali Farka Toure (Mali)
> Kazuhito Yamashita (Japan)

---

[7] Erkan Oğur, *Bir Ömürlük Misafir* (A Guest for this Life) [1996], Kalan Müzik Yapim CD184 (2000). See www.kalan.com for a selection of Erkan Oğur's recordings.

Although the names of these guitarists are known to very many serious guitar players throughout the world, I question whether they have featured together in such a list and in such a widely available high-profile publication before. There are also several 'How to Play' guitar tutors that now claim to train the budding guitarist in a range of 'world guitar' styles, for example, *World Guitar: Guitarist's Guide to the Traditional Styles of Cultures around the World* (Herriges, 2006), *Guitar Atlas: Guitar Styles from around the World* (2008) and *Ethnic Rhythms for Electric Guitar: Five Continents, Twenty-Seven Countries, Two Hands* (Belkadi, 2005), as well as occasional features in guitar magazines on African guitar (there are several by Banning Eyre in *Guitar Player* magazine). A range of demonstrations of guitar styles from around the world are now readily available on the Internet, especially YouTube, as well as instruction DVDs featuring guitarists playing in a wide range of styles, from Hawaiian slack-key to Indian slide guitar (see, for example, www.shanachie.com). Moreover, it is not just learning to play that informs an interest in the widely based cultures of the guitar. Mike de Jager has created his own website, guitarsaroundworld.com, which is devoted to his video captures of what he calls 'guitarist cultures'. Jager's brief biography provides some explanation for his activities: 'UK based internet TV video producer, guitarist and multimedia bandit Mike de Jager is on a mission. Armed with his JVC ProHD video camera, seven years in the pit and a few other tricks, he aims to document the many guitarist cultures that exist in our world today' (www.guitarsaroundtheworld.com).

Several guitar manufacturers also make the claim to an international outlook; see, for example, Fender International (www.fender.co.uk/international/). Beyond developing business links and franchises outside North America, though, one wonders what Fender's concept of 'international' means as Fender guitars move across cultures to Brazil and Japan, some instruments also having been made in Japan and Mexico. I have already mentioned in Chapter 3 the localizing strategies of some guitar manufacturers, emphasizing links to place of manufacture and evoking a sense of place in their advertising. This endeavour not only distinguishes their guitars from many other guitar manufacturing firms in the marketplace, but also emphasizes and roots their distinctive sound.

Just as space and place come to bear in any discussion of the aesthetics and marketing behind guitar manufacture, so also must the concept of travel be interrogated in relation to the guitar. In the new guitarscape, travel is a concept that informs not only the lifetime of many guitars but also their very *raison d'être*. Notions of travel are explored not just in rhetoric and a business sense by guitar manufacturers: they are now also making guitars especially designed for travelling or, rather, the travelling guitarist. These guitars are, as one might expect, highly portable, lightweight, often foldable and capable of being stowed away in the overhead lockers of passenger airliners, in a backpack or sometimes both.

As noted already, the travel guitar phenomenon is part of a broader phenomenon of travel, of which the guitar is not merely a facet but a solid constituent. The forces and complex notions that inform a concept of twenty-first-century travel also attend, surround and propel the guitar around the world. Not that the guitar instigates a journey into just the twenty-first century; it may also be seen to offer encounters with worlds past, present and future. As argued elsewhere in this book, the increasing intensity of the guitar's mobility – not just its physical mobility but its mobility across a wide range of media and ideas – is fundamental to the concept of the new guitarscape.

The guitar's portability, of course, has been a crucial factor in shaping its travelling existence, its ability to move with musicians into in a wide range of cultures and musical traditions, since its earliest appearance and development in the sixteenth century (see Tyler and Sparks, 2002). Victor Coelho notes that 'The cross-cultural migration and naturalization of the instrument is a process that began in the sixteenth century, and continues to have far-reaching implications on current guitar styles and techniques' (Coelho, 2003:6). Some of the musical implications of the travel guitar have been picked up earlier in this book, and there are other publications (especially Coelho, 2003) that look at guitar styles and techniques) in detail in a range of music cultures, the outcomes often demonstrating the sonic and design results of travel.

Coelho draws attention to several important issues in relation to the ways in which the travelling guitar is implicated in cultural relations and the kind of questions one might ask of the instrument in any endeavour to gain an understanding of its cultural significance as a travelling medium (and a medium for travel). Coelho notes the 'global seeding of guitar cultures through human migration, colonialism, post-colonialism, technology and revival' (Coelho, 2003:6). The list shows the wide range of social and historical processes and forces which have borne down upon the guitar, picked it up and carried it elsewhere. Moreover, they remind one of the complex cultural interactions that have taken place through the guitar and of which the guitar has been a part.

Equally important, Coelho notes, is the way in which 'the guitar has acted as an important conduit for the transmission of culture and ideology' (Coelho, 2003:6). As an instrument of globalization – its omnipresence fuelled by North American and East Asian manufacturers (but not exclusively) – it could be seen as an instrument of neo-colonialism (or re-colonization), representing a vision of culture and society at odds with visions of cultures and societies found elsewhere in the world as it comes up against local music traditions. One might posit what is surely a contentious view, that the new guitarscape is still as much an agent of colonization as the guitar was in past eras. Such a view might lead conspiracy theorists to argue that aspects of its performance might act as a means of social control. For example, the disciplining of the body involved in guitar playing could be a priority for any neo-colonial 'governmentality' (see Foucault, 1970, 1979) that was based on the dissemination of guitars from powerful centres to less powerful (or de-centred) peripheries (or via networks controlled by powerful centres).

The notion or idea of a disciplined body (used in a non-repressive sense by Foucault within the context of state policy) might also bring with it a censoring of 'skin knowledge, ear knowledge, eye knowledge' (Howes, 2005:6) as well as the means to overcome these potential prohibitions eventually. Such perspectives make me nervous but not paranoid, though they have helped to keep in check any idealistic notions I had of the guitar as the irreproachable arbiter of democracy and freedom. However, even if it is, some musicians across the world still find it hard to get hold of a proper guitar, let alone a recording contract. The following comment from Paul Lashmar is hardly objective, but it is telling:

> In a small bar in Basupa, the Guinea Boys play for afternoon beers. Their three guitars are a marvel of salvage, held together with packing tape, nails and bits of wire, the fretboard of one is so warped it's been converted into a bass ... they launch into some virtuoso playing. In a fairer world – and given an electric guitar – the lead guitarist, Antonio, would be a Paris recording star. (Lashmar, 1994:334)

Are we to lament the predicament of our fellow guitar players around the world who cannot afford what might be considered the luxury of a roadworthy guitar? It would be difficult not to empathize with the Guinea Boys' predicament.

Guitarist at the Interculture

I have already referred to Lysloff and Gay's 'illustrations' of the global industrial interculture, 'its use of media and information technologies and its overlapping, often colliding domains that reflect both local traditions and international conventions' (Lysloff and Gay, 2003:11). One guitarist who can be seen to be working in the spaces where local traditions and international conventions meet is Bob Brozman. Given Brozman's creation of a foundation to help musicians in Third World countries, he would certainly be able to empathize with the Guinea Boys' predicament as described above. His recordings and concerts with Tau Moe (Hawaii), Djelimady Moussa Diawara (Mali), Takashi Hirayasu (Japan), Debashish Bhattacharya (India) and Papua New Guinea stringbands (among others) have received particular attention in the press (see www.bob.brozman.com for extensive access to reviews of his work).

When Bob Brozman embarks on recording expeditions to places as far apart as La Réunion and Okinawa, or Hawaii and Mali, is it because he wishes to get closer to the musicians involved? Is it that he wants to try and understand the meaning and role of their music in their home environment? Trained in ethnomusicology and a virtuoso performer on several instruments, is Brozman able to work his way into a local cultural context, immerse himself in local music traditions and engage with the insider's point of view more effectively than other outsiders (especially given his prowess as a musician)? For sure, an engagement with the local value and meaning of music has been the primary goal of ethnomusicology. So the ethnomusicologist might question Bob Brozman's view that the guitar can function as a 'portable culture translator', but might ultimately concede that he is in the best position to know. However, there are at least four big questions that

Figure 9.1   Bob Brozman

arise: What is the guitar capable of translating? What is the guitarist capable of understanding? How is he or she received locally? What is it that audiences take away from cross-cultural productions?

Having seen Bob Brozman in concert three times, and having met and talked with him, I am convinced that he has little interest in exploiting anybody. I can think of many more intrinsically or potentially exploitative musical productions than those made by him. However, it is my claim here that he sails a difficult course through the uncharted waters of World Music. Moreover, evidence suggests that some commentators on his work have their own particular agenda for him. For instance, what is one to make of the following review, which is both thoughtful and seemingly dismissive of aspects of his work?

> Today a conversation with Brozman, who has studied and lectured on ethnomusicology and been called a 'musical anthropologist', might lead to a soliloquy on the distinct differences between the music of the 'colonizers and the colonized' or 'patterns of musical behavior in the human race ... the frontier between what's cultural and what's biological'. But all of that lofty talk aside, Brozman is no cultural imperialist. He is conscious that he is leaving a lasting impression on the people he encounters around the world. 'I establish within the first 30 minutes that I'm not some big American,' he said. 'I'm just a travelling musician, just a working guy. I haven't arrived with a giant entourage and we stay in the same shack and eat the same food.' The musicians on *Songs of the Volcano* became the first benefactors of Brozman's Global Music Aid Foundation, which donates instruments to musicians in Third World countries. He figures that's the least he can do to thank them. 'I'm either the hardest-working lucky guy in the world or the luckiest hard-working guy,' he said. Or maybe both. (Tamarkin, 2006)

The topics making up what is described as 'lofty talk' in the quotation above cannot so easily be brushed aside as the author suggests. These are fundamentally important in any contextualization of the travelling guitar and are contingent upon Brozman's work. Why, as the author suggests, should they ever be put aside? But these are not Brozman's words. In fact, he has talked about ethmomusicological topics many times before (see the well-documented interviews on his web pages, www.bobbrozman.com). At least the guitarist has the chance to explain his approach of working in the field in the above interview. This does sound like fieldwork (for however short a period). But does his fieldwork involve the deep immersion in the field and prolonged investigation into the music culture in question that defines the ethnomusicologist? Bob Brozman's web page claims that he is a 'tireless researcher in ethnomusicology' (www.bobbrozman.com). But whose words are these? If Brozman claims to be an ethnomusicologist, do we need to assess the definition of the field of ethnomusicology carefully to include professional musicians like him? Were they ever excluded? If he is a quasi-ethnographer, rather than a full-time ethnographer, surely he does not qualify for recognition as an ethnomusicologist. But since when did an ethnomusicologist need a licence to practice?

But one is also moved to ask the question: Why make records of a virtuoso guitarist playing with musicians around the world in the first place? Surely this leaves the musician open to comparison with potentially less able musicians and also with mass media productions with little interest in anything but musical tourism? Clearly, some clarification of Brozman's aims and motivations would be beneficial. His early recordings of blues and Hawaiian music set a precedent for his later work, as he notes:

> Blues was the first 'non-conventional' music I heard as a child. I was drawn to the improvisatory qualities of the music, and also very deeply moved by the timbres, grooves, and general emotional cry of the human soul. With my youthful interest in National guitars, I discovered Hawaiian music, which from 1900–1935 shared the same qualities. From there I branched out to other cultures, and it gradually dawned on me that there is so much great guitar music at the fringes of colonialism! Another common thread that turned me on was the concept of open tunings, found in all of these cultures. It yields unconventional ways of playing guitar, which has little to do with rock guitar or contemporary Western pop. And yet another common thread was interesting rhythms in colonized cultures again in contrast to much conventional music.[8]

But clearly, the collaborative recordings that Brozman has made cannot just be seen as an act of cultural preservation, because several of the musical traditions that he encountered have already been well documented by ethnomusicologists, though not all of them, of course. For instance, the stringband music of Papua New Guinea, examples of which feature on Brozman's *Songs of the Volcano*, has been reasonably well-researched and recorded by such academic fieldworkers as Steven Feld and Denis Crowdy, but according to the liner notes this is the first time these specific Tolai stringbands have been documented.[9] There is little doubt that Brozman's recordings add to this body of work as a further documentation of stringband music then (and will probably be viewed and listened to much more than any documentary or CD of field recordings by an ethnomusicologist). A short description of a performance by Brozman as found on his *Song of the Volcano* DVD recordings (2005) below shows something of his ability to propose and demonstrate a 'common thread among global musical cultures', but also dmonstrates his encyclopedic knowledge of the guitar styles that he rallies to support his claims. It is clear that he is an engaging presence and a confident field worker.

---

[8]   David Atkinson, November 2006: http://www.bluesinlondon.com/interviews/int_ brozman.html.

[9]   'The pattern of a lot of stringband music in Papua New Guinea is that there is just one song in Tok Pisin, the lingua franca, and the rest are in local languages. So all these guitar bands are at some level very much celebrating their language and their locality' (Feld, 1994b:323).

The recording studio in the radio station in Rabaul, New Britain (Papua New Guinea), comes alive as Bob Brozman is interviewed about his trip to the country to play with local guitarists. Here, he talks about the guitar's travels and its unique ability to accommodate the needs of particular music cultures: 'And it's funny because [the] Spanish, they call it standard guitar tuning. And you hear the sound of standard tuning everywhere. Everywhere the colonizers went they left guitars. And the local people they went like this [strums open strings, low to high]. And said, "Man, that does not sound good". So the least number of turns of the least number of tuning pegs gets you here [detunes E to D, A to G, top E to D] and suddenly you have something a little sweeter. And you find this tuning in blues culture in Mississippi, you find it in Mexico, and Hawaii, and the Philippines ... here, I know there are some variations here too, sometimes there is ... [tunes up sixth string]. And you find this in Hawaii also. Let me play a little Hawaiian music.'

Brozman opens up a Hawaiian tune on the guitar laid flat across his lap. Soulful lead lines and melodic fills are produced by the metal bar in his left hand. The right hand performs a multifaceted role, with its thumb pick and two finger picks. It acts as the means of plucking the strings, provides melodic embellishment and picked harmonics, and adds chord, bass, and rhythmic accompaniment. The soundboard of the instrument is also hit for percussive effect. Left and right hands, as well as fingers, dampen the strings when the need arises.

For a guitarist who plays with musicians across the world, Brozman is remarkably self-contained musically. He is also a vocalist and an able showman, injecting wit and good humour into his performances. In Papua New Guinea, during the making of *Songs of the Volcano*, Brozman is to be found extending further his links as an international musician. But he is not the only university affiliate with an interest in the guitar-based stringband music of Papua New Guinea. In the Southern Highlands region, Steven Feld has conducted extensive research among the Kaluli people of Mount Bosavi, for example, where he notes: 'Unquestionably, the guitar band movement continues and embellishes the Bosavi tradition of valuing song for its emotional power and poetic appeal.'[10] Bob Brozman comes away from Papua New Guinea similarly optimistic about the 'youngest guitar culture on the planet'.[11] His enthusiasm and optimism are certainly catching. But he is also clearly aware of the problems involved, not just as a world-travelling guitarist but as a collaborating

---

[10]   Steven Feld, *Bosavi: Rainforest Music from Papua New Guinea* (3CDs), Smithsonian Folkways Recordings/Institute of Papua New Guinea Studies SFWCD40487 (2001). Steven Feld is a Distinguished Research Professor at the University of New Mexico.

[11]   Bob Brozman, *Songs of the Volcano: Papua New Guinea Stringbands with Bob Brozman*, DVD/CD, Riverboat Records/World Music Network TUGCD1040 (2005). Bob Brozman is a Professional Associate at Macquarie University, Sydney (see Macquarie University Music Department web pages), but is described as Adjunct Professor of Music on the liner notes to *Songs of the Volcano*.

and recording guitarist with musicians around the world from very different social and economic contexts. David Atkinson of bluesinlondon.com asks what must be regarded as a key question:

> Q. Is it tricky to avoid cultural imperialism when you visit places?

> Bob Brozman: Not for me, I am very respectful and humbled by great musicians, and I make it clear right away that my name is second and that my goal is for the musical and personal benefit of my collaborators. We sleep in the same accommodation, eat the same food, carry all the gear, and share all the rewards equally. I only work with people I would share my home and table with … in other words, all of my musical and business relationships are with people who love their work, are kind and intelligent, and very dear friends. Life is too short![12]

But compare Bob Brozman's honest but perhaps idealistic claims above with Richard Henderson's more critical approach:

> Given the assertive, fundamentally show business types who have made their names as professional collaborators with 'world' musicians, slide guitarist Bob Brozman has always stood apart from the East-meets-West gang, probably owing to the adaptable nearly self-effacing character of his playing. The notes to this collection of stringbands from Papua New Guinea stress that Brozman is present as merely an ensemble player, not a collaborator. Still, his National steel is in the mix from the beginning .., Whispers of other Brozman projects on other islands – Okinawa or La Réunion — inform the proceedings, but these tracks stand as unique. Should the thought of a gentler version of Rhys Chatham's '70s guitar ensembles playing in fractured waltz time under palm trees prove enticing, *Songs of the Volcano* takes that dream and runs all the way to the bank with it. (Richard Henderson, *The Wire* (December 2005)).

Although Bob Brozman is as much an expert on the blues as he is on Hawaiian music, he has come to represent a new phenomenon among guitar players: a global guitarist or a world guitarist. The global or world travelling guitarist is a musician at the 'global industrial interculture of commodified music' (Slobin, 1993:61), exposing audiences to refreshingly new sounds from distant lands, whilst consistently drawing their attention to the issues posed by these commercial music ventures.

The final words on the matter should go to Bob Brozman. Here is part of an interview that I conducted with him online:

---

[12] David Atkinson, November 2006: http://www.bluesinlondon.com/interviews/int_brozman.html.

Q. You have been quoted as saying that you believe the guitar to be a 'portable culture translator'. Can you tell me a bit more about your ideas behind that phrase, please? It surely is portable. But how does the guitar function as a translator, and what is it able to translate?

Bob Brozman: Even better, it often serves as an imperfect translator, accidentally creating interesting forms of music, as a result of incomplete or partially misinterpreted translation of musical ideas. It serves also as a translator/transmitter of musical ideas, because it is a fairly easy instrument to make progress on in the earliest stages of playing, even if there is little or no accompanying information or instruction as to its tuning and playing techniques. As a roving guitarist/explorer I have seen this phenomenon repeatedly.

Q. I really enjoyed *Songs of the Volcano*. Here is another instance where you go into a very different cultural context and make great music, with the string bands in this case. But one wonders why you would want to do that?

Bob Brozman: 1. To get inside the music and the process, to learn and enjoy the music; 2. To help the musicians materially with the international release of the music; 3. Playing within each band provides deeper insights than simply observing.

Q. I can see your fascination for studying these cultures, but why make a record with these guys?

Bob Brozman: Well, as mentioned in #2 above, to help musicians in a country where there are few opportunities for musicians to be paid for their work. Each band has so far received the equivalent of 5–10 years of per capita income, from this project alone. The other important reasons: to preserve this fragile music before it disappears, and to expose the outer world to this naïve and beautiful music.

Q. Why is the guitar such an important medium for a cross-cultural encounter like this? I mean I can see why PNG with its stringbands, but why a guitar-based encounter over any other?

Bob Brozman: Because I am a guitarist! Also the PNG music is related to Hawaiian music, not in style, but in process, and Hawaiian music was a big part of my development.

Q. How does your ethnomusicology figure in this, if at all? What is your opinion of ethnomusicologists?

Bob Brozman: My process involves long-term experience, but this experience enables me to work quickly and insightfully, in the heat of the moment. I guess you could call it living ethnomusicology rather than studying ethnomusicology. I have no strong opinion about ethnomusicologists. I just prefer my own hands-on methods because playing the music forces other parts of the brain to work in concert with the intellect. Playing the music also confirms proof of understanding a particular music.

To my mind, Bob Brozman demonstrates an extremely considered approach. It would also seem that no questions that are off limits. There are signs of an ethnomusicologist at work in his comments, especially in his championing of a hands-on approach to learning another culture's music. But in contrast to the ethnomusicologist, Brozman seems to relish the fact that the guitar 'often serves as an imperfect translator, accidentally creating interesting forms of music, as a result of incomplete or partially misinterpreted translation of musical ideas'. This is surely an interesting phenomenon that ethnomusicologists might study as part of the cross-cultural encounters in which Brozman engages. Problems in translation might well yield new musical material in the real world. But if translation is only partial or incomplete in a commercial context, surely this is going to not only mislead those who buy the recordings but also misrepresent the music of locals? Moreover, partial or incomplete translation of local musical ideas is a high price to pay, even if locals may recoup some of their loss through their royalties. The fact remains that these are 'difficult encounters' even for a musician as experienced as Bob Brozman. Because the guitar has gone around the world, so does Bob Brozman. His encounters with locals are there for all to see on the *Songs of the Volcano* DVD. There is little pretence or ceremony. Brozman is an amiable, well-informed and genial host who has the ability to get to grips with much of the music he engages with, even if he does not try to re-create it exactly every time. He is to be seen mostly in the background of the stringband recordings, adding his own instantly recognizable sound to the mix.

The claim is that the cross-cultural encounters described above are 'difficult encounters'. They are difficult encounters even for the most experienced and enlightened musicians. But perhaps global or world guitarists and their audiences will benefit from the greater dialogue now in evidence between guitarists and locals as locals take centre stage, as evidenced on *Songs of the Volcano*. After all, these are not samples or pale imitations but real musicians playing. It would be a great pity if the work of the global or world guitarist was lost in translation, misunderstood or carried on without any attempt at translation, or if such projects were reduced to struggles couched in terms of cultural authenticity versus foreign influence (Inda and Rosaldo, 2006:3–4). Clearly, 'specific structures of race and culture, class and caste, gender and sexuality, environment and history' cannot be shed even in the heat of the moment, and perhaps there is 'no cure for the troubles of cultural politics in some new vision of consensus or universal values. There is only more translation' (Clifford, 1997:12–13).

Concluding Remarks

This book is composed largely of a series of observations made at a particular period in the life of guitars and guitarists, teachers, manufacturers, engineers, designers, technicians, producers, promoters, journalists and audiences. It is a thin slice through the history of the instrument, even if it represents wide, though variable, coverage of the current state of the guitar phenomenon.

After many decades of engagement with the guitar in various forms, encounters with guitarists around the world and three years of focused research on particular issues in relation to the instrument, I am more than a little surprised by the sheer size and complexity of the guitar phenomenon as it currently stands. However, this book was written at a time of looming global economic crisis, the full effects of which no one seems to be able to predict. The guitarscape is part of something much larger than itself, inextricably linked to political and economic forces that ultimately sustain, mute or silence it in the hands of musicians.

From the evidence presented here, but also the wider guitar literature now available, there can be little doubt that the guitar is profoundly significant in the lives of many different people the world over. Earlier pioneers providing such evidence include Frederic V. Grunfeld (1969), David George (1969), Harvey Turnbull (1974), and Tom and Mary Anne Evans (1977), some of the main writers to draw attention to the multifaceted role of the guitar in music, culture and society. Later studies by Waksman (1999), Chapman (2000), Bennett and Dawe (2001) Coelho (2003) and Noonan (2008), among others, have helped confirm the guitar's importance as not only a sound-producing object but as a part of material culture and the technology of globalization, in which roles it is both agential and meaningful in a great many ways and in a variety of social and cultural settings around the world.

It is clear that the guitar and its associated paraphernalia of sound-enhancing and sound-manipulating devices enable musicians to make music and consume technology in ways in which guitarists could only have dreamt of even a few decades ago. These developments not only present fundamental challenges to our understanding of musical instruments, but also demand that a study of the contemporary world of the guitar consider such far-reaching ideas and issues as materiality and immateriality, real and virtual, time and space, body and mind, self and others, senses and society, identity and ethnicity, gender and sexual orientation, places and peoples, local and global, old and the new, tradition and modernity, and so on. Not that this list represents a list of simple binary opposites. But is does represent something of a new approach in musical instrument research.

Moreover, it is clear that the guitar is able to preserve its own identity as an instrument of music, culture and society, whilst those who play it thoroughly engage with new technologies, communication systems and forms of travel and business practices, as well as new techniques and styles of playing. But debates rage about the value of video games, such as *Guitar Hero*: Does it undermine 'real' guitar playing, or does it draw attention to it? Yet there is no reason to assume that musical instruments should be any less empowering or empowered than at any other time in human history, despite the ways in which guitars have been taken into new realms of human experience. In fact, there is every reason to suggest that they might not only retain a fundamental role in human cultures and societies, but also extend their influence through a variety of new channels. The argument in this book is that the guitar is pre-eminent among musical instruments in this respect at the time of writing.

I have taken contemporary and cross-cultural perspectives, including a survey of the traditions of the guitar that has been international, at least in scope, and I have drawn from a limited range of ethnographic studies. I have engaged in theoretical discussion as well as description of playing techniques and musical technologies. But the emphasis in this book has been upon the development of a theoretical and methodological framework which could provide something of a kind of research companion for further work, connecting the literature of the academic with that of the journalist, the work of the ethnomusicologist with that of the anthropologist of material culture, the sociology of sensual culture with studies in music cognition, studies of globalization with studies in gender and sexuality and so on. All of these, I argue, are needed in any study that attempts to understand the early twenty-first-century guitar phenomenon. The hope is that this book will encourage those interested the guitar to take up research on any one of a number of potential subjects.

In an interview with Glen Campbell, Steve Lukather notes how honoured he is to be in the presence of one of his all-time guitar heroes (see the YouTube clip 'Steve Lukather and Glen Campbell jamming'). The legend that is the veteran guitarist Glen Campbell – his playing skills and individual style still recognized among guitarists – combined with the eclecticism and studied approach of the younger Steve Lukather (not to mention the obvious camaraderie between the musicians) makes for captivating viewing. It also shows that the baton has passed on to a new generation of guitarists who seem set to take the instrument in any number of possible directions in the early part of the twenty-first century. These musicians acknowledge their past but also embrace the future with both hands, along with a great many other people connected to the guitar, such as musical instrument manufacturers, designers, inventors, software engineers and video games specialists. Coming from quite different generations, musical traditions and musical periods, Campbell and Lukather establish common ground whilst exchanging guitar licks and nostalgic anecdotes.

Most African countries, as well as India, Myanmar, Indonesia, Japan, Brazil, Argentina and so on also have their guitar heroes. The pantheon of guitar heroes now includes women guitar players, such as Jennifer Batten, Kaki King, Vicki Genfan, Sharon Isbin, Lily Afshar and Xuefei Yang. Lesbian, gay, bisexual, transgender and transsexual guitarists are increasingly accepted as part of the new guitarscape, some of them as guitar heroes. There is also common ground established between musicians and manufacturers, guitar magazines and the Internet, guitar manufacturers and forestry commissioners, and so on. These are developments driven by aesthetic, economic, political, ethical and environmental imperatives.

Musicians, however, suggest that they have yet to find common ground in terms of their relationship with an ever-changing music industry. It is also difficult to see more than atoll-sized common ground being established as *cultures* meet through the guitar. These are difficult exchanges that depend on careful translation. The claim is that in the ways that guitar is sometimes used to depict culturally distant others, it becomes an object of symbolic violence. So although I have focused on the ways in which the various elements that make up the new guitarscape are interconnected, this does not mean that points of convergence are without contest and negotiation, trouble or conflict: the guitar has been used as the outer shell of a bomb, guitar cases have been used to disguise firearms. I have discussed fatal and near-fatal encounters with a guitar. For some singer-writers the guitar was a part of their musical activism, involving them in protests that led to their murder.

The new guitarscape is a reflection of the wider world as embodied by guitars in all its forms and guitarists of all ages, colours, genders, beliefs and nations. A host of characters base their lives around the guitar, some much closer to the instrument in body and mind than others, but all using the instrument in often singular and idiosyncratic ways, for both pleasure and empowerment. Such is the legacy and potential of the guitar as an instrument of music, culture and society in the early twenty-first century.

Bibliography

Abreu, Mauricio and Alamo Oliveira (1988), *Azores*, 2nd edn, Setubal, Portugal: Edition Abreu and Figueiredo.

Ackerley, Charlotte (1978), 'Women and Guitar', in Jim Ferguson (ed.), *The Guitar Player Book*, New York: Grove Press, pp.259–61.

Appadurai, Arjun (1992), 'Disjuncture and Difference in the Global Cultural Economy', *Public Culture*, 2/2:1–24.

—— (ed.) [1986] (1990), *The Social Life of Things: Commodities in Cultural Perspective*, Cambridge: Cambridge University Press.

Arora, Shirley L. (1995), 'A Woman and a Guitar: Variations on a Folk Metaphor', *Proverbium*, 10:21–36; also in *De Proverbio*: *An Electronic Journal of International Proverb Studies*, 1/2, http://info.utas.edu.au/docs/flonta/.

Bacon, Tony (1991), *The Ultimate Guitar Book*, London: Dorling Kindersley.

Baily, John (1977), 'Movement Patterns in Playing the Herati Dutar', in John Blacking (ed.), *The Anthropology of the Body*, London: Academic Press, pp.275–330.

—— (2001), 'Learning to Perform as a Research Technique in Ethnomusicology', *British Journal of Ethnomusicology*, 10/2:85–98.

—— (2006), 'John Blacking and the "Human/Musical Instrument Interface": Two Plucked Lutes from Afghanistan', in Suzel Reily (ed.), *The Musical Human: Rethinking John Blacking's Ethnomusicology in the Twenty-First Century*, Aldershot: Ashgate, pp.107–23.

—— and Peter Driver (1992), 'Spatio-Motor Thinking in Playing Folk Blues Guitar', *The World of Music*, 34/3:57–71.

Bannister, Matthew (2006), *White Boys, White Noise: Masculinities and 1980s Indie Guitar Rock*, Aldershot: Ashgate.

Bayton, Mavis (1997), 'Women and the Electric Guitar', in Sheila Whiteley (ed.), *Sexing the Groove: Popular Music and Gender*, London and New York: Routledge, pp.37–49.

—— (1998), *Frock Rock: Women Performing Popular Music*, Oxford and New York: Oxford University Press.

Belkadi, Jean Marc (2005), *Ethnic Rhythms for Electric Guitar: Five Continents, Twenty-Seven Countries, Two Hands*, Los Angeles: Musicians Institute Press.

Bennett, Andy (2001), '"Plug in and Play!" UK Indie Guitar Culture', in Andy Bennett and Kevin Dawe (eds), *Guitar Cultures*, Oxford and New York: Berg, pp.45–61.

—— and Kevin Dawe (eds) (2001), *Guitar Cultures*, Oxford and New York: Berg.

——, Barry Shank and Jason Toynbee (eds) (2006), *The Popular Music Studies Reader*, London and New York: Routledge.

Berger, Harris, and Cornelia Fales (2005), '"Heaviness" in the Perception of Heavy Metal Guitar Timbres: The Match of Perceptual and Acoustic Features over Time', in Paul D. Greene and Thomas Porcello (eds), *Wired for Sound: Engineering and Technologies in Sonic Cultures*, Middletown, CT: Wesleyan University Press, pp.181–97.

Berliner, Paul (1978), *The Soul of Mbira: Music and Traditions of the Shona People of Zimbabwe*, Chicago: University of Chicago Press.

Bernstein, Arthur, Naoki Sekine and Dick Weissman (2007), *The Global Music Industry: Three Perspectives*, Abingdon and New York: Routledge.

Bhabha, Homi K. (1994), *The Location of Culture*, London: Routledge.

Blackett, Matt (2007) 'Different Strings: Alex Lifeson Gets out of his Comfort Zone to Craft his Biggest Tones Ever', *Guitar Player*, September: 80–92.

Blau DuPlessis, Rachel (2006), *The Pink Guitar: Writing as Feminist Practice*, Tuscaloosa: University of Alabama Press.

Born, Georgina and David Hesmondhalgh (eds) (2000), *Western Music and its Others: Difference, Representation and Appropriation in Music*, Berkeley: University of California Press.

Bourdieu, Pierre (1977), *Outline of a Theory of Practice*, Cambridge: Cambridge University Press.

—— (1993), *The Field of Cultural Production*, Cambridge: Polity Press.

Brabazon, Tara (2008), *Thinking Popular Culture: War, Terrorism and Writing*, Aldershot: Ashgate.

Bream, Julian (1985), liner notes to *Guitarra: The Guitar in Spain*, 2 cassettes, RCA Records, RK85417(2).

Brett, Philip, Elizabeth Wood and Gary C. Thomas (eds) (1994), *Queering the Pitch: The New Gay and Lesbian Musicology*: New York and London: Routledge.

Broughton, Simon, Mark Ellingham, James McConnachie and Orla Duane (2000), *World Music: The Rough Guide*, vol. 2: *Latin and North America, Caribbean, India, Asia and Pacific*, 2nd edn, London: Rough Guides Ltd.

Butler, Judith (1990), *Gender Trouble: Feminism and the Subversion of Identity*, New York and London: Routledge.

Cardoso, Jorge (1973), *Science and Method in Guitar Technique*, Madrid: Didactic Book, Acordes Concert.

Carman, Richard (2006), *Johnny Marr: The Smiths and the Art of Gun-Slinging*, Church Stretton, Shropshire: Independent Music Press.

Carson, Mina, Tisa Lewis and Susan M. Shaw (2004), *Girls Rock! Fifty Years of Women Making Music*, Lexington, KY: University Press of Kentucky.

Cezar, Robert (2005), *La Guitarra: An Autobiography of a Guitar. Opus One*, Bloomington, IN: Authorhouse.

Chapman, Richard (2000), *Guitar: Music, History, Players*, London: Dorling Kindersley.

Charry, Eric (2000), *Mande Music: Traditional and Modern Music of the Maninka and Mandinka of Western Africa*, Chicago: University of Chicago Press.

Chase, Gilbert [1941] (1959), *The Music of Spain*, New York: Dover Publications Inc.

Chuse, Loren (2003), *The Cantaoras: Music, Gender, and Identity in Flamenco Song*, New York and London: Routledge.

Clapton, Eric (2000), 'Foreword', in Richard Chapman, *Guitar: Music, History, Players*, London: Dorling Kindersley.

Clarke, Eric (2005), *Ways of Listening: An Ecological Approach to the Perception of Musical Meaning*, New York: Oxford University Press.

Classen, Constance (ed.) (2005), *The Book of Touch*, Oxford and New York: Berg.

Clayton, Martin. (2001), 'Rock to Raga: The Many Lives of the Indian Guitar', in Andy Bennett and Kevin Dawe (eds), *Guitar Cultures*, Oxford and New York: Berg, pp.179–208.

Cleveland, Barry (2007), 'Riffs: Bleeding Edge: Erdem Helvacioğlu', *Guitar Player*, September: 32–3.

Clifford, James (1988), *The Predicament of Culture: Twentieth Century Ethnography, Literature and Art*, Cambridge, MA: Harvard University Press.

—— (1992), 'Travelling Cultures', in Lawrence Grossberg, Cary Nelson and Paula Treichler (eds), *Cultural Studies*, New York: Routledge, pp.96–116.

—— (1997) *Routes: Travel and Translation in the Late Twentieth Century*, Cambridge, MA: Harvard University Press.

Clinton, George (1989), 'Escuela Granadina de Luthiers' (Granada School of Guitar Making), *Guitar International*, London: Musical New Services Ltd.

Coelho, Victor (1997), *Performance on Lute, Guitar and Vihuela: Historical Practice and Modern Interpretation*, Cambridge: Cambridge University Press.

—— (ed.) (2003), *The Cambridge Companion to the Guitar*, Cambridge: Cambridge University Press.

Corbain, Alan (1998), *Village Bells: The Culture of the Senses in the Nineteenth Century French Countryside*, trans. Martin Thom, New York: Columbia University Press.

Corr, Richard (2000), *Guitar Academy*, vol. 1, London: Academy Music Publications.

Davidson, Lyle and Bruce Torff (1992), 'Situated Cognition in Music', *The World of Music* 34/3:120–39.

Dawe, Kevin (2003): 'The Cultural Study of Musical Instruments', in M. Clayton, T. Herbert and R. Middleton (eds), *The Cultural Study of Music: A Critical Introduction*, London: Routledge, pp.274–83.

—— (2007), *Music and Musicians in Crete: Performance and Ethnography in a Mediterranean Island Society*, Lanham, MD: Scarecrow Press.

—— with Moira Dawe (2001), 'Handmade in Spain: The Culture of Guitar Making', in Andy Bennett and Kevin Dawe (eds), *Guitar Cultures*, Oxford and New York: Berg, pp.63–87.

Delauney, Charles (1961), *Django Reinhardt*, trans. Michael James, New York: Da Capo Press.

DeVale, Susan C. (1990), 'Organizing Organology', in Susan C. DeVale (ed.), *Issues in Organology: Selected Reports in Ethnomusicology*, vol. 8, Los Angeles: Ethnomusicology Publications, Department of Ethnomusicology and Systematic Musicology, University of California, pp.1–34.

deWaal Malefyt, Timothy. (1998), 'Gendering the Authentic in Spanish *Flamenco*', in William Washabaugh (ed.), *The Passion of Music and Dance: Body, Gender and Sexuality*, Oxford and New York: Berg, pp.51–62.

Diamond, Beverley, M. Sam Cronk and Franziska von Rosen (1994), *Visions of Sound: Musical Instruments of First Nations Communities in Northeastern America*, Chicago: University of Chicago Press.

Diehl, Keila (2002), *Echoes from Dharamsala: Music in the Life of a Tibetan Refugee Community*, Berkeley: University of California Press.

Doubleday, Veronica (2008). 'Sounds of Power: An Overview of Musical Instruments and Gender', *Ethnomusicology Forum*, 17/1:3–39.

Eliade, Mircea [1964] (1989), *Shamanism: Archaic Techniques of Ecstasy*, New York: Pantheon.

Erlmann, Veit (1993), 'The Politics and Aesthetics of Transnational Musics', *The World of Music*, 35/2:3–15.

—— (ed.) (2004), *Hearing Cultures: Essays on Sound, Listening and Modernity*, Oxford and New York: Berg.

Evans, David (2001), 'The Guitar in the Blues Music of the Deep South', in Andy Bennett and Kevin Dawe (eds), *Guitar Cultures*, Oxford and New York: Berg, pp.11–26.

Evans, Tom and Mary Anne (1977), *Guitars: Music, History, Construction and Players from the Renaissance to Rock*, New York: Paddington Press.

Ewans, Graeme (1994), *Congo Colossus: The Life of Franco and OK Jazz*, North Walsham, Norfolk: Buku Press.

Eyre, Banning (2000), *In Griot Time: An American Guitarist in Mali*, Philadelphia: Temple University Press.

—— (2003), 'African Reinventions of the Guitar', in Victor Coelho (ed.), *The Cambridge Companion to the Guitar*, Cambridge: Cambridge University Press, pp.44–64.

Fairley, Jan (1994), 'Nueva Canción: The Guitar is a Gun; The Song as Bullet', in Simon Broughton, Mark Ellingham, David Muddyman and Richard Trillo, eds, *World Music: The Rough Guide*, 1st edn, London: Rough Guides Ltd, pp.569–76.

—— (2001), 'The "Local" and the "Global" in Popular Music', in Simon Frith, Will Straw and John Street (eds), *The Cambridge Companion to Pop and Rock*, Cambridge: Cambridge University Press, pp.272–89.

Farrell, Gerry (1997), *Indian Music and the West*, Oxford: Oxford University Press.

Fast, Susan (2001), *In the Houses of the Holy: Led Zeppelin and the Power of Rock Music*, New York: Oxford University Press.

—— (2006), 'Rethinking Issues of Gender and Sexuality in Led Zeppelin: A Woman's View of Pleasure and Power in Hard Rock', in Andy Bennett, Barry Shank and Jason Toynbee (ed.), *The Popular Music Studies Reader*, New York and London: Routledge, pp.361–76.

Feld, Steven (1994a), 'Notes on World Beat', in Charles Keil and Steven Feld, *Music Grooves: Essays and Dialogues*, Chicago and London: University of Chicago Press, pp.238–46.

—— (1994b), 'From Schizophonia to Schismogenesis: On the Discourses and Commodification Practices of "World Music" and "World Beat"', in Charles Keil and Steven Feld, *Music Grooves: Essays and Dialogues*, Chicago and London: University of Chicago Press, pp.257–89.

—— (1996), 'Pygmy POP: A Genealogy of Schizophonic Mimesis', *Yearbook for Traditional Music* 28:1–35.

—— and Keith H. Basso (eds) (1996), *Senses of Place*, Santa Fe: School of American Research Press.

Fikentscher, Kai (2003), '"There's Not a Problem I can't Fix, 'Cause I can do it in the Mix": On the Performance Technology of 12-Inch Vinyl', in René T.A. Lysloff and Leslie C. Gay Jr (eds), *Music and Technoculture*, Middletown, CT: Wesleyan University Press/University Press of New England, pp.290–315.

Fischer, Hans [1958] (1986), *Sound-Producing Instruments in Oceania: Construction and Playing Technique – Distribution and Function*, rev. edn, Boroko: Institute of Papua New Guinea Studies.

Foucault, Michael (1970), *The Order of Things*, London: Tavistock Press.

—— (1979), 'Governmentality', *Ideology and Consciousness*, 6:5–22.

Francis, Patrick (2008), 'Ibanez EWN28 Bubinga' (guitar review), *Acoustic Guitar*, July: 28–9.

Frith, Simon (1996), *Performing Rites: Evaluating Popular Music*, Oxford and New York: Oxford University Press.

—— (2001), 'The Popular Music Industry', in Simon Frith, Will Straw and John Street (eds), *The Cambridge Companion to Pop and Rock*, Cambridge: Cambridge University Press, pp.26–52.

Frost, Matt (2008), 'Tech That: Erich Gormley: Ministry's Guitar Tech', *Performing Musician*, 10, July: 70–75.

Gannon, Louise (2007), 'I'm a Dirty Blonde. We have more Fun' (interview with Avril Lavigne), *Live Night and Day*, supplement to *The Mail on Sunday*, London: Associated Newspapers Ltd, 1 April: 12–14.

García Lorca, Federico (1922), 'La guitarra' from *Cante Jondo*, in Luis F. Leal Pinar, *Retazos de guitarra*, Madrid: Editorial Alpuerto, S.A., 1989, p.29.

Garofalo, Reebee (1993), 'Whose World, What Beat? The Transnational Music Industry, Identity and Cultural Imperialism', *The World of Music*, 35/2:16–31.

Gell, Alfred (1998), *Art and Agency: An Anthropological Theory*, Oxford and New York: Oxford University Press.

—— [1999] (2006), *The Art of Anthropology: Essays and Diagrams*, ed. Eric Hirsch, New York and London: Berg.

George, David (1969), *The Flamenco Guitar. From its Birth in the Hands of the Guitarrero to its Ultimate Celebration in the Hands of the Flamenco Guitarist*, Madrid: Society of Spanish Studies.

Gerken, Teje (2003), 'Global Lutherie', *Acoustic Guitar*, March: 59.

Gibson, James J. (1986), *The Ecological Approach to Visual Perception*, Hillsdale, NJ: Lawrence Erlbaum Associates.

Gibson, Ralph (2008), *State of the Axe: Guitar Masters in Photographs and Words*, New Haven and London: Yale University Press.

Gill, Chris (1995), *Guitar Legends: The Definitive Guide to the World's Greatest Guitar Players*, London: Studio Editions Ltd.

—— (2009), 'Of Wolf and Man', *Guitar World*, February: 64–74.

Gilmore, David (1990), *Manhood in the Making: Cultural Concepts of Masculinity*, New Haven, CT: Yale University Press.

Givan, Benjamin (2003) 'Django Reinhardt's Left Hand', in E. Taylor Atkins, ed., *Jazz Planet*, Jackson: University of Mississippi Press, pp.19–39.

Gould, Rick and Michael Molenda (2008), '15 Sensational Superstar Rigs', *Guitar Player*, Holiday: 48–79.

Green, Lucy (2001), *How Popular Musicians Learn: A Way Ahead for Music Education*, Aldershot: Ashgate.

Greene, Paul D. and Thomas Porcello (eds) (2005), *Wired for Sound: Engineering Technologies in Sonic Cultures*, Middletown, CT: Wesleyan University Press.

Grunfeld, Frederic V. [1969] (1974), *The Art and Times of the Guitar: An Illustrated History of Guitars and Guitarists*, London: Collier Macmillan Publishers.

Guilbault, Jocelyne (1993), *Zouk: World Music in the West Indies*, Chicago: University of Chicago Press.

—— (2001), 'World Music', in Simon Frith, Will Straw and John Street (eds), *The Cambridge Companion to Pop and Rock*, Cambridge: Cambridge University Press, pp.176–92.

Guitar Atlas: Guitar Styles from around the World (2008), Van Nuys, CA: Alfred Publishing Company.

Hall, Stuart (1991), 'The Local and the Global: Globalization and Ethnicity', in Anthony King (ed.). *Culture, Globalization and the World System*, London: Macmillan, pp.19–40.

—— and Tony Jefferson [1976] (2006), *Resistance through Rituals: Youth Subcultures in Post-War Britain*, London: Routledge.

Harrison, Charles, Francis Frascina and Gill Perry (1993), *Primitivism, Cubism, Abstraction*, New Haven and London: Yale University Press.

Harvey, David (1989), *The Condition of Postmodernity*, Cambridge, MA: Blackwell Publishers.

Harvey, Steve (2009), 'Ovation iDea' (guitar review), *Guitarist*, 314, April: 92–4.

Hawking, Stephen [1988] (1990), *A Brief History of Time: From the Big Bang to Black Holes*, New York and London: Bantam Books.

Heatley, Michael (2008), 'In God he Trust', *Guitar and Bass Magazine*, 19/7, July: 22–8.

Hebdige, Dick (1979), *Subculture: The Meaning of Style*, London: Routledge.

Heck, Thomas (1998), 'Guitar-Related Research in the Age of the Internet: Current Options, Current Trends', *Soundboard*, 25:61–8.

Herriges, Greg P. (2006), *World Guitar: Guitarist's Guide to the Traditional Styles of Cultures around the World*, Milwaukee, WI: Hal Leonard Corporation.

Hill, Robin (2001), *The Guitar Gymnasium: A Mental and Physical Workout, Designed to Develop Flawless Technique*, Pacific, MO: Mel Bay Publications.

Hine, Christine (2000), *Virtual Ethnography*, London: Sage Publications Ltd.

Hodgkinson, Will (2006), *Guitar Man: A Six-String Odyssey*, London: Bloomsbury Publishing Plc.

Hooper, John (1986), *The Spaniards: A Portrait of the New Spain*, Harmondsworth: Penguin.

Howes, David (ed.) (2005), *Empire of the Senses: The Sensual Culture Reader*, Oxford and New York: Berg.

Hughes, James (2006), 'What Comes after Homo Sapiens?', *New Scientist*, 18, November: 70–72.

Hunter, Dave (2004), *Guitar Effects Pedals: The Practical Handbook*, San Francisco and London: Backbeat Books.

—— (2005), *Guitar Rigs: Classic Guitar and Amp Combinations*, San Francisco and London: Backbeat Books.

—— (2008), 'All about Tonewoods', *Guitar Player*, February: 192.

Hurrell, Andrew (2007), *On Global Order: Power, Values and the Construction of International Society*, New York: Oxford University Press.

The Illustrated Encyclopedia of Guitar Heroes (2008), London: Flame Tree Publishing.

Inda, Jonathan Xavier and Renato Resaldo (eds) (2006), *The Anthropology of Globalization: A Reader*, Malden, MA, and Oxford: Blackwell Publishing.

Jara, Joan (1983), *Victor – An Unfinished Song*, London: Jonathan Cape.

Jara Ortega, Juan (1953), *Mas de 2.500 refranes relativos a la mujer: Soltera, Casada, Viuda y Suegra*, Madrid: Instituto Editorial Reus.

Jeffery, Brian (1995), 'Preface' to Fernando Sor, *Method for the Spanish Guitar* [1832], London: Tecla, No. 389.

Jenkins, Henry (2006), *Convergence Culture: Where Old and New Media Collide*, New York: New York University Press.

Jorgensen, John (1996), 'Gypsy Guitar Primer', *Acoustic Guitar*, February: 40–42.

Joyner, Gary Lee (2008), 'Great Guitar Towns', *Acoustic Guitar*, December: 59–70.

Kartomi, Margaret (1990), *On Concepts and Classifications of Musical Instruments*, Chicago: University of Chicago Press.

Kaye, Andrew (1998), 'The Guitar in Africa', in Ruth Stone (ed.), *The Garland Encyclopedia of World Music*, vol. 1: *Africa*, New York: Garland Publishing, pp.350–69.

Keil, Charles and Steven Feld (1994), *Music Grooves: Essays and Dialogues*, Chicago and London: University of Chicago Press.

Keil, Charles, Angeliki Vellou Keil, Steven Feld and Dick Blau (2002), *Bright Balkan Morning: Romani Lives & The Power of Music in Greek Macedonia*, Middletown, CT, and London: Wesleyan University Press.

Kies, Thomas (2006), 'Ethnoaesthetics, Labor Process, and the Political Economy of Guitar Artisans in a Mexican Community', Ph.D. dissertation, University of New Mexico, Albuquerque, 2006.

Kingsbury, Paul and Alanna Nash (eds) (2006), *Country Music: The Complete Visual History*, London: Dorling Kindersley Ltd.

Kubik, Gerhard [1995] (2003), *African Guitar: Solo Fingerstyle Guitar Music from Uganda, Congo/Zaire, Central African Republic, Malawi, Namibia and Zambia. Audio-Visual Field Recordings, 1966–1993*, videotape, Rounder Records/Vestapol Productions 13017, MB95446G (video, 1995), GW13017 (DVD, 2003).

Labajo, Joaquina (2003), 'Body and Voice: The Construction of Gender in Flamenco', in Tullia Magrii (ed.), *Music and Gender: Perspectives from the Mediterranean*, Chicago: University of Chicago Press, pp.67–86.

Laing, Dave (1986), *One Chord Wonders: Power and Meaning in Punk Rock*, Milton Keynes: Open University Press.

Lashmar, Paul (1994), 'Equatorial Guinea Boys: Music of Bioko Island', in Simon Broughton, Mark Ellingham, David Muddyman and Richard Trillo, eds, *World Music: The Rough Guide*, 1st edn, London: Rough Guides Ltd, pp.333–5.

Leal Pinar, Luis F. (1989), *Retazos de guitarra*, Madrid: Editorial Alpuerto, S.A.

Leonard, Marion (2007), *Gender in the Music Industry: Rock, Discourse and Girl Power*, Aldershot: Ashgate.

Leal Pinar, Luis F. (1989), *Retazos de guitarra*, Madrid: Editorial Alpuerto, S.A.

Lévi-Straus, Claude [1962] (1966), *The Savage Mind (La pensée sauvage)*, Chicago: University of Chicago Press.

Lysloff, René T.A. (2003), 'Musical Life in Softcity: An Internet Ethnography', in René T.A. Lysloff and Leslie C. Gay Jr. (eds), *Music and Technoculture*, Middletown, CT: Wesleyan University Press/University Press of New England, pp.23–63.

—— and Leslie C. Gay Jr. (eds). (2003), *Music and Technoculture*, Middletown, CT: Wesleyan University Press/University Press of New England.

MacAuslan, Jana and Kristan Aspen (1997), *Guitar Music by Women Composers: An Annotated Catalogue*, New York: Greenwood Press.

MacFarlane, John (1989), 'International Festival of the Guitar – Córdoba', *Classical Guitar*, December: 20–22.

Magrini, Tullia (ed.) (2003), *Music and Gender: Perspectives from the Mediterranean*, Chicago: University of Chicago Press.

Manuel, Peter (1989), 'Andalusian, Gypsy, and Class Identity in the Contemporary Flamenco Complex', *Ethnomusicology*, 33/1:47–65.

Marcos (1991), 'Cuaderno *Flamenco*: The 1991 *Flamenco* Annual and a New *Flamenco* Bulletin from the *Flamenco* Foundation in Jerez', *Guitar International*, October: 13.

McGovern, Charles (2004), 'The Music: The Electric Guitar in the American Century', in André Millard (ed.), *The Electric Guitar: A History of an American Icon*, Baltimore and London: Johns Hopkins University Press, pp.17–40.

McIver, Joel (2008), 'Sub Bass: Charlotte Cooper of the Subways Reveals that when it Comes to Bass, it's All or Nothing', *Bass Guitar Magazine*, 37, July/August: 18–19.

Mead, David (2004), *Talking Guitars: A Masterclass with the World's Greats*, London: Sanctuary.

Meintjes, Louise (1990), 'Paul Simon's *Graceland*, South Africa and the Mediation of Musical Meaning', *Ethnomusicology*, 34/1:37–73.

—— (2003), *Sound of Africa! Making Music Zulu in a South African Studio*, Durham, NC, and London: Duke University Press.

Millard, André (ed.) (2004), *The Electric Guitar: A History of an American Icon*. Baltimore and London: Johns Hopkins University Press.

Miller, Daniel (ed.) (2005), *Materiality*, Durham, NC: Duke University Press.

Miller, Kiri (2007), 'Jacking the Dial: Radio, Race and Place in Grand Theft Auto', *Ethnomusicology*, 51/3:402–38.

Minhinnett, Ray and Bob Young (1995), *The Story of the Fender Stratocaster: Curves, Contours and Body Horns: A Celebration of the World's Greatest Guitar*, San Francisco: GPI Books/Miller Freeman Books.

Molenda, Michael (2008a), 'Guitar Player's Guitar Superstar 2008', *Guitar Player*, Holiday: 16–24.

—— (2008b), '15 Sensational Superstar Rigs', *Guitar Player*, Holiday: 56–7.

—— (2009), 'My Ruin', *Guitar Player*, April: 38–42.

—— (ed.) (2007), *The Guitar Player Book*, New York: Backbeat Books/Hal Leonard.

Napier, John (1971), *The Roots of Mankind*, London: Allen and Unwin.

Narvaez, Peter (2001), 'Unplugged: Blues Guitarists and the Myth of Acousticity', in Andy Bennett and Kevin Dawe (eds), *Guitar Cultures*, Oxford and New York: Berg, pp.27–44.

Neuenfeldt, Karl (1997a), 'The Didjeridu in the Desert: The Social Relations of an Ethnographic Object Entangled in Culture and Commerce', in Karl Neuenfeldt (ed.), *The Didjeridu: from Arnhem Land to Internet*, John Libbey and Company Pty Ltd/Perfect Beat Publications, pp.107–22.

—— (ed.) (1997b), *The Didjeridu: From Arnhem Land to Internet*, John Libbey and Company Pty Ltd/Perfect Beat Publications.

—— (1998), *Old Instruments in New Contexts*, special issue of *The World of Music*, 40/2.

Nicholson, Geoff (1998), *Flesh Guitar: A Novel*, London: Victor Gollancz.

Noble, Douglas (2008), 'Play Like: Newton Faulkner', *Guitar and Bass Magazine*, November: 136–40.

Noonan, Jeffrey J. (2008), *The Guitar in America: Victorian Era to Jazz Age*. Jackson: University of Mississippi Press.

Norman, Donald A. (2000), *The Design of Everyday Things*, 3rd edn, London: MIT Press.

Noyes, Jan (2001), *Designing for Humans*, Hove and New York: Psychology Press/Taylor and Francis.

Nygaard, Scott (2008), 'Gipsy Fire' (Robin Nolan), *Acoustic Guitar*, December: 44–57.

Oldfield, Mike (2007), *Changeling: The Autobiography*, London: Virgin Books.

Olsen, Dale A. (2002), *Music of El Dorado: The Ethnomusicology of Ancient South American Cultures*, Gainesville: University of Florida Press.

Orsenna, Érik (1996), *Historie du monde en neuf guitares*, Paris: Librairie Arthème Fayard.

—— with Thierry Arnoult (1999), *History of the World in Nine Guitars*, trans. Julia Shirek Smith, New York: Welcome Rain Publishers.

Osborn, Clive (2008), 'Faking Acoustics with Piezo Bridges', *Performing Musician*, 10, July: 42–3.

Palan, Ronan (ed.) (1996), *Global Political Economy: Contemporary Theories*, London: Routledge.

Palmer, Douglas (2005), *Seven Million Years: The Story of Human Evolution*, London: Weidenfeld and Nicholson.

Patoski, Joe Nick and Bill Crawford (1994), *Stevie Ray Vaughan: Caught in the Crossfire*, London: Time Warner Books.

Pepper Rodgers, Jeffrey (2009), 'Endorsement Deals: How Pro Players and Manufacturers Work Together to Promote the Music and a Brand', *Acoustic Guitar*, March: 74–7.

Pinnel, Richard (1980), *Francesco Corbetta and the Baroque Guitar, with a Transcription of his Works*, 2 vols, UMI Studies in Musicology, No. 25, Ann Arbor: UMI Research Press.

—— (1993), *The Rioplatense Guitar*, vol. 1: *The Early Guitar and its Context in Argentina and Uruguay*, Westport, CT: Bold Strummer Ltd.

Pohren, Don E. [1962] (1990), *The Art of Flamenco*, Madrid: Society of Spanish Studies.

—— (1992), *Paco de Lucía and Family: The Master Plan*, Madrid: Society of Spanish Studies.

Polak, Rainer (2000), 'A Musical Instrument Travels Around the World: Jenbe playing in Bamako, West Africa, and Beyond', *The World of Music*, 42/3:7–46.

Pujol, Emilio [1956] (1983), *Escuela razonada de la guitarra*, Book 1, published also as *Guitar School: A Theoretical-Practical Method for the Guitar*, 2 vols (1982), trans. Brian Jeffery, Boston: Editions Orphée.

—— (1960), *El dilema del sonido en la guitarra* ('The Dilemma of Timbre on the Guitar'), Buenos Aires: Ricordi (written in Spanish, French and English).

Ramírez III, José (1993), *Things about the Guitar*, Madrid: Soneto Ediciones Musicales.

Reddington, Helen (2007), *The Lost Women of Rock: Female Musicians of the Punk Era*, Aldershot: Ashgate.

Rey, Juan José and Antonio Navarro (1993), *Los instrumentos de púa en España: bandurria, citole y 'laúdes españoles'*, Madrid: Alianza Editorial, S.A.

Riley, Suzel (2001), 'Hybridity and Segregation in the Guitar Cultures of Brazil', in Andy Bennett and Kevin Dawe (eds), *Guitar Cultures*, Oxford and New York: Berg, pp.157–77.

Robson, Ian (ed.) (1991), *Picasso Museum, Paris: The Masterpieces*, Munich: Prestel-Verlag.

Romanillos, José (1987), *Antonio de Torres, Guitar Maker*, London: Element Books.

Ross, Andrew (2001), *Strange Weather: Culture, Science and Technology in the Age of Limits*, London and New York: Verso.

Rothenberg, David (1993), *Hand's End: Technology and the Limits of Nature*, Berkeley: University of California Press.

Russell, Craig (1995), *Santiago de Murcia's 'Códice Saldívar No. 4': A Treasury of Guitar Music from Baroque Mexico*, 2 vols, Urbana and Chicago: University of Illinois Press.

Ryan, John and Richard A. Peterson (2001), 'The Guitar as Artifact and Icon: Identity Formation in the Babyboom Generation', in Andy Bennett and Kevin Dawe (eds), *Guitar Cultures*, Oxford and New York: Berg, pp.89–116.

Rycroft, David (1961–2), 'The Guitar Improvisations of Mwenda Jean Bosco', Part 1: *African Music*, 2/4:81–9; Part 2: *African Music*, 3/1: 86–101.

Sachs, Curt [1942] (1977), *The History of Musical Instruments*, London: J.M. Dent and Sons Ltd.

Scaramanga, Jonny (2008), 'Washburn W150 Pro E' (guitar review), *Total Guitar*, 181, November: 138.

Schafer, R. Murray (1969), *The New Soundscape: A Handbook for the Modern Music Teacher*, Don Mills, Ontario: BMI Canada.

—— [1977] (1994), *The Tuning of the World*, New York: Knopf; republished as *The Soundscape*, Rochester, Vermont: Destiny Books.

Schechter, John (1996), 'Latin America/Chile, Bolivia, Ecuador, Peru', in Jeff Todd Titon (ed.), *Worlds of Music*, 3rd edn, New York: Schirmer Books, pp.428–94.

Schmidt, Cynthia (ed.) (1994), 'The Guitar in Africa: The 1950s–1990s', special issue of *The World of Music*, vol. 36/2.

Schwartz, Nancy L. (1988), *The Blue Guitar: Political Representation and Community*, Chicago: Chicago University Press.

Serres, Michel (1998), *Les cinq sens*, Paris: Hachette.

Sexton, Jamie (ed.) (2007), *Music, Sound and Multimedia: From the Live to the Virtual*, Edinburgh: Edinburgh University Press.

Shaar Murray, Charles (2008), 'I, Cooder' (interview with Ry Cooder), *Guitarist*, 306, Summer: 53–6.

Shapiro, Greg (2006), 'Lesbian Guitar Virtuoso Kaki King Takes her Acclaimed Third Album on the Road', *Lesbian and Gay Times*, 978, 21 September.

Shaw, Robert (2008), *Hand Made, Hand Played: The Art and Craft of Contemporary Guitars*, New York and London: Lark Books.

Shelemay, Kay Kaufman (2006), *Soundscapes: Exploring Music in a Changing World*, 2nd and rev. edn, London: W.W. Norton & Co.

Shilling, Chris (2005), *The Body in Culture, Technology, and Society*, London: Sage Publications Ltd.

Simmons, Sylvie (2009), 'The Man with No Name' (interview with Ry Cooder), *Mojo*, 184, March: 55–61.

Slash with Anthony Bozza (2007), *Slash*, London: HarperCollins Publishers.

Slobin, Mark (1993), *Subcultural Sounds: Micromusics of the West*, Hanover, NH: Wesleyan University Press.

Sloboda, John (2004), *Exploring the Musical Mind: Cognition, Emotion, Ability, Function*, New York: Oxford University Press.

Smith, Christopher J. (2003), 'The Celtic Guitar: Crossing Cultural Boundaries in the Twentieth Century', in Victor Coelho (ed.), *The Cambridge Companion to the Guitar*, Cambridge: Cambridge University Press, pp.33–43.

Smyth, David (2008), 'Funny-Haired Troubadour Returns to his Spiritual Home' (review of Newton Faulkner concert at Hall for Cornwall, Truro), *Q* magazine, 259, February: 136.

Sor, Fernando [1832] (1995), *Method for the Spanish Guitar*, trans. Brian Jeffery, London: Tecla Editions.

Stearns, David Patrick (1993), 'The Gentle Touch' (interview with Julian Bream), *BBC Music Magazine*, 18, July: 16–19.

Stimpson, Michael (ed.) (1988), *The Guitar: A Guide for Students and Teachers*, Oxford and New York: Oxford University Press.

Stokes, Martin (2004), 'Music and the Global Order', *Annual Review of Anthropology*, 33/1: 47–72.

—— (2007), 'On Musical Cosmopolitanism', in Institute for Global Citizenship, The Macalester International Roundtable, http://digitalcommons.macalester.edu/intlrdtable/3.

—— (ed.) (1994), *Ethnicity, Identity and Music: The Musical Construction of Place*, Oxford and Providence: Berg.

Strohm, John (2004), 'Women Guitarists: Gender Issues in Alternative Rock', in André Millard (ed.), *The Electric Guitar: A History of an American Icon*, Baltimore and London: Johns Hopkins University Press, pp.181–200.

Stump, Paul (2000), *Go Ahead John: The Music of John McLaughlin*, London: SAF Publishing Ltd.

Summerfield, Maurice J. (1996), *The Classical Guitar: Its Evolution, Players and Personalities since 1800*, 4th edn, Newcastle-upon-Tyne: Ashley Mark Publishing Company.

Tallis, Raymond (2003), *The Hand: A Philosophical Enquiry into Human Being*, Edinburgh: Edinburgh University Press.

Tamarkin, Jeff (2006), 'Bob Brozman: Man of the World', *Relix Magazine*, April/May: 17–19.

Tamm, Eric (1990), *Robert Fripp: From King Crimson to Guitar Craft*, London: Faber.

Tanenbaum, David (2003) 'Perspectives on the Classical Guitar in the Twentieth Century', in Victor Coelho (ed.), *The Cambridge Companion to the Guitar*, Cambridge: Cambridge University Press, pp.182–206.

Tapscott, Don and Anthony D. Williams (2006), *Wikinomics: How Mass Collaboration Changes Everything*. New York: Portfolio, Penguin Group.

Taylor, Mick (2009), 'Editorial', *Guitarist*, 314, April: 3.

Taylor, Timothy (1997), *Global Pop: World Music, World Markets*, New York and London: Routledge.

—— (2001), *Strange Sounds: Music, Technology and Culture*, New York and London: Routledge.

—— (2007), *Beyond Exoticism: Western Music and the World*, Durham, NC: Duke University Press.

Théberge, Paul (1997), *Any Sound You Can Imagine: Making Music/Consuming Technology*, Middletown, CT: Wesleyan University Press.

Thomas, Nicholas (1991), *Entangled Objects: Exchange, Material Culture, and Colonialism in the Pacific*, Cambridge, MA, and London: Harvard University Press.

Thrift, Nigel (2005), 'Beyond Mediation: Three New Material Registers and their Consequence', in Daniel Miller (ed.), *Materiality*, Durham, NC: Duke University Press, pp. 231–55.

Titon, Jeff Todd (ed.) (1996), *Worlds of Music*, 3rd edn, New York: Schirmer Books.

Titon, Jeff Todd and Mark Slobin (1996), 'The Music-Culture as a World of Music', in Jeff Todd Titon (ed.), *Worlds of Music*, 3rd edn, New York: Schirmer Books, pp.1–16.

Toynbee, Jason (2000), *Making Popular Music: Musicians, Creativity and Institutions*, London and New York: Arnold/Oxford University Press.

Turino, Thomas (2000), *Nationalists, Cosmopolitans, and Popular Music in Zimbabwe*, Chicago: University of Chicago Press.

Turnbull, Harvey (1984) 'Guitar', in Stanley Sadie (ed.), *The New Grove Dictionary of Musical Instruments*, vol. 2, London: Macmillan, pp.87–109.

—— [1974] (1991), *The Guitar from the Renaissance to the Present Day*, Westport, CT: Bold Strummer Ltd.

Tyler, James (1980), *The Early Guitar: A History and Handbook*, Oxford: Oxford University Press.

—— and Paul Sparks (2002), *The Guitar and its Music: From the Renaissance to the Classical Era*, New York: Oxford University Press.

Vernon, Paul (2003), *Jean 'Django' Reinhardt: A Contextual Bio-Discography 1910–1953*, Aldershot: Ashgate.

Vines, Adi (2008), 'All Hands-on Tech', *Guitar and Bass Magazine*, 19/2, February: 42–8.

Vitebsky, Piers (1995), *The Shaman. Voyages of the Soul: Trance, Ecstasy and Healing from Siberia to the Amazon*, London: Duncan Baird Publishers/ Macmillan.

Wade, Graham (1980), *Traditions of the Classical Guitar*, London: John Calder.

—— (1983), *Segovia: A Celebration of the Man and his Music*, London and New York: Allison and Busby.

—— (2008), *The Art of Julian Bream*, Blaydon on Tyne: Ashley Mark Publishing.

Wade, Graham and Gerard Garno (1997), *A New Look at Segovia: His Life, his Music*, 2 vols, Mel Bay Publications.

Waksman, Steve (1999), *Instruments of Desire: The Electric Guitar and the Shaping of Musical* Experience, Cambridge, MA: Harvard University Press.

——, Omar Corrado and Sergio Sauvalle (2003), 'Guitar', in John Shepherd et al. (eds), *The Continuum Encyclopedia of Popular Music of the World*, vol. 2, New York: Continuum.

—— (ed.) (2003), 'Reading the Instrument: An Introduction', *Popular Music and Society*, 26/3:251–62.

Walser, Robert (1993), *Running with the Devil: Power, Gender, and Madness in Heavy Metal Music*, Hanover, NH, and London: Wesleyan University Press/ University Press of New England.

Ward, Peter (1978), *The Oxford Companion to Spanish Literature*, Oxford: Oxford University Press.

Washabaugh, William (1994), 'The Flamenco Body', *Popular Music*, 13/1:75–90.

—— (1995), 'Essay Review', *Popular Music*, 14/3:65–71.

—— (1996), *Flamenco: Passion, Politics and Popular Culture*, Oxford: Berg.

—— (ed.) (1998), *The Passion of Music and Dance: Body, Gender and Sexuality*, Oxford and New York: Berg.

Waterman, Christopher (1990), *Jùjú: A Social History and Ethnography of an African Popular Music*, Chicago: University of Chicago Press.

Weissman, Dick (2006), *Guitar Tunings: A Comprehensive Guide*, New York and London: Routledge.

Welton, Russell (2008), 'Brook Tamar 010' (guitar review), *Acoustic*, 21, June/ July: 66–8.

Wenders, Wim (2003), *The Soul of a Man* (film, directed by Wenders and part of the series *The Blues*, presented by Martin Scorsese), Reverse Angle Productions and Vulcan Production Inc.

Wheeler, Tom (2007), 'Introduction', in Michael Molenda (ed.), *The Guitar Player Book*, New York: Backbeat Books/Hal Leonard, pp.x–xii.

Whiteley, Sheila (ed.) (1997), *Sexing the Groove: Popular Music and Gender*, London and New York: Routledge

—— (ed.) (2000), *Women and Popular Music: Sexuality, Identity and Subjectivity*, London and New York: Routledge.

—— and Jennifer Rycenga (eds) (2006), *Queering the Popular Pitch*, New York and London: Routledge.

Wise, Sam (2008), 'Steve Toon "Montpellier" Hybrid' (guitar review), *Acoustic*, 24 October/November: 56–8.

Wong, Deborah (2003), 'Plugged in at Home: Vietnamese American Technoculture in Orange County', in René T.A. Lysloff and Leslie C. Gay Jr. (eds), *Music and Technoculture*, Middletown, CT: Wesleyan University Press/University Press of New England, 2003, pp.125–42.

Wood, Abigail (2008), 'E-Fieldwork: A Paradigm for the Twenty-First Century?', in Henry Stobart (ed.), *The New (Ethno)musicologies*, Lanham, MD: Scarecrow, pp.170–87.

Woodward, Ian (2007), *Understanding Material Culture*, London: Sage.

Yates, Henry (2008a), 'Ovation Mick Thomson MT37–5' (guitar review), *Total Guitar*, 178:26.

—— (2008b), 'The New Rock Revolution? Video Games', in *Classic Rock*, 122, August: 50–53.

Yung, Bell (1984), 'Choreographic and Kinesthetic Elements in Performance on the Chinese Seven-String Zither', *Ethnomusicology*, 28/3:505–17.

Index